HOW TO DISAPPEAR FOR AN HOUR

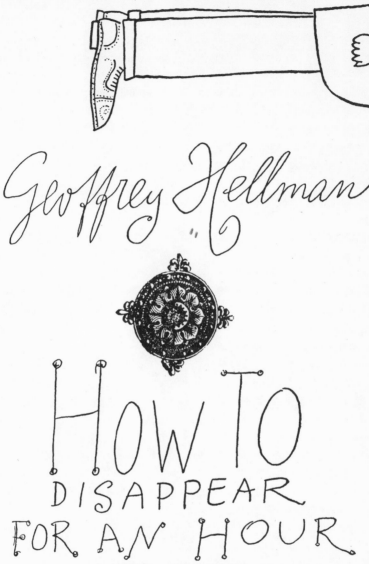

Geoffrey Hellman

HOW TO
DISAPPEAR
FOR AN HOUR

Illustrations by STEINBERG

Biography Index Reprint Series

 BOOKS FOR LIBRARIES PRESS
FREEPORT, NEW YORK

INTERNATIONAL STANDARD BOOK NUMBER:
0-8369-8095-6

LIBRARY OF CONGRESS CATALOG CARD NUMBER:
71-179727

PRINTED IN THE UNITED STATES OF AMERICA
BY
NEW WORLD BOOK MANUFACTURING CO., INC.
HALLANDALE, FLORIDA 33009

Acknowledgments

Except for "How to Solve the Servant Problem," "How to Be a Secret Agent," "Major George Fielding Eliot and the Aqua Velva Club," "The Coordinator's Cufflinks," and "The Strange Behavior of Mr. A. Bryan, of Monolith, California," the first four of which appeared in *Promenade*, all the material in this book was originally published in *The New Yorker*.

Contents

HOW TO DISAPPEAR FOR AN HOUR

HOW TO DISAPPEAR FOR AN HOUR

Reading Maketh
A Full Man
I

How to Write Your Autobiography

PUBLISHERS, inviting me to write my autobiography, have found me depressingly unresponsive, lacking in the confidence essential for such an enterprise, modest to the point of lethargy. "Who," I invariably ask them over the cigars and coffee in the Oak Room of the Ritz, "outside of my wife and a few morbidly curious friends, could possibly be interested in the simple facts of my life?"

But the other day, browsing amid the stacks of the New York Society Library, an establishment I frequent because the taps in its washroom stay on without your holding them, I picked up a copy of "Grover Cleveland: A Study in Courage," by Allan Nevins, and read, of the period of Cleveland's early youth:

American families were usually large, and the children were soon pushed from the edge of the nest, while the work of pioneering in every field demanded young men of energy and initiative. The prairies of the West were broken and the battles of the Civil War were fought, in the main, by lads hardly out of their teens. In an age which read Samuel Smiles on self-help, and produced innumerable counterparts of Horatio Alger's self-reliant heroes, the fact that Grover Cleveland was forced to strike out for himself at sixteen could not be regarded as a great misfortune. Were Dick Whittington listening to the London bells ring "Turn Again," and runaway Ben Franklin munching his penny-roll as he walked down Market Street, to be pitied? . . . "Cast the bantling on the rocks," Emerson was writing—and in Cleveland's case the rocks had their edges somewhat smoothed.

I took a deep breath, cast a bantling and two Parmachenee Belles on the smoothed rocks of East Seventy-ninth Street, pulled in a muskellunge, skipped twelve pages, and read:

The moment Cleveland entered the office of Rogers, Bowen, and Rogers he began adjusting himself to a wholly new world.

This period of the late fifties and early sixties was preëminently one which inspired youth to action. Many young men of Cleveland's generation—Garfield, Randall, Hayes, McKinley—plunged into the smoke of the Civil War. Others, like Henry James, Howells, and Henry Adams, were enriching their experience amid European scenes, or like Mark Twain and Clarence King, found adventure in the Far West. Cleveland was almost of the same age as John Hay, who throughout the war was with Lincoln in the White House and shortly afterwards went gaily off to a diplomatic post in Spain; as Winslow Homer, who was drawing pictures of battle scenes for *Harper's Weekly*, and later studying art in Paris; as J. Pierpont Morgan, who was carrying out financial operations . . . on two continents. It was a time when home-keeping youths feared homely wits, and when even the future poets and novelists, like Sidney Lanier and George W. Cable, were drawn by the bright face of danger into the full current of events. . . . Millard Fillmore had long been at the head of the [Buffalo] city bar.

All at once an autobiography looked entirely feasible to me. I was born on February 13, 1907; Theodore Roosevelt was in the White House, probably playing medicine ball in the gymnasium with Ik Hoover, the Chief Usher. J. Pierpont Morgan,

seventy years my senior, was husbanding his strength for the
Pujo Investigation of 1912; Mark Twain, busy with his autobiography, was almost a year older than Winslow Homer;
Henry James was fiddling around preparing a collected edition
of his novels. Home-keeping youths were hiding under the
dining-room table, in mortal terror of homely wits. All this I
happened to have at my finger tips, and a little research in the
old-newspapers branch of the Public Library on West Twenty-
fifth Street has fortified me in the conviction that the circumstances surrounding my birth would make a capital opening
for *any* man's autobiography. I herewith submit same, just to
show what a fool I was to be so modest all those years.

February 13, 1907, the date of my birth, was Ash Wednesday; in Manhattan, the borough of my birth, it was uncom-
monly cold that day, the temperature hovering around five
above zero. Theodore Roosevelt was in the White House (the
lower floors of which I was to inspect many years later on a
guide-conducted tour), standing pat on railroad legislation and
refusing to alter one jot or tittle of his demands on Congress for
government control of Big Business. James J. Hill, president
of the Great Northern, charged the President with trying to
shackle the progress of transportation expansion. It was announced that the Chief Executive, Secretary Root, and Senator
Lodge had evolved a complete solution of the Japanese problem, whereby the exclusion of Japanese coolies would be ac-
complished by legislation, to which the Japanese government,
through its Ambassador here, had already given its consent.

In New York thefts of watches and cash from lockers of
members of the Seventh Regiment baffled detectives; three
men were killed when a scaffold at the new Public Library
building on Forty-second Street collapsed; Mrs. Archer Huntington, whose home was to become headquarters of the National Academy of Design, shipped a thirty-five-horsepower

Panhard automobile to Europe to be used in a tour of England
and France; and Dr. Britton D. Evans, expert alienist for the
defense in the Harry K. Thaw trial, then in full swing, called
the jury's attention to a peculiar conformation at the back of
Mr. Thaw's head, consisting of a depression and a protuberance
unlike anything he had previously encountered in his experience. Joseph H. Choate delivered an address in Cooper Union
on Lincoln; Anna Held, Eleanor Robson, George M. Cohan,
and David Warfield were appearing in Broadway shows; Professor George Santayana of Harvard checked in at the Buck-
ingham; Heinrich Conried, director of the Conried Opera
Company, lay ill with a severe attack of sciatica; and Mme.
Sembrich and Caruso, appearing in "La Traviata" at the
Metropolitan, played to an audience that included Mrs.
Cadwalader Jones, Mr. and Mrs. Lewis Iselin, Mr. and Mrs.
William G. Rockefeller, Mr. and Mrs. Jacob Schiff, Mr. Mon-
cure Robinson, and Miss Alice Van Rensselaer. Miss Edith
Deacon, in pale-blue satin and a corsage of pink roses, was in
Box 2; Box 12 was embellished by Mrs. Moses Taylor Camp-
bell, in coral-pink gauze and satin, and Miss Ethel LeRoy De
Koven, in white satin and lace. In the Bronx Zoo, Norah, said
to be the handsomest baboon in captivity, had a baby. Lady
Clarke, wife of Sir Casper Purdon Clarke, superintendent of
the Metropolitan Museum of Art, sailed for Europe on the
Baltic, announcing that on her return she would hold a salon
to stimulate interest in art, music, and literature.

The cold weather was even colder in Connecticut (where I
was to go to school thirteen years later), and Robert E. Peary,
the arctic explorer (who was to reach the North Pole about
twenty-six months later), delayed by snowdrifts, missed a train
in Hartford and was thus prevented from fulfilling a lecture
engagment in Norfolk, Connecticut. Elsewhere in that state,
in Winsted, a jury of his peers assessed Charles Seymour, a

janitor at the Hartford Public High School (who was never to become President Charles Seymour of Yale), $79.50 for attempting to kiss Miss Annie B. Cambridge, a Winsted resident; while the Savings Bank of New Britain closed its doors, short $560,000 and with its treasurer, William F. Walker, a man with a beard and a long record of activity in church circles, pointedly missing. It was a terrific day to be born on.

February 14th dawned cold and clear, with Lady Clarke and Mrs. Huntington's Panhard on the high seas, Roosevelt still in the White House, and Norah's baboon and me in our second day. The era of rag-paper editions had not yet set in, and those 1907 newspapers are in frightful condition, but the sense of history is running in me like wine. A nod from Simon & Schuster, and the first volume of my autobiography ("Formative Years, 1907–1909") will be theirs.

How to Become a Terrible Bore

IT seems like another aeon, but less than a month ago I was a popular, or at least a widely tolerated, extra man, dining out five or six nights a week, having my dinner coat pressed every other day, the recipient of innumerable cigars, and the pawn of married women, some of whom called me up as late as six in the afternoon of a day on which they were giving a dinner party to ask me to fill in, and fill up. I was way behind on my stamp collection; I had to snatch precious hours from my work during the day to catch up on *Time, Life,* and the monthly letter of the National City Bank; I was constantly exposed to conversation about world affairs; my house slippers, which I like to put on when I dine at home, were rigid with disuse and my nerves, like my dinner coat, worn to a frazzle. I had drifted into this way of life gradually—to what extent I realized only one night this January when the butler of a house where I had long been a familiar figure said to me, as he helped me off with my coat, "It's common gossip at the Staff Club, sir, that you're getting to be the Henry James of your generation—in point of dining out, that is."

I am able to mention this in a carefree way because all of it now has the aspect of an implausible nightmare. My telephone hasn't rung for ten days, my mail consists exclusively of appeals from charities, I sit home night after night in slippered comfort conversing easily to myself about trivialities, my laundry bill has been cut in half, I have read an entire book and bought several Hoyo de Monterreys on my own, my stamp albums are in apple-pie order, and I understand that the Staff Club has gone back to talking about Lauder Greenway, Nicky de Gunzburg, and George Jean Nathan.

The vehicle of my salvation is a book called "Mastering Your Nerves," by Peter Fletcher, a volume which has made me the laughing-stock of hostesses all over town and as composed as a cat. I picked it up at my neurologist's two weeks ago and, in a chapter entitled "The Discovery of Things," read:

We are dull, bored, uninterested and uninteresting, tired and disillusioned, in a world brimming with mysteries and thrills, because we have never opened the eyes of our minds to see the wonders on our own thresholds. . . . Here is a list of common things, about most of which most people know nothing at all.

Furniture	Rivers	Chemicals
Postage stamps	Roof tiles	Skeletons
Flowers	Thatch	Carpets
Birds	Grasses	Windows
Trees	Pollens	Carvings
Insects	Flies	Dogs
Clocks	Aeroplanes	Telescopes
Pictures	Children	Pond life
Printing	Books	Worms
Buildings	Butterflies	Salads
Music	Embroidery	Snakes
Jewellery	Statues	Pencils
Microscopes	Matches	Porcelain
Stars	Silks	Newspapers
Rocks	Wireless sets	Fungi

It struck me that children are not really "common things" and that most persons do know a little more than "nothing at all" about books, newspapers, radios, and dogs, but I was desperate and my neurologist was tied up with another extra man, so I read on. "Go through that list," I read on, "and choose from it the three items you know least about. Walk round to your local free library before you have time to change your mind, and from the catalogue there pick out the titles of the most interesting book on each of these three subjects."

Like a man in a dream, I walked to the Public Library and looked up "Clocks," "Fungi," and "Worms," three subjects about which I know next to nothing, or .000000000000001. It is hard to tell from a title whether a book is interesting or not, and I proceeded on the theory that what Mr. Fletcher meant was to pick out the title which looked the most interesting. Under "Clocks," therefore, I selected "Die Hemmungen der Uhren, ihre Entwicklung, Konstruktion, Reparatur und Behandlung vor de Reglage, nebst Zugehörigen Tabellen, Zahlreichen Abbildungen und 6 Porträts. Allgemein verständlich für Uhrmacher, Ingenieure, Techniker u. s. w.," by C. Dietzschold. Under "Worms," the obvious choice seemed to be "Some Common Bagworms and Basketworms," by Claude Fuller. When I looked up "Fungi" in the card index, however, my troubles began. "The Yeastlike Fungi of the Human Intestinal Tract," by Harry Warren Anderson, and "Sooty Blotch of Pomaceous Fruits," by Arthur Samuel Colby, sounded promising, but they turned out to be mere pamphlets and thus not strictly within the scope of Mr. Fletcher's scheme. I had just about resolved to abandon "Fungi" and look up "Pond Life," another item on Mr. Fletcher's list, when I recalled a note I had seen on the first card, or one of the first few cards, in the "Fungi" section of the index. I flipped back to it and read:

Fungi—See also Actinomycetes, Ascomycetes, Ascotricha, Aspergillus, Bacteriology, Balansia, Basidiomycetes, Blastomycetes, Cynomorium Coccineum, Diaporthe, Discomycetes, Endogoneae, Erysipheae, Fermentation, Fimetariales, Giberella Saubinetti, Gasteromycetes, Hydinaceae, Hymenomycetes, Hyphomycetes, Lacteria, Lentinus, Lycoperdaceae, Macrosporium, Meliola, Micromycetes, Mildew, Mycosis, Molds, Mucorineae, Mushrooms, Mycorhiza, Myxomycetes, Nidulariaceae, Peronosporaceae, Phycomycetes, Phytophthore, Plants—Diseases, Pleurotus, Polyporaceae, Protomycetaceae, Pyrenomycetes, Rhizoctonia, Russula, Saprophytes, Sclerotinia, Septobasidium, Septoria, Smut, Sordariaceae, Sticta, Stilbum, Torula, Tuberaceae, Tulasmellaceae, Truffles, Tylastomaceae, Uredineae.

Well, I walked over to the "S" section of the index, looked up "Smut," and, after studying the various titles in this fungoid subdivision, picked out "Rust, Smut, Mildew, and Mould," by M. C. Cooke, perhaps because it sounded like a rather interesting law firm. I ordered the three books from the stacks and turned to "Mastering Your Nerves" for further instructions. "Take the three books home and look through them," these ran. "Select of the three the one subject you find most attractive on closer acquaintance, and set about the task of mastering it thoroughly."

The Library people wouldn't let me take the books home, so I read them right there, in the reading room, having sandwiches sent in every few hours. I found Mr. Cooke's book more attractive than the clock and worm volumes and by nightfall I had mastered it thoroughly. I went home, took a long, hot bath, and proceeded jauntily to a small dinner party, the sort of thing that always used to make me feel jumpy. "Why, your hand doesn't shake a bit this evening," said my hostess as I confidently downed a Martini. We went in to dinner and I turned briskly to the girl on my right. "Four diseases in wheat of fungal origin are known and recognized in the popular language of the farm as mildew, rust, smut, and bunt," I said.

"You live in Westport?" said the girl.

"According to Mordecai Cubitt Cooke," I continued, "if we break open a grain of wheat infested with the stinking rust or bunt and then place some of the powder in a drop of water on a glass slide and submit this to the microscope, we shall find that this minute dust consists of myriads of globose brown bodies termed spores, which possess certain reproduction functions."

"Lucky spores," said my dinner partner, with a glazed expression.

She turned rather quickly to her partner on the other side, and I nudged the woman on my left, a Mrs. Appleby, who is a leader in my set. "You'll be interested in this," I said. "Winchell hasn't had it yet, but bunt or stinking smut is caused by two species of microscopic fungi which live as parasites in the wheat plant." I went on to discuss *Tilletia tritici* and *Tilletia foetans.*

As I said, Mrs. Appleby is a leader in my set. Word of my new interest spread like wildfire. By the next day my telephone was humming with rescinded invitations; around three in the afternoon I began to hum myself. I haven't been out of the house since, except to go to a bookshop and order a copy of Daniel McAlpine's "The Smuts of Australia, Their Structure, Life History, Treatment, and Classification."

Winter Comes to Nantucket

IN Nantucket last September, according to the *Nantucket Inquirer & Mirror*, Chief of Police Mooney tendered his resignation as dog officer; Professor Jim, the island bootblack, closed up his place and went to New Haven for the winter; Arthur Weeks had a piece added to his garage; the Yacht Club closed for the season; the local schools opened; and a number of native prophets predicted there wouldn't be much of a scallop season. Mrs. Ernest Thomas announced she was agent for Spencer Corsets, Sea Cliff Inn closed, cranberry picking began on the Nantucket Cranberry Company's bog, bluefish struck at both the west and east ends of the island, Walter G. Pollak caught sixteen squeteagues in one afternoon, and on the twenty-fifth the Executive Committee of the Civic League met to consider plans for the elimination of ragweed, a pest which causes many hay-fever-ridden summer visitors to shorten their stays. "Poison ivy, tent caterpillars, and the new threat to our elm trees," said the *Inquirer & Mirror*, "is also included within the scope of this committee's activity."

I subscribed to the *Inquirer & Mirror* this fall because it has the largest pages of any newspaper in the country, with a wing-spread of forty-four by twenty-eight inches, and because, having several times visited Nantucket in the summer, I was vaguely curious as to what went on there during the time of year when there weren't any hotel arrivals, bus tours of the island, or monodramas by Cornelia Otis Skinner at the Yacht Club. I had mentioned this curiosity in conversation with a native woman whom I met on a fishing-boat excursion last August, and she had begun to tell me how busy she was kept all fall and winter, what with meetings of the Daughters of Nantucket Lighthouse Keepers and other orders, but in the middle of it she had pulled in a balloonfish and in the ensuing excitement we never got back to the topic. Catching a balloonfish is exciting, because when you tickle it, it swells up into a kind of ball. Then you can bounce it, gently, on the ship's deck.

The *Inquirer & Mirror* hasn't fully satisfied my curiosity about winter in Nantucket, but it does give a considerably better-rounded picture of the life of the community than, say, the *Times* does of New York. In September, in addition to the events already mentioned, a large school of porpoises was plainly seen not far from shore; Edward B. Rideout, meteorologist, predicted the coming winter would be "colder than normal"; the schooner Coral unloaded a hundred barrels of road oil at the South Wharf for John C. Ring, the road contractor; the Maddequet Admiralty Association formally dedicated its new clubhouse; and a small, civic-minded group met in Leeds Mitchell's boathouse to discuss transportation facilities, which had been seriously impaired by the folding, last summer, of the old Fall River Line. On Tuesday, September 7th, Harry Gordon and Irving Bartlett each caught a bluefish in Smith Point opening, and exactly a week later Dewey Sandsbury got two large bass at Great Point, each weighing about thirty pounds. A few days later, Dewey, apparently one of the most active men on the island, received a fifty-dollar check for returning to its owner some jewelry he had found while beachcombing, but the check bounced back and Dewey had to pay the bank's charge of two dollars. On the last day of the month the steamer Naushon took fifty-two cars away from the island, thus polishing off the summer trade except for Mr. and Mrs. Emory Buckner, who left for New York early in October.

October was a busy month for Nantucket's Board of Selectmen. Among other things, they voted to allow the Senior Club to hold a costume cabaret at Red Men's Hall, cabled the Duke of Windsor inviting him and his wife to come to the island if they were looking for a quiet place, and authorized the sale of the coal stoves formerly in the town-office building, these having been replaced by gas heaters. This manifestation of progress was not appreciated by Town Treasurer Tirrell, who complained that the disposition of crows' heads which people brought in to him for the twenty-five-cent bounty, hitherto simply a matter of popping them into the stove, was now getting to be an irritating problem. After a few days, the Duke of Windsor cabled his regrets and appreciation.

Apart from the Selectmen's activities, October saw several ladies contributing jars of beach-plum jelly to the reunion in Boston of the Sons and Daughters of Nantucket; the opening of the season on cock pheasants, excluding only Melanistic Mutant, otherwise known as black pheasants; the laying of a new gas main under Main Street; and the unexpected appearance, in the garden of Alvin E. Paddock on Lily Street, of a sweet potato ten inches long and two and a half inches in diameter. Captain Everett B. Coffin of Seattle, a Nantucketer born, revisited his boyhood home after an absence of forty-five years; Miss Carrie J. Long, for many years in the ladies'-and-infants'-furnishings business, announced her retirement; and fifteen citizens petitioned the Honorable Board of County Commissioners to relocate that part of the Polpis Road between Pole No. 90 of the New England Telephone & Telegraph Company and Pole No. 30-158, "convenience and necessity requiring the same."

The island's schools were by now well under way, with seven hundred and nine children attending. At Academy Hill, Mr. Maloney, the drawing master, brought in some brilliant autumn leaves for the class to copy. Small animals cheered the lives

of many children and adults. Mrs. Field sent a canary to the
'Sconset School, causing a pupil to report, "He has a very nice
voice and sings all the songs with us," and on October 27th, at
a Halloween party at the Cyrus Pierce School, "the appearance
of a little gray mouse which was soon frightened away added
to the excitement of the evening." The major academic event
occurred at the end of the week, when the first Nantucket high-
school football team in history played Provincetown, on the
home grounds. The Cape Cod boys, who had raised the necessary eighty dollars for the trip by a public sale of cakes and
doughnuts baked by their mothers, sisters, and female friends,
proceeded to trounce Nantucket 40–0. This defeat enlisted the
sympathy and imagination of the *Inquirer & Mirror*, which
observed, "The cold figures of the score mean absolutely nothing as regards the merits of the local boys. . . . To begin with,
although the sky was fair and the sun high, there was a strong
southwest breeze blowing, and the Nantucket boys found themselves facing it. One can well imagine how they felt, with the
roar of the crowd in their ears, a set of determined new faces
gazing at them from across a yard stripe, a strange thing called
a football in their hands that felt as big as a bushel basket one
minute and as small as a baseball the next."

The October sitting of the Superior Court at Nantucket was
heralded by a salute from the cannon of the Wharf Rat
Club as District Attorney Crossley and other court officers
approached on the Naushon. Although these gentlemen were
ceremoniously greeted at the pier by Sheriff Larkin, who got
himself up in the sheriff's traditional silk hat and swallowtails
for the occasion, there was little for them to do, as, according
to the *I. & M.*, "No cases are scheduled for trial at the October
sitting of the Superior Court at Nantucket." The court met
this situation calmly. "No one," remarked the *I. & M.*, "could
blame the judge and other court officers for bringing business

to a prompt close Tuesday and then leaving posthaste for a trip out through the rips after bluefish. It was a delightful balmy day—just right for an outing."

The scallop season found twenty-six boats out on the first of November. During this month the Nantucket Lightship, having been in port preparing for winter service, was returned to her station on the South Shoals; the fishing schooner Annie Perry put into market with 19,000 pounds of groundfish, her crew getting $203 each, and the Abiah Folger Franklin Chapter of the D.A.R., named after Benjamin Frankin's Nantucket mother, appointed Mrs. Orville Coffin chairman of the committees on Americanism, Correct Use of the Flag, Junior American Citizenship, and Motion Pictures. On November 15th, at a special town meeting, it was voted to change the name of Pearl Street back to its original one of India Street. The Selectmen authorized Superintendent Tice to overdraw the "snow and sand" account, which stood at nine dollars, in case of emergency due to heavy snowfall during November and December, several persons reported rambler roses still growing on their places, and Orin Coffin picked strawberries from his vines on North Liberty Street on Saturday, November 13th.

First snow of the winter fell November 21st. Two cows were brought over on the steamer for Matthew Jaeckle; the Maddequet Admiralty Association held a Thanksgiving dance enlivened by the appearance of a black-and-white kitten, and the first Christmas tree of the season was seen November 30th in the window of Congdon's Pharmacy. The freshman-English high-school class was taking up "the subject of an adequate vocabulary," while the Civics class held a debate on "Leisure Time Should Be Spent for Individual Enjoyment," which was given twice "because it was not very successful the first time." The negative won. In football, Provincetown beat Nantucket 20–0 in a return engagement at Provincetown, and on the home field Lawrence High School of Falmouth beat them 57–0 "in a much more interesting encounter than the score indicates." This holocaust found the *Inquirer & Mirror,* from which I have just quoted, as chipper as ever. "The score does not measure the actual worth of the contest," it stated, adding that Falmouth made its first touchdown by executing "the sleeper play" on Nantucket's ten-yard line. "Rabeca, Falmouth's right halfback," it explained, "had not joined his team as they lined up at the scrimmage line, but lay at full length far across the field, where none of the local players noticed him. When the ball was snapped, it was a comparatively easy matter for Rabeca to get to his feet, scramble across the goal line, and catch a perfect pass thrown to him by Mills, the left halfback."

The deer season opened December 6th, with twenty-five killed the first day, and the Nantucket Anglers' Club voted to notify the sporting-goods stores in Boston and New York that the pollock were running. In December, also, a rabbit appeared one evening on Main Street, Mrs. Pearl Miko won the electric toaster at the complimentary lottery which celebrated the opening of David MacMillan's new drugstore, Mr. and Mrs. Frederick R. Currie bought a new Studebaker coupé, and the shutters on the Whaling Museum were painted a brighter green than before. Robert Seevrens, the town trumpeter, played his usual carols from the South Tower on Christmas Eve; the Nantucket Gas & Electric Company's prizes for the best Christmas lighting effects were awarded to Earl S. Ray, Leroy H. True, and Robert Wilson; and Archibald Cartwright was reported quite pleased with his wife's Christmas present, a new Chevrolet truck. The only untoward event was a fire which occurred in the 'Sconset Post Office a few days before Christmas, doing $450 damage. Ordinarily tested every day at noon, the fire-alarm system had gone uninspected that day in the flurry of excitement preceding a Community Club banquet in the evening, and the alarm failed to work. "It appears that a most unusual coincidence has occurred by the fact that a fire should break out on the only day of the year when the fire alarm was not tested," commented the *Inquirer & Mirror*. "Naturally, the person who rings in the noon test feels badly over the incident, and everyone sympathizes, realizing what a busy day in the life of the village Monday happened to be."

I subscribed to the *Inquirer* for a year, beginning with September, and intend to keep on reading it every week, but this probably gives you a sufficient idea of what is going on. In any case, 1938 has started off pleasantly, with Mrs. John Santos, of Codfish Park, 'Sconset, getting the paper's annual five-dollar prize for the first baby of the year, a daughter born January 13th, and the return from Boston of Nantucket's delegation to the annual meeting of the Massachusetts Selectmen's Association with the aluminum gavel awarded to the town having the largest representation and coming from the longest distance. Captain Augustus E. Folger, of Long Beach, California, who is better known as "Whale Oil Gus," is planning to revisit his boyhood home in Nantucket this spring, and the young people are coasting down Dead Horse Valley every moonlit night.

Thanks to the *Inquirer & Mirror*, I am, along with most of the people on the island, looking forward to the Annual Town Meeting in Legion Hall next Monday, when a Tree Warden will be elected and sums appropriated, among other things for the support of the Moth Department, the Shellfish Department, two comfort stations, replacing buoys and new spar buoys, care of the town clock, and the ringing of the town bell. I haven't any idea how these things are handled in New York, and although I read three or four Manhattan papers daily I couldn't tell you whether there is a tree warden in all of Central Park.

How to Disappear for an Hour

LAST Tuesday, stopping in at my dentist's to have my porcelain fillings exchanged for platinum as a hedge against inflation, I picked up a copy of *Your Life, The Popular Guide to Desirable Living*, as I walked through the anteroom. I tossed the magazine out of the window to an accomplice I had stationed below and sauntered in to the dentist's chair, whistling nonchalantly as though nothing were the matter. "Why all this idiotic whistling?" said my dentist. "You didn't just throw a magazine out of the window, did you?"

I put him off with a jest, and later on, secure in a hideout where I read purloined magazines and print counterfeit membership cards to the Museum of Modern Art, I examined the contents of *Your Life* in the hope of gaining some hints on self-improvement. I was sustained in this hope by the knowledge that small magazines, around five and a half by seven and a half inches, usually are full of improving matter and by the fact that *Your Life* was almost exactly five and a half by seven and a half inches. For a while, as I leafed through the magazine's various departments—"Your Life," "Health," "Love," "Fortune," "Charm," and so on—my expectations were realized. In an article entitled "Ways to Outwit Your Habits," I learned that when Geraldine Farrar feels a temper coming on, she counts up to ten "to prevent herself from acting or expressing herself with undue precipitancy"; that a certain young husband, finding that he is cranky on rising, makes it a rule to breakfast downtown instead of at home, since "in this way he obviates the possibility of anything disagreeable occurring at the breakfast table"; and that Arthur Hays Sulzberger, publisher of the *Times*, kept himself "from behaving in ways that he wished to avoid" at a recent Labor Board hearing by tucking into his vest pocket a slip of paper on which he had written "(1) Keep calm. (2) Don't be smart. (3) Smile." I was a little puzzled at learning that Herbert Bayard Swope keeps his nose to the grindstone by putting on a dressing gown when he gets up and by not dressing until he has finished his work. Mr. Swope's formula for outwitting his non-work habits struck me as something less than foolproof, considering all the extracurricular practices one can get into in a dressing gown, but I dismissed this thought as captious.

An article by Dr. Paul Popenoe which said, "Look for the best in people," and one by Nina Wilcox Putnam warning the reader not to blame all his troubles on God had just about convinced me that I ought to lead a better life when, on page 84, in an article by Carol Carroll about jealousy, I read the following passage:

Every man with a jealous wife should form this simple little habit—whenever he is with his wife in the presence of a group of people, he should ask her to supply some information for a story he is telling or ask her to tell something as though he felt that she told it well. He can disappear for an hour after that and she will not be jealous.

Coming in a magazine otherwise devoted to material of an uplifting nature, these are strangely cynical words, and I wonder what Mr. Wilfred Funk, editorial director of *Your Life* and former editor in chief of the *Literary Digest*, was thinking of when he let them slip into his publication.

They are not only cynical words, conducive to loose rather than desirable living, but they are misleading ones. I know they are misleading because I tried out Carol Carroll's advice on a jealous girl I know. I took this girl to a party at a friend's house the evening after I read the article, and as I felt her fix a madly possessive gaze on me, I launched into an anecdote about two Negroes and President Roosevelt. "These darkies were walking up Pennsylvania Avenue," I said, "when a large, open, black touring car sped by, followed by several cars of police with screaming sirens. One of the Negroes asked the other who was in the car and the second Negro replied, 'Dat's President Roosevelt.' " At this point I faltered, intentionally, and turned to my jealous companion, who was watching me like a hawk. "Sweetie," I said, "what was it that the first Negro then said? I can't seem to remember." My girl's expression relaxed and she looked at me lovingly. " 'What he done?' " she said.

Scarcely were the words out of her mouth when, taking my cue from the piece in *Your Life*, I grabbed a girl who had been sitting in a corner with another guest, whisked her through the door, and disappeared. When I returned, precisely an hour later, the girl I had brought to the party, far from seeming mollified, was looking more jealous than I had ever seen her look before. "What *you* done, you rascal, you?" she shouted, throwing a plate of cold turkey at my face. This isn't a pretty story, but it's apposite, and if this is the reaction Miss Carroll's technique inspires in a jealous friend, you may be sure it would be even worse in the case of a jealous wife.

Perhaps the trick is to leave your wife in the middle of an anecdote that will take her an hour to finish, but *Your Life* doesn't say so and in any case my supply of such stories is too meagre to be of practical use. A man who wants to settle his wife with a group of people and disappear for an hour would do better to provide himself with a short-wave radio, announce a police-car report of a robbery taking place in Harlem, and rush off. He should return with a slip of paper in his vest pocket bearing the message "(1) My, what a complicated robbery! (2) We had to stick around nearly an hour till they got through with it, and (3) I *think* the police may want me to appear as a witness this time tomorrow night."

How Lovely Are Your Planet Aspects?

THE trouble with astrology, from the point of view of a man who would like to check up on it—a point of view which I have been entertaining, wildly, for years—is that its practitioners usually either couch their prophecies and advice in general terms (everyone born on January 9th better think twice before petting a mad dog next Wednesday) or else deliver their prognostications privately to individuals who can scarcely be expected to report on them in public. In a recent issue of *Stage*, however, Miss Myra Kingsley, a horoscopist who enjoys a fashionable clientele here and in Hollywood, came right out and published thumbnail forecasts, covering dates in last November and December, for a number of theatrical critics around town. She started with the *Herald Tribune's* man:

Richard Watts, Jr., probably doesn't know what he'll be doing on Saturday, November 30th, but he is in for something upsetting or I don't know how to read horoscopes. I am extremely unhappy when I am obliged to tell someone such things.

Well, I wrote Mr. Watts, in the interest of science, asking him how he felt that Saturday, and he answered:

Outside of the fact that my hangover that morning being slightly more violent than usual I found everything about as usual on Saturday, November 30th, and I suggest that Miss Kingsley adopt an old custom of General Hugh Johnson's and eat her *Stage* piece on astrology.

Watts' reply isn't terribly grammatical, but the truth is in it; he wasn't upset, and Miss Kingsley, by her own admission, doesn't know how to read horoscopes and shouldn't get unhappy about fancied upsets of others.

Not wishing to come to a conclusion on the basis of one man's evidence, I subsequently addressed similar queries to Brooks Atkinson, Burns Mantle, Walter Winchell, Sidney Whipple, and George Jean Nathan, all of whom were included in Miss Kingsley's peeks into the future. "Brooks Atkinson's date of birth," she reported, "shows that Saturday, November 23rd, will be upsetting because of the conjunction of the planets Saturn and Mars." Mr. Atkinson's letter to me tended to confirm this. "The lady was terribly right about November 23rd," it ran. "That was the day my careful and responsible son ripped two wheels off my car. But if she had wanted a ten-strike, she should have forecast the tragic burning of my fine old barn in the country on the 20th." Miss Kingsley wasn't so good about Burns Mantle. "November 22nd is a very ominous day for Mr. Mantle," she wrote. I asked Mr. Mantle about this, and he replied that nothing special happened to him that day and that he had felt O.K. Mantle is not a Pollyanna type, and I am inclined to believe him. Mr. Whipple, who was promised an enjoyable Monday, November 25th, failed to answer my letter, and Mr. Winchell, whom Miss Kingsley had down for two black Fridays, November 1st and November 22nd, wrote me that Fridays are usually black for him.

All this left me with the feeling that Miss Kingsley, and the science of which she is a leading exponent, get things right about a third of the time, thus approximating the record I used to make in geometry exams. I regret to state that her average was appreciably lowered by her performance on George Jean Nathan. "George Jean Nathan," her forecast ran, "will have so lovely a Venus aspect on Friday, November 22nd, that his whole world may be colored with a roseate hue. He should watch his health this Fall. November 12th–14th will bring cheer with Mars smiling at the Sun and Venus." Mr. Nathan's comment on this, which he penned to me on hotel stationery nostalgically inscribed "Visit the World's Fair—New York," should bring cheer to those who prefer tea leaves, cards, and numerology to the stars. "Friday, November 22nd," it reads, "was, Kingsley to the contrary, and unfortunately, notwith-standing, a peculiarly bleak day for me. I spent the whole of it groaning at my writing table, and cursing the world. Nov. 12–14 was an even duller span. The only symptom of Venus discernible during it was a telephone call from a colored woman in Brooklyn—Mrs. Ruby Johnson—who has stage ambitions and asked me to introduce her to Gilbert Miller, whose fash-ionable first-night audiences she deemed a suitable background for the display of her talents. So far as my health went and goes, no man over thirty-eight ever, if he tells the truth, has a day in which he feels wholly and completely fit. That is, unless he takes a couple of drinks."

Miss Kingsley isn't the only astrologer in the world, of course, but as far as I am concerned, the fact that I have a cold today is the result of sitting in a draft last night and not of a temporary conjunction of Saturn and Uranus afflicting all persons born at three o'clock in the morning on February 13th, 1907. Moreover, in my opinion, the Titanic sank because it hit an iceberg, and Evangeline Adams had nothing to do with it.

Mr. William Saroyan
and the Public Library

EVER since reading an article by the late Evangeline Adams which stated that people who, like myself, were born between the twentieth of January and the nineteenth of February are Aquarians, and are more likely to fall in love with an institution than with a private individual, I have realized that I have a crush on the Public Library. I am fond of Cooper Union, Sailors' Snug Harbor, and the New York Historical Society, and I once had a brief, unhappy affair with the Metropolitan Museum of Art, but for a real, lifelong flirt give me the Public Library, Central Building. I like the Library because it contains such paintings as "Deer Drinking," by Rosa Bonheur; "Grandmother's Birthday," by V. Brožik; "Lesson in Embroi-

dery," by Em. (J. B. Antoine Emile) Béranger; "The Petition
to the Doge," by Carl Becker; "The Foundling," by H. Salen-
tin; "Sheep in Snow Storm," by A. Schenck; "Thoughts of Liberia," by Edwin White; "Milton Aveugle Dictant 'Le Paradis
Perdu' à Ses Filles," by M. Munkácsy; "Pigs in a Fodder Yard,"
by George Morland; "A Boy in a Red Velvet Dress Leaning
Forward on a Green Cushion, Holding a Pen and Paper in His
Hand," by Sir Joshua Reynolds; and "A Romantic Woody
Landscape, with a Peasant and Two Horses Crossing a Pool of
Water, and Sheep on a Rising Ground," by Thomas Gains-
borough. I like it, too, because some of these pictures are hung
at least eighteen feet high, where no one can really see them.
Many of the paintings, along with a large collection of shells,
minerals, tea cups, and paper cutters, were left to the Library
by Mrs. Robert L. Stuart, widow of a president of the Museum
of Natural History, who revoked a bequest in her will leaving
most of the contents of her house to that Museum when,
shortly before her death, she suspected that this institution
would soon succumb to public pressure and open up Sundays. I
admire the Library the more for accepting and displaying these
implausible objects, and for keeping the gallery which contains
them closed on Sundays, although the rest of the Library is
open then.

Other features which make it difficult for me to dismiss
the Library from my thoughts are its impressive selection of
United States stamps, from 1840 to 1890, on exhibition on the
third floor; the two "Ancient Roman Busts" on the second-
floor landing; and the fact that the push buttons have been
removed from the elevator entrances, since the elevators are
continually going up and down anyway. I like it, too, for its
many prints (most of them presented by Mr. Isaac Newton
Phelps Stokes), which, if you consult one of the Library's
catalogues, you will find include "The Patriotick Barber of

New York, or the Captain in the Suds," "A Correct View of the Old Methodist Church in John Street, N. York," "View of an Unidentified Town of Considerable Size, Showing Large Church and Factories," and "View of a Monument Erected in Milwaukee, Wisconsin, by the Sunday School Children of the United States to the Memory of Emanuel Dannan, a Sunday School Scholar Who Chose to Suffer a Cruel Death Rather than Tell a Lie." I particularly admire the Library for hanging "V. o. a. M. E. i. M., W., b. t. S. S. C. o. t. U. S. t. t. M. o. E. D., a S. S. S. W. C. t. S. a C. D. R. t. T. a L." in view of the fact that it admits, in this same catalogue, that Mr. M. S. Dudgeon, librarian of the Milwaukee Public Library, has written of it, "The picture . . . is, in a sense, a fake. No such monument was ever erected," and goes on to say that in his opinion it is not a view of Milwaukee at all. The Library's attitude on this is straightforward and engaging, and one well calculated to win the heart of any moderately susceptible Aquarian.

The other day, though, my affection for the Library received an unexpected setback. I was browsing through the "S" section of the card index in Room 315—a gesture which Miss Adams would probably have considered the institutional equivalent of ruffling a loved one's hair. Reading a card which listed "The Coming Reality," an article by William Saroyan which was published in *Theatre Arts Monthly* last December, I noticed, in the lower left-hand corner, the typed words "No subj." I asked one of the young men at the information desk what this meant, and he said that, in the indexing of magazine articles, this space was ordinarily reserved for a brief description of the subject matter and that he had never before heard of a catalogued item being dismissed with the phrase "No subj." Now, I am no authority on Mr. Saroyan, especially in his more obscure manifestations, but I have taken the trouble to read this particular piece and I am at a loss to account for the

Library's bewilderment, not to mention downright rudeness to the Pulitzer Prizewinner. Mr. Saroyan's subject is apparent right from the start:

It is incredible how unimaginative a whole age can be. Our age has been inventive, but always unimaginative. If we have had anything new it has been shabby and pointless and clinical, like da-da or dada, surrealism, et cetera. All feeble. All unhealthy, or rather non-healthy. The operation of imagination in the realm of the normal is practically unknown. Implements, gadgets, and so on: plenty. Anything that has to do with matter: plenty. Anything that has to do with spirit, rhythm, and so on: none. We have plenty of reporters. Practically no creators. There is no imagination.

Obviously, Mr. Saroyan's premise is that this is an unimaginative age, and his conclusion, as well as his choice of title, is made clear in the following passage:

The reason for all this sorrow in behavior everywhere is that we've had no real imagination. No one has behaved freshly and spontaneously, excepting he was crazy, which doesn't count in the record. I mean to behave freshly and spontaneously and supernormally.

The coming reality is the coming fresh, spontaneous, and supernormal behavior of Mr. Saroyan. The Library may not believe that this is the coming reality, and I am not sure that I do either, but that is no excuse for saying Mr. Saroyan has no subject. "This unimaginative age" or "The coming fresh, spontaneous, and supernormal behavior of William Saroyan" is what should have been typed on that card.

The trustees of the Public Library include Vincent Astor, William Adams Delano, J. P. Morgan, Frank L. Polk, Elihu Root, Jr., John M. Schiff, Myron C. Taylor, Bronson Winthrop, Mayor LaGuardia, and President of the City Council Newbold Morris—a competent group of men; not one to be easily baffled, one would suppose. Considering the extraordinary problem involved in the cataloguing of the Saroyan article, it is safe to assume that they were consulted and, unless they take their responsibilities lightly, did all they could to prevent such a public exhibition of their corporate perplexity. Their failure, like a beautiful woman's inability to understand the funny papers, has left me with a slightly let-down feeling. It may be, of course, that they were thrown off by Mr. Saroyan's remarks about the lizard. "All things influence all things," he writes. "A boulder in a desert influences a lizard. Once in a while, though, comes a lizard who influences a boulder, *the* boulder, and therefore all boulders, and everything else." Well, it is true that Mr. Saroyan strays from his subject now and then, but this is one of his chief charms and one that a library which goes in for shells, minerals, postage stamps, and prints of nonexistent monuments certainly ought to understand.

The Strange Behavior of Mr. A. Bryan,
of Monolith, California

O NE night, a couple of months ago, I was lounging in my well-stocked library—a hookah at my ankles, a box of chewing gum at my elbow, a neighbor at my throat—trying to make up my mind which of my favorite books I really liked best: the *Summer Social Register*, 1929, *All Cities*; "The ABC of Social Credit," by E. S. Holter; "The Sexual Life of Savages," by Bronislaw Malinowski; "Decorating Is Fun!," by Dorothy Draper; "The Action of the Living Cell," by Dr. Fenton B. Turck; the 1891–92 Annual Report of the New York Chamber of Commerce; or the 1940 *World Almanac and Book of Facts*. A rather stimulating experience, dating from that evening, has made me feel that my first desert-island choice would be the *Almanac*, and has supplied me with a minor mystery that is going to keep me thumbing and ruffling this work whenever I can, in search of further excitement. On page 53A of the current edition, in a section devoted to Classified Advertisements, I found, under the heading "Lists," an advertisement reading, "Millionaires Names—Names and Addresses of Seven Millionaires Sent Anywhere for $1.00. A. Bryan, Box 1, Monolith, California."

I have long wanted to know the names and addresses of seven millionaires, so that I could bandy them about in conversation, and at once I mailed a dollar bill to Mr. Bryan, asking him to send me the list. The only millionaires' names and addresses I have ever been able to think of are those of John D. Rockefeller, Jr., J. P. Morgan, and George Blumenthal. My friends had been getting terribly tired of hearing me say, "You know, George Blumenthal, the president of the Metropolitan Museum of Art, lives in a roomy house at 50 East Seventieth Street built by McKim, Mead & White and has one of the best art collections on East Seventieth Street" or "Since John D. Rockefeller's house at 10 West Fifty-fourth Street was razed two years ago by the Albert A. Volk people to make room for the Museum of Modern Art's sculpture garden, he and Mrs. Rockefeller have been living at 740 Park Avenue, the northwest corner of Seventy-first Street." I figured that with Mr. Bryan's help I would be in a position, at small expense, to brighten up my conversation with some new blood.

Well, nothing of the sort. Three weeks after sending in my dollar, I got it back, along with my letter to Mr. Bryan, on the back of which he had written, "Due to the lack of inquiries for said list we have been forced to discontinue said list. Inclose we are returning your money. Thank you." Much as I appreciate Mr. Bryan's honesty (I had not marked the dollar bill and there was nothing for which he could have been apprehended had he kept it), his actions puzzled me. The envelope in which he returned the bill bore a letterhead reading, "Bryan Publications, Post Office Box Number One, Monolith, California," indicating that his was no fly-by-night business but one whose advertised products might reasonably be expected to exist. Moreover, the fact that he answered me on the back of my own letter showed him to be no stickler for form but an unceremonious Western type—one, I would have thought, who would not have hesitated to scribble down the list of seven millionaires and send it to me even if the lack of demand had discouraged him from getting out printed or mimeographed copies.

It costs money to advertise in the World Almanac, and it

seems strange that Mr. Bryan should have inserted his notice without making more of an effort to get back his investment. To be precise, it costs twenty cents a word to place a classified ad in the *Almanac* if you use small letters, and twenty-five cents a word if you use capital letters. Every word in the Bryan ad is printed in capitals. There are a hundred and fifty-eight such advertisers in the 1940 edition, but Mr. Bryan, with one exception, is the only one to cry his wares exclusively in large, costly letters. His offer is couched in seventeen words, if you count the name A. Bryan as one word, and must therefore have set him back $4.25, a fairly stiff price for a practical joke.

I do not believe that Mr. Bryan is a practical joker, and I do not think the *World-Telegram*, which publishes the *World Almanac*, would be party to his pranks if he were. I have two conflicting theories about my experience with Bryan Publications, and as time will probably show which one is right, I may as well set both of them down, before time seizes me by the forelock. One is that there was something in my note, or the way I signed my name, that convinced Mr. Bryan I was an agitator of some kind and not the sort of person who should be encouraged to buy millionaires' names for 14²⁄₇ cents apiece. The other theory—and I am inclined to favor it—is that Mr. Bryan is simply in the market for a list of people who are willing to pay a dollar for the names and addresses of seven millionaires because, in next year's *World Almanac*, he wants to run an advertisement reading, "Names of Inquisitive People—People Willing to Pay a Dollar for the Names and Addresses of Seven Millionaires—Sent Anywhere for $2.00." This will doubtless net him a handsome profit, for almost everybody knows the names and addresses of seven millionaires and will be willing to pay $2 for a list of people willing to pay $1 for same.

How to Solve the Servant Problem

(With thanks to Marcia Davenport, who has done it nicely in "The Valley of Decision").

IT was the spring of 1837, and Nora O'Rourke held her breath as she rang the back doorbell of Joseph Dodd's house on Stuyvesant Square. She was dressed in an old potato sack, and her hair was neatly growing out of the top of her head.

"Och, *begor!*" she said. "This wud be it." The butler showed her to the living room, where Sarita Dodd was feeding her goldfish. The fish jumped out of the bowl, and Nora swallowed in fright. "Oh dear, you've swallowed my goldfish," Mrs. Dodd said. Nora burst into tears. "Don't cry, child," said Sarita. "The work is easy, just making the beds and helping wait on table, and besides, if you play your cards right, you can probably get engaged to my son, Robert. We don't let him see any girls in his set, you know, and he's a fool for propinquity. I don't say you can marry him, but you can damn well get engaged to him, and that would be something, wouldn't it?" She patted Nora's hand reassuringly. "*Would?*" said Nora. "Not *wud?*" "*Would*, dear," Sarita said gently. I must polish up on my English, Nora thought as she went upstairs to her room.

(1837—*Continued*)

Passing the watercress salad, Nora thought she had never seen such striking people. Old Joseph Dodd, head of the great counterfeiting plant which bore his name, sat at one end of the table, solid as a rock; he was, in fact, slowly turning into stone, but no one knew it except his doctor, who as a matter of professional etiquette was keeping mum. Robert Dodd was sitting toward the center of the table, looking terribly queer. Nora understood that. Opposite him was his sister, Gladys, furtively writing a letter to the third duke of Northumberland. The other guests included August Belmont, James Gore King, one of the Brown brothers of the banking family of that name, and several rich, worried couples whom Nora, who had only gotten up to the letter L in Moses Beach's "Wealth and Biography of the Wealthy Citizens of the City of New York," couldn't quite place. "How are conditions?" old Joseph asked. "Shaky," said King, "shaky. Of course, they won't affect you." A carrier pigeon flew in the window and dropped a coded message at Belmont's plate. "Waterloo!" said Belmont slowly. "Pigeon's twenty-two years late. That means—" He mumbled an apology and left. One of the men at the far end of the table looked up shrewdly, walked into the conservatory, and shot himself. "Holy Mother o' God!" said Nora, passing the Baked Alaska, "It's the panic of 1837!"

(*March, 1865*)

The Civil War was over, and Nora had been engaged to Robert for twenty-seven years. He had been married for twenty-five of these years to his second cousin, Laura Bogart, by whom he had eleven children, but he and Nora were still engaged, and Nora felt more engaged than ever as she and Robert walked through the heavy snowstorm on the hill overlooking the Dodd plant. Twenty-dollar bills were flying out of the main smokestack, and Robert's eyes narrowed as he took in the scene. Old Joseph was dead, and Robert was running the plant alone, driving himself hard and often lunching at his desk. " 'Tis me sister, Begorra, thinks we ought to be married, Mister Robert," Nora said quietly, "but I know me place, ye may be sure." "Call me Mister Bob," Robert said harshly. He took her in his arms and looked her full in the eye. "If it weren't for Laura and the kids," he said, "I'd ask you to have lunch with me some day. By God, I would!" "How about the plant?" Nora said slowly. "Ye've clean forgot the plant. Ye mus'na', Mister Robert." Robert Dodd leaned forward eagerly. "We're branching out into stamps, Nora," he said. "A man called Russell Davenport gave us the idea. This very minute the presses are turning out Andrew Jackson two-cent blacks. The Postmaster General doesn't know what to make of it." Nora nodded. "I know," she said. "Scott's Number Seventy-three. Yere father wud be proud of ye." Robert laughed. "I'm giving you 50,000 shares of the company's common stock and Wednesday afternoon off, in addition to your regular day," he said noiselessly. "We're friends, aren't we, Nora?" A soft laugh was the only reply.

(*December, 1902*)

It was Nora's day off, and she and Gladys were in the latter's house in London, signing proxies. Gladys had married one of the Barings, causing old Joseph, who detested Englishmen, to cut her off with $500,000, but Nora had stuck to her. Gladys was the particular friend of a certain exalted party, and while Nora did not approve of this, she kept her trap shut. "I keep me trap shut, Gladys," she said, reddening.

The bell rang, and Gladys' second man fired a salute of twenty-one guns. A heavy bearded man stroke into the room, followed by Sir Ernest Cassel. "Sire," said Gladys.

It was Gladys' turn to blush now, but she didn't.

"Blush, ye spalpeen," said Nora, refusing to be bulldozed.

"Won't," said Gladys.

"It's your *turn* to blush," Nora insisted.

"Won't, won't, won't!" Gladys screamed.

The heavy bearded man reached for his crown and turned to Gladys slowly. "You're not playing the game, my dear," he said as he left the room. Nora followed Cassel to the door. "I've a little loose cash, Sir Ernest," she began.

(November, 1943)

Nora was tidying up the study in Robert's old house on Stuyvesant Square. She was 121 years old, and Robert had died the year before. Dear Robert, she thought, they had been engaged to each other for 105 years; probably a record of some sort. The president of the counterfeiting plant was now one of Robert's great-grandsons, Joseph Dodd, 3d, and the firm was doing more business than ever, dropping bogus money all over Germany and bringing the end of the war just that much closer. Young Joseph came into the room and sat down.

"Nora," he began. "You've been with us quite a while. We wondered whether perhaps a new maid—"

Nora's lips began to tremble. " 'Tis not me ye'll be turning out into the streets, Master Joe," she barked slowly. "Ye may be the prisidint o' the company, but 'tis Nora O'Rourke that owns fifty-one per cent o' the voting stock, thanks to yere great-gran'pappy and me owl' frind Sir Ernest Cassel.

"Moreover, macushla," said Nora, straightening her faded hair, "I can speak the King's English, thanks to a certain exalted party, and I could have for some time had I thought it would get me anywhere. Give me the gate, and I'll form a syndicate that will vote you right to a fare-thee-well."

Young Joseph smiled the smile of a minority stockholder. "You win, Nora," he said. "You can stay, and there's a ten-dollar raise for you, as of today."

Nora blushed with pleasure. She thought of a girl in a potato sack ringing the back doorbell; of Mr. Lincoln and the Civil War; of all the interesting proxies she had signed and still would sign; and she laughed out loud, for the first time, as she turned up the carpet, looking for buffalo moths.

How to Take History in Your Stride

(After Being Tipped Off by John P. Marquand)

Iᴛ was very hard for Roger to remember what he had been
thinking about Tuesday, now that it was Wednesday. It was
one of those weeks that passed like a dream, and you could not
tell, from the flowers at Schling's, the mansard roof of the
Union Club, or the barred windows of the old George Blumenthal house across the Avenue, that the Russians were entering
Kiev, that Tom Dewey was back from Mackinac, and that the
Pope was in the hands of the Germans. There were more uni-
forms in the streets, of course, and the Whitelaw Reid house
was a club for service women, but Johnny Farrar was still publishing books, Hank Hansen was still reviewing them, and
Roger was not able to understand how this sort of thing could
go on, in October of 1943, just as though nothing were the
matter. The Madison Avenue shoe stores were full of shoes,
and you could not tell, from their appearance, how soon the
war would be over. At any rate, Roger could not tell, and Peggy
was no help. "Shoe stores are always full of shoes, Roger," she

41

had said. "Don't stand there gaping." He could see her the day of their marriage, standing in her father's house in Stockbridge without the slightest knowledge of world affairs, and he knew he would have to go to Washington for the answer. He had taken the Congressional and he had seen Jack Leffingwell in the Pentagon Building. Jack had been commissioned a major soon after Pearl Harbor, but during his first week at the Pentagon he had walked into the general officers' dining room and they had made him a brigadier, to get him past the cashier on his way out.

"We don't know, Rodge," he had said. "We just don't know. Come back again tomorrow."

"What?" said Roger.

"Come back again tomorrow," said Jack.

"Where?" said Roger.

"Here, Rodge," said Jack, "here."

"Oh, here," said Roger, "tomorrow. Well, it's been swell seeing you, Jack."

"It's been swell seeing you, Roger," said Jack. "I particularly enjoyed it because I looked you up in *Who's Who* and found you were listed. Any time you want to become a private first class, let me know. We've got Bill Saroyan, you know, and we're working on Frank Crowninshield. He was down here the other day, shopping around."

"Thanks, Jack," Roger answered. "You'll be in the next edition. They're listing all Army officers above colonel and all Navy men above captain."

Roger tried to recall this conversation as he and Peggy stood in the elevator. The garage had delivered the car at the door and Peggy had given Herbert and Nora Betty and Ed's telephone number in Connecticut, but there was no gas and they had decided to spend the weekend in the elevator, riding up and down.

"Roger," Peggy asked, "did you remember your watch? Are you wearing your garters? What time is it, Roger?"

"What?" said Roger.

"What time is it?" Peggy asked.

"It is later than you think," said Roger.

"Stop worrying about the war," said Peggy.

The elevator stopped between the second and third floors and a midget got on. Roger felt Peggy give him a terrible pinch. "Roger," said Peggy, "isn't that Henry Bernstein?"

"What?" said Roger. "Who?"

"The man on your right," Peggy said, "isn't it Henry Bernstein?"

"No," said Roger. "This is a restricted apartment house. Sometimes I think we ought to move."

"It's Coolidge Weld," said Peggy. "Hello, Coolidge."

"Thought I remembered you from last night's dinner," said Coolidge. "I sat on your right. Isn't your son my godchild? What's the news?" Coolidge asked. Coolidge was wearing a Poole blazer and he had a custody account of three million dollars at John Monroe & Co., a firm that had gone out of existence many years before.

It was like Coolidge to keep his money in a bank that no longer existed. Coolidge's whole life, Roger reflected, was an anachronism. Coolidge lived in the old Peter Cooper house, which had, of course, been torn down, but old Mrs. Weld, Coolidge's mother, had lived there, and Coolidge had never felt like moving—not even when his wife did, taking the children with her. Old Mrs. Weld had slipped into the house in the seventies; the house was so large that Peter Cooper and his son-in-law, Abram S. Hewitt, had never even noticed. Roger sometimes wondered what the stuffed peacocks on the Stanford White marble balustrades had to do with the German retreat in Russia, but Coolidge was his best friend and he usually dismissed this speculation as disloyal. He could not help wondering, however, how many times Poole's had been bombed out and why Coolidge had never proposed him for the Union Club.

"Rodge," said Peggy, as the elevator went up. "Don't you remember?"

Roger did not answer.

"Don't you remember, Roger?" said Peggy.

"Remember what?" Roger asked.

"Just remember," said Peggy.

"No, Peggy," said Roger. "No, I don't remember."

Roger had been born in New Hampshire, in the general store, and although he had forgotten all about it, it filled him with a sense of futility. He knew he had been born somewhere, and he sometimes tried to recall where it had been and where he had passed his boyhood, but the radio kept interfering with his thoughts. *President Roosevelt announces the resignation of Sumner Welles as Undersecretary of State* (it ran). *Edward Stettinius . . .* Roger could see his father bending over the sundial and saying, "It's time you were a man, Roger," and he could see the sunflowers in the yard, but that was as far as he could get. That was the way he felt about his boyhood. He sometimes wished he had spent it in the old Peter Cooper house, like Coolidge Weld, but his family had never come to New York, and he knew this was out of the question.

The elevator started down again, and it made Roger think of Krasnograd, where there probably weren't any elevators. He pulled out a cigarette and Peggy offered him a match.

"Match?" he heard Peggy saying.

"What?" said Roger.

"Match," said Peggy.

"Oh," Roger said, "thank you," and he carefully lit the cigarette end which was not in his mouth.

"Roger," said Peggy. "Don't you think—"

"No, Peggy," said Roger. "I don't think. There isn't time to think, dear."

It all tied up together somehow—not thinking, smoking cigarettes, the war, the flowers at Schling's, the Pope, Jack Leffingwell, Coolidge Weld, Sumner Welles's resignation, Krasnograd, Dewey back from Mackinac. Still, it was hard to see exactly how. He wished they had enough gas to get to Betty and Ed's. There would be Martinis, he knew, and grace before lunch.

How to Be a Secret Agent, Or, Consult
Your Neighborhood Irredentist

WHEN, in a civilian capacity, I joined the Washington office of Major General William J. Donovan's Office of Strategic Services during the war, I was given a very severe security lecture by a young naval lieutenant and warned never, never to tell anyone what the organization was up to, in case I found out. I was urged to read certain sections of the Espionage Act (wherein the phrase "thirty years in Leavenworth" still sticks in my memory) and informed that my obligation to keep my trap shut would terminate not with the end of the war but only upon specific notice of release from our ultimate boss, known locally as "the General." Should anyone ask me what OSS did, or what I did in its employ, I was instructed to say either "Research" or "Filing." My office contained a safe, in which I was directed to keep my papers locked up not only at night and during lunch, but whenever I went down the hall to the watercooler for a drink, unless I could persuade a properly security-checked secretary to keep an eye on them in the interval. The secretaries were usually occupied with more pressing assignments, and the Washington heat made me terribly thirsty, so that I spent a good deal of time locking and unlocking my safe. I had been enjoined not to write the combination down anywhere, and at first I kept forgetting what it was. Apparently only one other individual in the agency was privy to it; he was, of course, forbidden to refresh my recollection over the phone, which was presumably tapped by the German *Abwehr*, the Japanese Imperial Home Rule Assistant Society, G-2, ONI, and J. Edgar Hoover. Since, as the sole co-repository of the similar secrets of other forgetful OSS employees he was kept busy making memory-prodding rounds, it sometimes took quite a while to get him to show up. One evening early in my new career I went home leaving one of my safe drawers open —only a crack, but enough for the inspecting guard to call me up just as I was sitting down to dinner and insist on my coming down to close it personally. Punishment for a transgression of this sort took the form of the offending party's having to serve as security officer of his branch until he caught a colleague in a comparable sin, when said colleague succeeded him. Security officers had to stay after hours and inspect the neighboring offices after their occupants had left for the day; a second check was then made by the guard.

On my first, and only tour, I rummaged through a number of unlocked desks and found—in addition to a surprising amount of candy, a collection of two hundred pennies, and a blotter jocosely stamped "Secret"—documents of a satisfactorily restricted nature in the drawers of two lieutenant colonels and one lieutenant commander, on whom I duly blabbed.

This experience sobered me, and I got to be so continuingly

mysterious and security-conscious that when I returned to New
York to my old job last summer I replied in monosyllables to
my boss, a notably inquisitive man, asked (vainly) for a safe,
and went around confiscating my associates' loose-lying candy.
I continued to be unfathomable about OSS after V-J Day,
since I had received no release from the General. Toward the
end of the year, however, I became increasingly conscious of
the fact that questions put to me during dinner parties—such
as "What was OSS doing in Burma?"—and countered with a
"Research" to the lady at my right and a "Filing" to the partner
at my left, were often answered more truthfully, and in more
interesting detail, on the first page of the New York *Times* the
following morning, or in articles, written by OSS men, in
Collier's or the *Saturday Evening Post* the following week.

Naming names and placing places, these revelations, as well
as more recent books by Corey Ford, Stewart Alsop and others,
have been so full of spies, saboteurs, guerillas, black propagan-
dists, limpeteers, and secret-agent grandsons of Thomas Fortune Ryan and Morgan and Sullivan & Cromwell partners as
to make a conversational fool out of me. I now propose to
discuss, openly and perhaps belatedly, certain aspects of my
rather sedentary wartime duties. While these never called for
my setting up a secret radio station on the roof of the Cosmos
Club or blowing up the offices of the *National Geographic*, I
did have access to a continuing flow of classified material
almost as arcane as the stuff Drew Pearson publishes from time
to time. The documents containing this intelligence were
housed in a large air-conditioned room for which I had special
clearance and which afforded respite from the Washington
climate; the room's battle-order wall maps were kept current,
with colored pins, by a detachment of well-spoken Grotonian
master sergeants; and there was always the chance of running
into a Sullivan & Cromwell partner who might come in handy

if I ever wanted to draw up a really crackajack will.

One of the first things I came across, filed in a confidential folder marked *India*, was a Helen Hokinson cartoon from *The New Yorker*, but most of the items I inspected were agents' overseas reports of a more legitimately restricted complexion and such notes as I took on them have, naturally, long since been either burned or swallowed. I would sometimes treat a carefully security-checked friend to an off-the-record swallow, so that he could go around—however briefly, as we shall see—saying he was a repository of secret data, but I would invariably watch him swallow, and I need hardly say that all such swallowers were liquidated within the week—or, in the case of Saturday swallowers, within the next week—since most of our guerillas, being in the armed forces, were allowed Saturday afternoon off for squash racquets at the University Club, or, in the lower echelons, squash tennis. As nearly as I can recall, a typical report read as follows:

Subject: Mortimer Maimonides, a Boer living in Asia Minor. Evaluation: E-5, or Watch Out.
1. Approximately 67.2 kilometers directly under Mossamedes there is a permanent water-hole where Mortimer Maimonides, an apostate Boer, lives.
2. Every afternoon Maimonides, whose code name is Mossamedes, goes 14 kilometers south and slightly east to a neighboring river, or drywash, where he engages in apostasy, light persiflage, and the smuggling of wolfram.
3. Maimonides' persiflage is considered inept by his neighbors, and his smuggling as only fair, and they regard him as a terrible Boer. They have reportedly advised him to move to a temporary water-hole.

I didn't make much of this report or its prototype when I read it, and here is another, or approximation thereof:

1. The Syrians in Liberia are disliked socially.
2. At times, there have been rumors that the Syrians in Liberia

are *not* disliked socially. A reliable source, X,[1] considers such rumors without foundation. However, an equally reliable source, Y,[2] states that these rumors have a foundation, and a concrete foundation at that.

OSS-Washington Comment: The name of a firm specializing in concrete foundations may be obtained from the Secretariat.

There are still some Syrians in Liberia, and maybe even some Liberians in Syria, so I will not divulge what I did with this scoop, but there can surely be no harm in concluding with an item which was undoubtedly red-hot when I came across it but which is now practically indistinguishable from junket, owing to the rapid course of events, or workings of the Heraclitan doctrine of Flux:

Subject: Personality Details of New Armenian Cabinet Ministers.
1. Maxim Donchian, Minister of Bottlenecks, is suspected of improper relations with Evdokia, an easy puppet.
2. A fanatic supremist and ruthless irredentist, Donchian is foolish and vain, but possesses a wolfram collection that would make your mouth water.
3. Three lieutenant-colonelcy slots are available to Young & Rubicam partners.

A new generation is growing up, and I suppose I should explain that there were a good many advertising boys on the staff, and that Evdokia, or Alice-Leone-Moats, was a Sullivan & Cromwell receptionist planted on Mount Ararat by General Donovan with a suitable array of forged documents, transformations and peasant costumes. Her relations were simply those of a patriotic American girl enjoying a good Civil Service rating and abundant vitality, and the fact that they were misconstrued, and her identity muffed, by a fellow-agent was the natural fruit of a cellular organizational policy which aimed at internal, as well as external, security. For example, I never knew

[1] *Corey Ford.*
[2] *Corey Ford.*

whether the man across the hall from me was busy with research or with filing, and I never even met the General. I used to see him trotting across the campus between invasions, followed by eager junior officers, and at times he seemed to glance at me rather sharply. I had joined the outfit disguised as a troupial, however, and I never had a moment's apprehension.

A Note on the Founder of the
Smithsonian Institution

CUT off for the past three years from the Museum of Natural History, the Metropolitan Museum of Art, the New York Historical Society; exiled from the Museum of the American Indian, the Museum of Science & Industry, and the Parke-Bernet Galleries; four hours by train from striking distance of the old George Blumenthal house, the Jumel mansion, not to mention the site of the old Peter Cooper house, at No. 9 Lexington Avenue, I have sought solace in the Smithsonian Institution, a multi-building hodgepodge of everything from an 1834 silk dress "made of silk produced from cocoons raised by Abigail Sherwood on her father's farm in Fairfield County, Connecticut" to the first jet-propelled airplane.

I have inspected not only the Smithsonian's treasures but also its history. This dates from 1846, when Congress belatedly voted to accept a bequest of $550,000 left in 1829 by James Smithson, an illegitimate son of the first Duke of Northumberland, to the United States of America "to found at Washington, under the name of the Smithsonian Institution, an establishment for the increase and diffusion of knowledge among men." Smithson had never visited this country. His unconventional connection with his father, who was married to a Lady Percy, may have given him a chip on the shoulder as far as England was concerned. "The best blood of England flows in my veins," he once wrote. "On my father's side I am a *Northumberland*, on my mother's I am related to kings, but this avails me not. My name shall live in the memory of man when the titles of the Northumberlands and the Percys are extinct and forgotten."

Approximately $1,500,000 has been added to the original Smithsonian endowment and the Institution has been entrusted with collections worth many times that sum. It is governed by a board of regents, headed by Chief Justice Stone, whose responsibilities, in addition to the exhibits already mentioned, include the Spirit of St. Louis, a good deal of sulphur from Gergenti, Sicily, an 1831 locomotive, a 1902 Franklin automobile, an 1876 hand-drawn steam fire engine known as the Lily of the Swamp, dresses of Presidents' wives, some rather faded Cecropia moths, a hell of a big stamp collection, the Alfred Duane Pell collection of spode, a bureau which used to embellish the studio of Eliphalet Fraser Andrews, founder of the W. W. Corcoran School of Art, a family group of Cocopa Indians, busts of Alice Longworth and P. T. Barnum, dinosaur and mastodon skeletons, one of James Smithson's visiting cards, a stuffed Jocose cactus wren (*Campylorhynchus Jocosus*), an upright spinet, or clavicytherium, and a cast of a seventy-eight-foot sulphur-bottom whale.

My passion for these and allied items has caused me to scratch up an acquaintance with a number of men prominent in Smithsonian circles. Dr. Alexander Wetmore, secretary of the Smithsonian and a crackajack avian paleontologist, has permitted me to finger some of his reconstructed birds; Dr. Charles Greeley Abbot, retired secretary of the Smithsonian and a noted astrophysicist, has described for me his solar cooker and, scarcely pausing for breath, sung a singularly passionate love song with which he regales the other members of his car pool, a group of young women; Dr. Gilbert Grosvenor, president of the National Geographic Society and editor of its magazine, has brightened my life in the nation's capital by telling me how, in 1903, when Smithson's body was about to be turned out of its grave in Genoa to make room for a quarry, or part of a quarry, Grosvenor's father-in-law, the late Alexander Graham Bell, a regent of the Smithsonian Institution, personally brought the remains and sarcophagus to Washington to be installed in the Smithsonian's main building.

Against this background of erudition and special knowledge, I hope it will not be necessary for me to pretend that I recently acquired a volume published in 1880 and entitled "James Smithson and His Bequest," by William J. Rhees, simply in order to fill a gap in the shelf on which I keep my dark-green books. I bought Mr. Rhees's book because of prior interest and I have been combing it for significant passages ever since. Smithson was something of a scientist—a bug for analytical chemistry and a member of the Royal Society of London—and it is a description of one of his experiments as outlined at the anniversary meeting of this society in 1830, the year after his death, that struck me as perhaps the most significant passage in the Rhees biography. This passage, which is a quotation from an address by the society's president, Sir Davies Gilbert, runs as follows:

He [Smithson] was the friend of Dr. Wollaston, and at the same time his rival in the manipulation and analysis of small quantities. Αγαθη δ' ερις ηδε βροτοισι. Mr. Smithson frequently repeated an occurrence with much pleasure and exultation, as exceeding anything that could be brought into competition with it; and this must apologize for my introducing what might otherwise be deemed an anecdote too light and trifling on such an occasion as the present.

Mr. Smithson declared that, happening to observe a tear gliding down a lady's cheek, he endeavored to catch it on a crystal vessel; that one half of the drop escaped, but having preserved the other half, he submitted it to reagents and detected what was then called microcosmic salt with muriate of soda and, I think, three or four more saline substances, held in solution.

In the interest of science, and in justice to Smithson's memory, I propose to clear up the circumstances of this experiment. Smithson never married, so the lady who furnished this useful tear, or half tear, could not have been his wife. Probably she was not even a friend, since apparently he was in a position to go after only one drop, and, having lost half of it, he surely would have liked more. Ladies, once they get started, produce quite a number of tears in sequence; had Smithson's source of muriate of soda been reasonably coöperative, she would have filled his crystal vessel, thus performing a fuller service to science. Clearly, then, Smithson and the lady were not on the best of terms. There remains the question of what got her started crying and how Smithson caught her at it. He may have stuck a pin in her, on purpose. This would have annoyed her and would account for her refusal of a second tear, but it appears to be ruled out by Smithson's declaration that he *happened* to observe a tear. More likely, he inadvertently said something that stimulated her ducts, and then, the scientist triumphing over the man, ruthlessly whipped out his crystal vessel rather than a decent handkerchief. I gather from the movies that many interesting scientific discoveries have originated in some such unpremeditated fashion, and I suspect that Smithson was sitting next to a young woman at a dinner party, around a hundred and twenty years ago, and the following scene was enacted:

YOUNG WOMAN: Who you leaving your money to, Mr. Smithson?

SMITHSON: To the United States of America, to found at Washington, under the name of the Smithsonian Institution, an establishment for the increase and diffusion of knowledge among men.

YOUNG WOMAN: The States? Why, we were at war with them only a few years ago! Why not leave it to a British institution, such as Boodle's? After all, the best blood of England flows in your veins.

SMITHSON (*moodily*): Avails me not.

YOUNG WOMAN: You *must* leave your money to England. On your father's side you are a *Northumberland*, on your mother's you are related to kings.

SMITHSON: Avails me not. However, my name shall live in the memory of man when titles of the Northumberlands and the Percys are extinct and forgotten.

YOUNG WOMAN: You *are* a difficult 'un!

SMITHSON: To hell with England.

YOUNG WOMAN: Mr. Smithson, you are a traitor!

SMITHSON: Another peep out of you and I'll leave my money to found the Chicago *Tribune*.

(*The young lady bursts into tears. Smithson pulls out his crystal vessel, clasps it to her cheek, and tries to catch a drop, only to have half of it escape.*)

SMITHSON: Damn! Mind if I take another drop?

(*His dinner partner shakes her head, sobbing, and Smithson, after a greedy look at her glistening cheeks, leaves the room for his laboratory while the other guests cry, "For shame!"*)

If my reconstruction of events is correct, Smithson was never asked to another dinner party. He died, a few years later, a kind of martyr to science, for, like many bachelors, he was very fond of dining out.

Birds of a Feather
II

Geography Unshackled

D R. GILBERT H. GROSVENOR, editor of the *National Geographic Magazine* and president of the National Geographic Society, which publishes it, is a kindly, mild-mannered, purposeful, poker-faced, peripatetic man of sixty-seven, endowed with the sprightly air of an inquiring grasshopper, with a clear, pink complexion, and with the mixture of business sagacity, intellectual curiosity, regard for tradition, and tolerance of temperate innovation that is sometimes found in the president of a fairly wealthy college. He is also, unlike most college presidents, a man after whom four babies, a fish, a sea shell, an island, a glacier, a trail, a lane, a mountain range, a mountain peak, a lake, and a plant have been named. His human namesakes are Gilbert Grosvenor II, a grandson; Gilbert Grosvenor La Gorce, a son of Dr. John Oliver La Gorce, who is the associate editor of the *Geographic* and the vice president and a trustee of the Society, and who has been Grosvenor's right-hand man for the past thirty-eight years; John Grosvenor Hutchison, a son of George W. Hutchison, who is the secretary and a trustee of the Society, who has been associated with Grosvenor and La Gorce for thirty-five years, and who impartially named his son after both of them; and Gilbert Grosvenor Edson, a grandson of the late John Joy Edson, a Washington banker who was an early trustee and treasurer of the Society. The National Geographic Society was founded in Washington in 1888 to promote "the increase and diffusion of geographic knowledge," and it finances, or helps to finance, expeditions which generally result in articles for its magazine. Many of Grosvenor's non-human namesakes were discovered in the course of such expeditions. Thus the fish named after Dr. Grosvenor, a blind specimen called *Bryconamericus grosvenori,* was extracted from the Urubamba River in southern Peru by the late Carl H. Eigenmann, an Indiana zoologist who had gone to South America on a grant from the Society. The Grosvenor sea shell is *Margarites grosvenori,* dredged up on a 1925 Society expedition carried out in the waters west of Greenland by the late William H. Dall, a paleontologist to whom it came as a surprise. "Since the Greenland seas have been industriously explored for mollusks since the time of Fabricius in 1780," he reported at a meeting of the Biological Society of Washington, "and not only the resident Danes but a multitude of Arctic explorers have paid particular attention to the shells, this (new one) was most unexpected." He went on to describe *Margarites grosvenori* as turbiniform, thin, translucent, and pearly white, with four and a half well-rounded whorls, a distinct suture, a minute nucleus, and a well-rounded base.

Gilbert Grosvenor Island, which is off the coast of Alaska, was discovered and christened by Vilhjalmur Stefansson, an old friend and admirer of Grosvenor's to whom the editor of the *Geographic* subsequently made a gift of the title of one of Stefansson's early books, "The Friendly Arctic." Stefansson had sent proofs of this volume to Grosvenor, beseeching him to suggest a title, and Grosvenor, who likes to look on the friendly side of geography, was pleased that after reading Stefansson's book he felt for the first time in his life that the Arctic was a friendly place. He made his recommendation accordingly. Stefansson thinks the title helped to sell the book, and in his preface he refers to Grosvenor as "that genius in editorship and public relations."

Grosvenor Glacier, in Peru, was officially sighted and named by Hiram Bingham during an expedition financed jointly by the National Geographic Society and Yale University. Grosvenor Trail and the Gilbert Grosvenor Mountain Range, both in the Antarctic, constitute a 1929 tribute to Grosvenor by Admiral Richard E. Byrd, to whom the Society had granted some $75,000 for exploration. Byrd later pressed upon Grosvenor a small rock from one of the Grosvenor Mountains, along with a card on which he wrote, "Presented to Gilbert Grosvenor with the highest regard from his friend Richard Byrd. This rock is from the Grosvenor Mountain System containing the Grosvenor Range." Grosvenor, who thinks that Byrd may have conjured up the Grosvenor Mountain System, which does not exist, simply in order to round out his sentence, feels that the range, which definitely exists, is enough of a good thing, and he has appreciatively placed the rock and card on a mantelpiece in his home in Bethesda, Maryland, which is on Grosvenor Lane, a road named after Grosvenor by his wife.

Mount Grosvenor, not to be confused with the Grosvenor Mountain Range, is in China, near the Tibetan border; it was named by Joseph F. Rock, an explorer who in 1927 headed a National Geographic Society expedition to southwestern China. The *Geographic* ran a color photograph of it in 1930, warmly describing it as "a mass of gneiss and granite which towers 20,000 feet above sea level." Grosvenor Lake, an Alaskan body of water twenty-eight miles long, was named by its discoverer, Dr. Robert F. Griggs, a Washington botanist and professor to whom the Society had granted financial assistance for several expeditions. Dr. Griggs, whose excursions have resulted in a number of *Geographic* articles, does not do things by halves, and he named an Alaskan mountain, somewhat smaller than the lake but adorned with pink granite slopes, after Dr. La Gorce. The Grosvenor plant, *Momordica grosvenori*, was discovered and named in 1937 in Kwangsi Province, China, by Walter T. Swingle, another Washington botanist benefiting from a Society grant. It is thought by the Chinese to possess aphrodisiac qualities, and Grosvenor's colleagues have subjected the editor of the *Geographic* to a certain amount of appropriate chaffing. Swingle did not stress this aspect of his plant, however, when he formally dedicated it. "I take pleasure in naming it *Momordica grosvenori*, in honor of Dr. Gilbert Grosvenor, who for many years has encouraged liberally the geographic and botanical exploration of China," he wrote in the *Journal of the Arnold Arboretum*, and he proceeded to describe it, in part, as follows:

Ab aliis speciebus Momordicae differt seminibus applanatis radialiter striatis sulcatisque, margine rima lata profunde percursis, embryone ovato-lenticulari quam semine multo minore, fructus pulpa dulcissima in sicco in massam fibrosam levem coalescente, tota superficie plantae (facie superiore folii excepta) pilis minutissimis nigris ornata, folii margine sparse irregulariterque hydathodibus instructo.

Dr. Grosvenor, who frankly confesses his inability to translate even the Grosvenor family motto, "*Nobilitatis virtus non stemma character*," which appears under the coat of arms embellishing his bookplates, enjoys these compliments as much as the next geographer, and he does not care to have anyone tamper with the Grosvenor names. He has, on occasion, made his attitude plain. In 1925, the United States Board on Geographic Names, established as part of the Department of the Interior by President Benjamin Harrison to standardize the names and spellings of geographic names on government maps, made a determined effort to change the names of Lake Grosvenor and Mt. La Gorce to something else, on the theory that topographical features should not be named after living persons. Grosvenor got wind of this scheme and, accompanied by La Gorce and Griggs, took the matter up at the White House with President Coolidge, who had been two classes ahead of him at Amherst. Coolidge instructed the board to leave the names alone, and moreover he chided the board, tersely, for even thinking of making the changes. Grosvenor is a modest man and he usually can't recall all of the things named after him, while La Gorce's attitude toward his mountain is so casual that he frequently calls it a lake, but the two men considered the Society's honor to be at stake and consequently became inexorable. "We felt that the suggested changes constituted a reflection on the Society," Grosvenor said recently when the incident was recalled to him. "The board was unfriendly to us at the time. It has since been revived by Secretary Ickes, and we now have a representative on it. It's a great compliment to have a lake named after you, and Mrs. Grosvenor and I hope to visit it some time." The Society was grateful to Coolidge for keeping the names of its two chief editors on the map, and in 1929 it elected him a trustee.

Grosvenor's friends feel that on the strength of his record he has every right to have a few topographical, zoological, and botanical items named after him. As editor of the *Geographic*, Grosvenor, whose doctorate (honorary) was conferred upon him in 1921 by Georgetown University and has since been buttressed by honorary degrees from Amherst, William and Mary, Lafayette, the University of Maryland, and the South Dakota State School of Mines, has done more than anyone else in the country to put geography on a broad, popular, and paying basis. In 1899, when Grosvenor, then twenty-three, came to the *Geographic* as assistant editor, the magazine, founded in Washington eleven years before, was a rather sedate and technical monthly which went to the one thousand members of the National Geographic Society, a rather sedate and technical group, many of them government scientists. It shared a single-room office in the capital with the American Forestry Association, and its outlook on geography was a narrow one, leading it to confine itself largely to such articles as "Geographic Methods in Geologic Investigation," "Studies of Glaciers," and so on. Its concept of finance was more flexible, and it had used up the proceeds of a good many life memberships, which then sold for fifty dollars, as working capital and was several thousand dollars in debt. Grosvenor, who belongs to an old Massachusetts family, was born on the European side of the Bosphorus, in Constantinople, where his father, the late Edwin A. Grosvenor, taught history at an American-endowed college; from his bedroom he could see Asia. Thus equipped with the financial perspective of a New Englander and the geographical insight of a man who had been brought up within sight of two continents, he had a more rigid view of money and a more limber view of geography than the Society had had up to then. He came to the conclusion that the magazine could be made profitable, and he came to another and not altogether unre-

lated conclusion that the science of geography covered practically everything there is and that a magazine devoted to its
interests should also cover practically everything there is. "A
revolutionary idea," he has since written. "Why not popularize
the science of geography and take it into the homes of the
people? Why not transform the Society's magazine from one
of cold geographic fact, expressed in hieroglyphic terms which
the layman could not understand, into a vehicle for carrying
the living, breathing, human-interest truth about this great
world of ours to the people? Would not that be the greatest
agency of all for the diffusion of geographic knowledge?"

Since 1903, when Grosvenor was promoted to the post of
editor-in-chief of the *Geographic*, it has treated its readers to
articles, many of them vividly illustrated in color, on aeronautics, the reindeer industry in Alaska, the tetrahedral principle
in kite structure, the geographical distribution of insanity in
the United States, snow crystals, the diamond mines of South
Africa, ostrich farming, elephant hunts in Siam, Chinese Jews,
"Queer Methods of Travel in Curious Corners of the World,"
Philippine head hunters, lighthouses, cancer in plants, pen-
ances in India, daily life in ancient Egypt, identification of the
stars, American battle monuments in France, the automobile
industry, "Prehistoric Telephone Days," the larger North
American mammals, the smaller North American mammals,
acorns as food, common mushrooms of the United States,
American berries, "Medicine Fakes and Fakers of All Ages,"
immigration, flags, dogs, cannibals, fish, turtles, lizards, birds,
butterflies, trees, flowers, the Alaskan brown bear, and the
Mellon Gallery, to name but a fraction of the subjects. Grosvenor once outlined his magazine's cosmic trend in the following words, which do only partial justice to it:

The subject matter covers almost the entire range of Nature, from
the ant to the elephant, from the humming bird to the trumpeter

swan, from tiny tropical fish to the gigantic whale, from the micro-scopic spores of mold to the mighty sequoia and eucalyptus trees. It deals with nearly every part of the earth, from the teeming pave-ments of New York and London to equatorial jungle and polar wastes.

Here, in a photograph, a solitary Moslem kneels beside his camel amid the dreary dunes of the desert, turns his face toward faraway Mecca, and strikes his turbaned brow against the sands in obei-sance at the hour of prayer. There, a handsome Romanian peasant girl, barefoot, in gaily embroidered dress, strides through the cool waters of a mountain stream, her water pitchers swinging from a stick across her shoulder, the joy of living in her eye and step; per-haps she is in love.

Even though Dr. Grosvenor blue-pencils all mention of cer-tain distasteful subjects sometimes associated with travel, such as bedbugs and poor hotel accommodations, the American Geographical Society, a more serious and technical geographi-cal group in Manhattan with which his organization is some-times confused by laymen, is inclined to think that his editorial policy is still a trifle too catholic, and professors of geography have occasionally protested to him that he is carrying things too far. The president of the National Geographic Society is calm and even triumphant in the face of such criticism. "Our interpretation of geography is very wide," he told a friend the other day. "When I see a subject that I think would be inter-esting to our million, two hundred thousand members, I don't scrutinize it to see if it's geographical." Grosvenor is a member of the American Geographical Society and a thoughtful student of this body's quarterly, which he pronounces excellent, authori-tative, and just the thing for its thirty-three hundred readers. Grosvenor's own position as a geographer has been adequately summed up by La Gorce, who once said, "Behind the term geography is exploration. Behind that is adventure, and just over the hill is romance. Under Dr. Grosvenor, these three elements are stepped into closer focus. The Chief has removed the technical padlocks from the science of geography."

Grosvenor's staff all call him Chief; they admire him as an intuitive idea man with a finger on the public's pulse. They also admire him for his scientific carpentry, which has blessed their Society with a million, two hundred thousand members at $3.50 a head annually; for a reserve fund, saved out of income, of nearly ten million dollars; and for just about the most commodious offices in Washington. The National Geographic Society is tax-free, by act of Congress, because it is considered an educational institution; its magazine is a membership rather than a subscription affair and the Society is owned by its members. It has a board, presided over by Grosvenor, of twenty-four trustees, including General Pershing, former Chief Justice Hughes, and Robert V. Fleming, president of the Riggs National Bank of Washington; it pays its editors and administrative officers generous salaries; and it has made contributions of nearly two million dollars toward expeditions, ranging from a thousand dollars for Admiral Robert E. Peary's trip to the North Pole in 1909 to two hundred thousand dollars spent on various stratosphere-balloon experiments in 1935, in the course of which Captains Albert W. Stevens and Orvil A. Anderson of the Army Air Corps piloted the world's largest balloon to a record altitude of 72,395 feet, or 13.71 miles, conversing easily with the earth by radio throughout the journey.

The Society has devoted another considerable portion of its income to the construction of several large, airy, modern buildings in which it is housed. Its circulation, paper-storage, and business departments, which together have five hundred employees, as many filing cabinets, and twenty-two electrically operated cash registers, occupy a five-story edifice on a railroad spur on the outskirts of the capital. As many as fifty thousand pieces of mail, mostly membership renewals, have come in there on a single day. The main editorial offices, as well as a library of fifteen thousand geographical books, which is open to the public, are in a row of buildings which stretch for two hundred and ninety-five feet and nine inches along Sixteenth Street, one of Washington's main thoroughfares. These quarters reflect some of the rewards of the Grosvenor policy of freeing geography from its shackles. The Chief's two-room office is a good deal larger than, say, the ballroom in the old Peter Cooper house on Lexington Avenue, and his four or five chief assistants, among them La Gorce, Hutchison, and his son, Melville Bell Grosvenor, occupy rooms almost as spacious. The Society's map-making division, whose annual output includes four or five ten-color wall maps, is quartered in a penthouse, and its photographic division has a plant which includes nine darkrooms, five printing and enlarging rooms, washing troughs equipped with water spigots that can be operated by treadles, and a twenty-by-twenty-four-inch camera built on a carriage that rolls on steel tracks.

The twenty or so editors of the *Geographic*, all of them notably polite individuals who are forever bowing one another through the sculptured bronze doors of their elevators, move in a leisurely welter of thick rugs, bookshelves stocked with British and American *Who's Who's*, encyclopedias, bound volumes of the *Geographic*, and geographical books published by the Society; interoffice memorandum slips with "Memorandum from Dr. Grosvenor," "Memorandum from Dr. La Gorce," or the like printed at the top; incoming correspondence stamped, in purple ink, "Commendation," "Criticism," or "Suggestions"; and photostatic copies of appreciative letters from generals, admirals, coördinators, and ex-Presidents to whom the Society has presented maps or turned over geographic research, much of it bearing on the war. The editors of the *Geographic* freshen up in rooms where the towels are hung under a hierarchy of name cards; in one room the cards read, from left to right, "Dr. Grosvenor, Dr. La Gorce, Mr. Fisher, Mr. M. B. Grosvenor, Mr. Simpich, Mr. Hildebrand, Mr. Bumstead, Dr. Williams, Mr. Borah, Mr. Riddiford, Mr. Canova, Mr. Vosburgh, Mr. L. J. Canova, Guests, Guests, Mr. Nicholas." For business errands around town, such as trips to the magazine's circulation annex or to its printers, the firm of Judd & Detweiler, the editors have a fleet of five chauffeur-driven cars. They lunch in three private dining rooms, drinking buttermilk, exchanging puns, and ordering excellent à-la-carte meals from menus on which prices are discreetly omitted. One of these dining rooms is reserved for Dr. Grosvenor, and he sometimes eats there alone, like the captain of a ship. This room adjoins a bathroom containing two marble shower baths, which in sticky weather are occasionally patronized not only by Dr. Grosvenor but other of the more important staff members. Next to the private dining rooms is a cafeteria where lesser employees lunch well and inexpensively but without access to as wide a selection of food as is afforded their betters. Here the sexes are segregated, a partition separating the men from the women. "We prefer not to mix 'em up," an officer of the Society once explained. "We feel the men are freer in their own room. If they want to swap a risqué anecdote or two, they can do it." Every now and then, private-dining-room delicacies are displayed, by mistake, in the cafeteria. On one of these occasions, a stenographer, sliding her tray along, pointed to a dish which had captured her fancy. "My goodness, no," said the counter maid. "That's the officers' liver."

The editors of the *Geographic*, few of whom have been with Dr. Grosvenor less than fifteen years, are, though grateful to the Chief for the perquisites of office which his successful stewardship has brought them, mildly vexed by what some of them suspect may be, professionally, his Achilles heel—a passion for birds. This interest is reflected in the magazine as often as they fail to talk him out of it. Two years ago, Grosvenor had the Society publish a cumulative index to the *Geographic* covering the period from 1899, when he became an editor, through 1940; this volume contained seventy-nine entries under the heading "Birds," as compared with forty-eight under "Volcanoes," thirty-two under "Deserts," nineteen under "Glaciers," and eighteen under "Earthquakes." Grosvenor fell in love with birds in 1913, when, in his thirty-ninth year, he acquired a hundred-acre farm in Bethesda, Maryland, and found that it was full of what the *Geographic* subsequently described, at one time or another, as "Nature's children," "feathered foragers," "masters of flight," and "winged denizens of woodland, stream, and marsh." In the issue of June, 1913, he ran a series of color photographs of "Fifty Common Birds of Farm and Orchard," and he followed this, in the same issue, with a reprint of an article in *Bird Life* by Frank Chapman, called "Birds May Bring You More Happiness than the Wealth of the Indies," and with an article of his own, entitled "Our Policemen of the Air," in which he pointed out that birds were man's best friends. Next year the March issue's table of contents included "Encouraging Birds Around the Home," the May issue contained "Birds of Town and Country" as well as "A Naturalist's Journey Around Vera Cruz and Tampico," in which Chapman again affectionately discussed birds, and the July number featured "Hunting with the Lens," a series of bird photographs accompanied by descriptive text.

The outbreak of the first World War late that July caused the *Geographic* to turn from birds to such timely subjects as "The France of Today," "Belgium: the Innocent Bystander," and "The German Nation," but birds continued to fascinate

Dr. Grosvenor. He installed a number of bird boxes on his farm, kept pans of fresh water around, and in general made things so attractive for birds that in 1915 the late Henry W. Henshaw, who was then chief of the Biological Survey of the Department of Agriculture, after an astonished look around the farm, delegated Dr. Wells W. Cooke of the Survey to make an official count of the nesting birds on an acre adjoining his host's farmhouse and barns. Dr. Cooke found fifty-nine pairs of birds with young or eggs in the nests on this acre, and he pronounced this the highest number of land birds inhabiting one acre in the continental United States that had yet been reported to the Department of Agriculture or to any Audubon Society. Grosvenor subsequently wrote about the incident, by invitation, in *Bird-Lore*, the bimonthly organ of the Audubon Societies of the United States, reporting:

I attribute our success primarily to shooting the Sparrows and driving all cats away. . . . We did everything we could for the comfort of our birds; for instance, we put on twigs little pieces of the oil-paper that our butter was wrapped in, and we left mud in convenient places for the Martins. The Catbirds used the oil-paper for their nests; in fact, they used all kinds of scraps. Imagine the delight of the family when, on examining one of the Catbirds' nests in the autumn, we found one of the children's hair-ribbons, and also a piece of the old dress of the baby!

Grosvenor lists his ornithological record in his account of his accomplishments in *Who's Who*, thus: "Country Home, 'Wild Acres,' at Bethesda, Md., is a bird paradise, holding Audubon Soc. and U.S. Biol. Survey record for greatest number of land birds nesting in one acre adjacent house in U.S., 59 pairs in 1915." This piece of information is retained in the current edition of *Who's Who*, although the editor of the *Geographic* is not positive that the record still holds. He tore down his farmhouse and barns in 1928 and built a larger stone house, and he gloomily suspects that around that time a flock of purple martins moved off to the nearby Chevy Chase Club, where he often plays golf and, he is afraid, recognizes his former guests. He is inclined to give himself the benefit of the doubt, however, partly on the theory that the continuing publicity in *Who's Who* may attract new birds to his place.

Five days a week and eight or nine months of the year, Dr. Grosvenor drives ten miles from his place in Bethesda to his Washington office. He has, besides, a winter cottage in Coconut Grove, Florida, and he spends a month or two of each summer on Cape Breton Island in Nova Scotia, in a large Victorian house which his wife inherited from her father, Alexander Graham Bell, inventor of the telephone. There, before the war, Grosvenor, often accompanied by his son Melville, did a lot of sailing in a fifty-seven-foot yawl—named the Elsie, after his wife—which his father-in-law gave him many years ago. He is a founder of the Cruising Club of America, which organized the Bermuda yacht races, and is an enthusiast about sailing picnics, as well as about golf and bridge. The *Geographic* is never far from his mind, however, and he is just as likely to generate an idea for it while on vacation in Florida or Nova Scotia as in his office. "Get piece on lend-lease," he will jot down in a memorandum to one of his associates, and three or four months later the *Geographic* will come out with a timely article on lend-lease, illustrated by photographs showing British children eating American vegetables and eggs and bearing such captions as "Who Wouldn't Share His Vegetables to Keep These Little Allies Healthy and Smiling!" and " 'Uncle Sam Is a Good Egg,' British School Children Agree."

As befits a man in his position, the president of the National Geographic Society has traveled a good deal to other places besides Florida and Nova Scotia. On his journeys, he is generally interviewed by reporters here and there, and he has taken advantage of this circumstance to disseminate propaganda in behalf of birds. In the spring of 1935, when Grosvenor, who has five daughters, went to Arizona to see one of them graduate from school, his visit was described by the Tucson *Daily Citizen* in a typical account:

Gilbert H. Grosvenor, president of the National Geographic Society and for thirty-five years editor of the Society's magazine, was concentrating on a house finch with the aid of high-powered binoculars, while sitting on the porch of a local inn this morning. Turning to a page on which there was a number of colored bird pictures, he remarked, "Color is a bit too vivid in the illustration but it is necessary in order to contrast the local finch with its eastern relation. You see, I am very interested in birds," he explained.

Grosvenor's affection for birds has been encouraged by one of his close friends, Dr. Alexander Wetmore, a trustee of the National Geographic Society, who is also the secretary of the Smithsonian Institution and one of the world's leading ornithological authorities. In 1937, just before Grosvenor and his wife left by Clipper for the Far East, Wetmore tipped him off to the fact that Wake Island, which was on their itinerary, was one of the rare habitats of the fairy tern, a small, snow-white bird which has the extraordinary habit of not building a nest but simply laying its eggs, precariously, on the branch of a tree. Grosvenor duly observed this phenomenon when he got to Wake and took several photographs of a nestless egg which he discovered there. Arriving in China, he was interviewed by the Peiping *Chronicle*, and said, "An interesting species of bird was found by the Clipper passengers on Wake Island. The bird lays its eggs on branches of trees about two fingers' width and hatches the egg there. There is no nest at all." Grosvenor, who rarely forgets either birds or the National Geographic Society, found journalists in China sympathetically disposed toward 'these interlocking interests, and he managed to plant in another Chinese paper, the *China Press*, an item which read in part:

"This is our first visit to China," Mr. Grosvenor said, "although we travelled through Manchuria in 1928. Our society has more than two thousand members in this country. . . . Among them is your Mr. E. S. Wilkinson, who has made such excellent studies of bird life. Birds are my particular interest."

The Grosvenors were the first married couple to fly across the Pacific as paying passengers. Four years later, Juan Trippe, president of Pan American Airways, after reflecting on the matter, sent them a congratulatory letter, along with a certificate which said:

Know Ye By All These Presents That: Dr. Gilbert Grosvenor and Elsie Grosvenor on the 8th day of May 1937 sailed on the wings of a Clipper of the Pan American Airways System across the Pacific Ocean from Alameda, California, to Hong Kong, China. . . .

And, therefore, for this good and sufficient reason let it be known that Dr. Gilbert Grosvenor and Elsie Grosvenor have been accepted into the Domain of Phoebus Apollo as the first revenue married couple to have flown from and to the places designated above.

Grosvenor has had this certificate framed, and he keeps it in one of his two offices at the *National Geographic*, together with several honorary degrees, a framed letter from Admiral Richard E. Byrd, signed photographs of Theodore Roosevelt, Lincoln Ellsworth, and General Pershing; an autographed picture showing Admiral Robert E. Peary, discoverer of the North Pole, shaking hands with Roald Amundsen, discoverer of the South Pole, on the occasion of a 1913 National Geographic Society banquet; a roll-top desk which used to belong to Alexander Graham Bell; a bundle marked "Books Autographed by Gen. Artemas Ward 1795, belongs to G.H.G.," and a few tins of Ovaltine. Around four or five in the afternoon, just before he leaves for the day, the editor of the *Geographic*, who does not touch alcohol or tobacco or accept advertisements for them in his periodical, pours some powdered Ovaltine onto a shoehorn, deposits it in a Lily cup filled with water, stirs it with a penholder, and drinks it down with a pleased expression.

Dr. Grosvenor, since his return from the Far East in 1937, has evolved a theory that the fairy tern glues its eggs to the branch. Dr. Wetmore disagrees with this. The two men have remained friends, however, and in 1939 they collaborated in editing "The Book of Birds," a two-volume collection of ornithological articles, most of which had appeared in the *Geographic*. The title pages of these books, which were published by the Society, contain the legend "Edited by Gilbert Grosvenor, LL.D., Litt.D., D.Sc., and Alexander Wetmore, Ph.D., D.Sc." Grosvenor's name is in slightly larger type than Wetmore's. Grosvenor, who does not claim to have done more work on the books than Wetmore, attributes this disparity to the fact that he was away when the books went to press. He believes that staff members who had been left in charge of the project simply put his name in bigger letters because he is ten years older than Dr. Wetmore. "It was a tribute to my age," he says. "I really wanted it smaller than Wetmore's." Grosvenor is regarded with considerable veneration in his office, and, according to those who know the Society well, the title pages were simply a reflection of the *National Geographic* state of mind, in which the Chief's name just naturally seems larger than anyone else's. All in all, the Society has done its best to make the name of Gilbert Grosvenor a household word, or two household words. His name appears three hundred and seventy-one times in the Society's "Cumulative Index to the National Geographic Magazine, 1899 to 1940 Inclusive," which credits the *Geographic*, during this period, with having run two hundred and sixty-nine pieces of text—including addresses at annual dinners, captions on maps, and so on—by Gilbert Grosvenor, two hundred photographs by Gilbert Grosvenor, and twenty-eight photographs *of* Gilbert Grosvenor.

The second World War, like the first, made the editor of the *Geographic* go easy on birds in his magazine, post-Pearl Harbor issues of which featured articles on United States food production, the Alaskan highway, the Coast Guard, Army dogs, convoys, aircraft carriers, women in uniform, and military and naval insignia, but he knows that wars are fleeting affairs compared to birds and he did not wait for the end of the conflict before threatening to resume doing justice, editorially, to his favorite topic. "The Chief has been begging us to run a series of color photographs on the wrens of Australia for the past three years," a *Geographic* recently told an acquaintance in mid-conflict. "Everyone conspires to keep him from using these goddam birds. We keep putting him off, but he'll sneak them in any month now." Birds are perhaps never completely off Grosvenor's mind; once, referring to Elisha Hanson, a *Geographic* trustee and the Society's lawyer, he said, "He's a warm personal friend, and furthermore he's intensely interested in pigeons." Hanson is a shrewd and capable attorney, whose other clients include the American Newspaper Publishers Association and the American Chemical Society, but a good many people around Washington think Grosvenor was glad to get him as a trustee in 1936 more because ten years before he had written a *Geographic* article entitled "Man's Feathered Friends of Longest Standing: Peoples of Every Clime and Age Have Lavished Care and Affection Upon Lovely Pigeons."

For all his preoccupation with birds Dr. Grosvenor tries to keep a clear head about them, and, in published descriptions of bird pictures, to avoid phrases which might be considered too fulsome or, as he puts it, "sob stuff." "These are very inter-

BIRDS OF A FEATHER

esting legends," he wrote a few years ago in an interoffice memorandum about the proofs of the captions for a series of photographs of birds which migrate between North and South America. " 'Perennial emissaries of friendship,' Plate 1, was a good phrase but strikes me as perhaps unlikely to occur in conversation. 'Mother' and 'her' should be used sparingly when referring to birds. See Plate V. G.H.G." Grosvenor is a polite and almost diffident man, with the outwardly gentle manner of a ninth-generation New Englander who knows precisely which Colonial governors and Salem witches were his forebears, but his interoffice communications, generally penned in a rather wavy longhand, can be outspoken and at times even sharp. In 1940, for example, he dispatched the following chit to Franklin L. Fisher, chief of the *Geographic's* illustration division:

I wonder if you realize the steady march of your department to the increasing use of half page illustrations, notwithstanding repeated protests by J.O.L. and myself.

The climax is reached in this . . . article for which 22 half page pictures are scheduled, and only 8 full pages. A black and white page costs $750 approximately, a half page $375. Picture on page 406 costs $375 to print. It is not worth five cents in this size; 30 years ago this plate would be permissible but used today it stamps the Nat Geog Mag as *out of date*. Several other plates . . . are as bad or worse; they should not have been used in any size.

Then again the use of half page plates as on pages 424, 429 etc. is increasing though setting plates thus kills the text alongside. I have been obliged, much to my regret, to allow this wretched assortment to go to press, as to change now would disrupt the printing schedule.

The "J.O.L." in the note is the *Geographic's* associate editor and right-hand man, Dr. John Oliver La Gorce. Mr. Fisher, who has been with the magazine only twenty-eight years as against La Gorce's thirty-eight and Grosvenor's forty-four, felt himself placed in the mortifying position of a censured junior partner when he received this communication. A year or so later, however, he had rallied to a point where, in discussing a projected article on "Fruitful Shores of the Finger Lakes," he suggested to Grosvenor that it include the picture of a memorial to Eugene Zimmerman, an old *Judge* cartoonist who signed himself "Zim" and who, like Fisher, used to live in Horseheads, New York, a town in the Finger Lakes region. Grosvenor, whose travels had never taken him to Horseheads, responded to this suggestion without much enthusiasm. He wrote:

In an area so packed with great achievers and great events and great factories etc etc, for the Nat Geog Mag to devote a half page to this artist, when so many more important matters must be omitted, seems to me contrary to my long standing policy and I must regretfully omit this local hero, Eugene Zimmerman, I say this with no disrespect to him. Lack of Space and a Proper Sense of Proportion must govern. This article is planned to interest and please all our members. Andrew D. White, First President and seer of Cornell University, L. H. Bailey, America's foremost botanical writer, also of Ithaca, are examples of residents of this region far more important than E. Zimmerman. Then there was our good friend Richtmyer. Really we'd make ourselves ridiculous to force him on our readers.

Mr. Fisher, who regards Zimmerman as the father of the comic strip, felt worse than ever after this, but a few months later his spirits were raised by the following interoffice message:

This working dog series, text and paintings, is one of the finest things the Geographic has ever published. I congratulate you on guiding this magnificent story to a most successful completion. I know how much time and thought you gave to it.

I want too to congratulate you on bringing through to the gratifying result the Hayes-Herget contribution in the October number. You directed this work from the beginning. The result is a masterpiece, and a great tribute to your ability in selecting contributors and human interest subjects for paintings. Also it is a tribute to your staying powers and tenacity, your Chevy Chase activities help all this along, so get as much on the golf course as you can.*

G. H. G.

* footnote: 18 holes limit for one day recommended.

"The Chief is no man to bear a grudge," Fisher has since remarked. "His only real interest is the *National Geographic*. I think he sort of sets the tone for the whole organization."

Grosvenor began setting the tone for the Society and its magazine from the day he joined them in 1899. He got his initial job as assistant editor as the result of an excellent undergraduate record at Amherst, romance, and the fact that he was an identical twin. Gilbert and his twin brother, the late Edwin Prescott Grosvenor, were born in 1875, in Constantinople, where their father, Edwin A. Grosvenor, was professor of history at Robert College. When the boys were three, their mother, who wanted to get them away from the Russo-Turkish War, took them to live at their maternal grandfather's house in Millbury, Massachusetts. They returned to Constantinople when they were seven. In 1890, when they were fifteen, their father came back to the United States to teach at Amherst, and the two boys, after a couple of years at Worcester Academy, entered Amherst in 1893. There they constituted the college tennis-doubles team, won many scholastic prizes, belonged to Phi Beta Kappa, dressed alike, and confused most of their classmates. In the summer of 1897, shortly after their graduation, the late E. S. Martin, one of the founders of the pre-Luce *Life*, wrote, in a department called "This Busy World," which he then conducted in *Harper's Weekly*:

Interest at the Commencement at Amherst seems to have been divided between President Gates and the Grosvenor twins . . . both of whom were graduated this year and both with distinction. Both of them were included in the eight Seniors who had Commencement parts. . . . At the alumni dinner the graduates had fun with the twins, and did their best to have them put on exhibition. It is a good plan to have as much seemly fun at Commencement as possible.

Mrs. Alexander Graham Bell, a lady with several marriageable daughters, read this passage with interest. Her husband was a friend of Professor Grosvenor, and she invited the twins to a houseparty at the Bell summer place in Nova Scotia. Her daughter Elsie, who was not confused by the twins, took a special fancy to Gilbert. A year or so later, she came to the conclusion that Englewood, New Jersey, where Gilbert was by then teaching languages, algebra, and chemistry at a boys' school, was too far from Washington, D.C., where the Bells lived, and she solicited her father's advice on this problem. Bell was then president of the National Geographic Society, which his father-in-law, Gardiner Greene Hubbard, the first man to organize a telephone company, had founded in 1888 as a sort of clearing house where government scientists, exploring this country in search of natural resources, might compare notes. Their meetings took place at the Cosmos Club, and the Society started its magazine as a means of keeping a permanent record of their discussions. Bell wrote Professor Grosvenor that he was looking for a capable young man to brighten up his magazine and asked, with tactful impartiality, whether either of the twins would be interested in such an assignment. Brother Edwin chivalrously shook his head, and Gilbert, animated by a sudden enthusiasm for geography, took the job. He married Elsie Bell the next year, and he has since commented, with some satisfaction, on the fact that his and Edwin's tastes were not invariably identical. "We were very much alike except we never fell in love with the same girl, which was very fortunate," he has said.

Edwin Grosvenor, who died in 1930, became a lawyer. He was a partner in Cadwalader, Wickersham & Taft, and divided

his time between New York and Washington, where he
occasionally posed as the editor of the *Geographic*. Unlike Gilbert, he loved to smoke, and he sometimes caused a certain
amount of confusion by strolling through the *Geographic*
offices puffing a large cigar and greeting editors in a proprietary
way. One morning the late George Judd, head of Judd &
Detweiler, the printing firm which the *Geographic* has patronized since 1888 and which it now provides annually with a
million dollars' worth of business, thought he recognized his
client on a Washington street. "Can I take you downtown,
Mr. Grosvenor?" he asked, stopping his car. "Why, yes," said
Edwin. "Now about these color plates of 'Fifty Common Birds
of Farm and Orchard,'" Judd began. His passenger answered
him rather offhandedly, and Judd, after dropping him at his
office, called up La Gorce in some anxiety. "What's the matter
with the Chief?" he said. "He didn't seem to want to discuss
the birds. Is he mad at me?"

As president of the National Geographic Society, Alexander
Graham Bell put the *National Geographic Magazine* on a
membership rather than a subscription basis. His son-in-law has
continued this practice, and although it is possible, by paying
fifty cents a year extra, to subscribe to the magazine without
joining the Society, most of the million, two hundred thousand
people who receive the *Geographic* prefer to be members and
have been nominated for the Society by other members. A few
have not been. "In the case of a police magistrate, of course, no
nomination is required," Dr. Grosvenor has said, by way of
giving an example. He does not care to say whether anyone has
ever actually been blackballed by the Society, but he still feels
that membership is more than just another word for a subscription. "Most people think our membership principle is
phony," he recently observed, without rancor, "but it is per-

fectly sound. The members really own the Society and, in addition to receiving the magazine, and the maps which we publish separately, share in the responsibility for the scientific expeditions which we sponsor." Grosvenor's attitude was made clear in a foreword he contributed to "The Valley of Ten Thousand Smokes," a book, published in 1922 by the Society, in which Dr. Robert F. Griggs described the study of a volcanic eruption in Alaska which he made on a Society expedition. The foreword says:

This remarkable exploration of Mt. Katmai by Professor Griggs and his associates, which continued for five years, was financed by the 750,000 members of the National Geographic Society, each of whom, millionaire and college professor, captain of industry and clerk, had an equal share in its support. Every member of the organization may thus derive considerable satisfaction that he or she has assisted to bring about such important additions to our knowledge of the young and active planet upon which we live.

The books the Society publishes, which can be bought only at headquarters, are generally illustrated in color and are about birds, dogs, fish, horses, insects, wildflowers, and the like. Their contents are usually taken bodily from the magazine, so the prices are very low. Reports on the results of the Society's expeditions, published in these books and in the magazine, help make Society members feel like members rather than subscribers, and Washington, D. C., members are put even more firmly in this state of mind by being invited to subscribe, at a nominal fee, to a series of weekly illustrated lectures, sponsored by the Society at Constitution Hall, from November to April. The hall seats four thousand, and the lectures, which in the past year have included first-hand reports on Java, the Philippines, Australia, Singapore, and Alaska, are invariably oversubscribed. The *National Geographic* people are proud of the fact that their members, of whom more than eighty per cent sign up year after year, represent many strata of society. In 1941 the Society analyzed its magazine's circulation in a booklet which, under the heading "How National Geographic Family Heads Earn Their Incomes," listed five hundred and twenty-nine categories of paid-up members, among them farmers (36,816), bankers (15,084), barbers (1,557), bartenders (39), clergymen (27,843), college presidents (456), senators (159), congressmen (123), dentists and dental surgeons (11,715), elevator operators (237), executives (13,710), clerks (32,589), college matrons (261), housewives (39,543), lighthouse keepers (126), masseurs (156), physicians and surgeons (53,514), poets (15), philanthropists (9), tropical-fish raisers (3), undertakers (3,000), politicians (228), road builders (207), roll-turners (33), and royalty (114). By means of the rather cozy editorial tone which pervades the *Geographic*, Grosvenor has managed to communicate to many of his readers a feeling that they are indeed members of a gigantic family. This notion has brought him many affectionate letters, but it has also let him in for a few severe family rebukes.

"I had the pleasure of having the *National Geographic Magazine* in my home a good many years," one of these ran. "All that met the eye was interesting and upbuilding. Therefore it was with surprise I read in the Feb. '43 issue the phrase, 'An occasional round American oath.' I never read such an expression in the *Geographic* before. I am very sorry to admit that some of our men do take God's name in vain, but it surely ought not be called an American trait."

In Grosvenor's early days with the Society, it was even more literally a family affair. In 1903 Grosvenor's in-laws presented the Society with a building which housed it for many years and now contains its library; they also put up the money for a decoration, known as the Hubbard Gold Medal, which the Society has awarded, "in recognition of outstanding achievements in the field of geography," to Peary, Amundsen, Sir Ernest Shackleton, Stefansson, Byrd, Lindbergh, Mrs. Lindbergh, Amelia Earhart, and Roy Chapman Andrews, among others. In the early nineteen-hundreds, Grosvenor used to invoke his wife's aid in reading manuscripts and proofs, and he published several articles by his father about Russia, Siberia, Constantinople, and other places. His relationship with his father-in-law, who died in 1922, was very close, and Bell was delighted with the way the *Geographic's* circulation grew under Grosvenor's direction. "I remember well," Bell said, on the occasion of the 1906 presentation of the Hubbard Medal, to Peary, "when the mantle of your first president, Mr. Hubbard, fell on my shoulders and we looked at this little seed that he helped plant. Could we ever suppose it could grow into the great national organization that we have today? That little seed! And yet I can still remember when we congratulated ourselves upon a thousand members, but today we number eighteen thousand members. This little seed has grown into a tree and covers the whole world. Wherever Americans are, there we find members of the National Geographic Society."

Grosvenor greatly admired his father-in-law, and when Bell, in whose life the telephone was simply one of a number of interests, sent the *Geographic* pieces on eugenics, longevity, the future of the airplane, "Our Heterogeneous System of Weights and Measures," and certain inventions of his—a man-lifting kite and a tetrahedral radio tower—the editor of the *Geographic* did not reject them. He even became a party to a little joke of Bell's; the inventor, venturing rather far afield, contributed three articles to the *Geographic*—"Extinct Reptiles Found in Nodules," "Notes on the Remarkable Habits of Certain Turtles and Lizards," and "Purple Veil: A Romance of the Sea," which was about fish—under the nom de plume H. A. Largelamb, an anagram of A. Graham Bell. Grosvenor's brother-in-law, David Fairchild, an outstanding botanist, who married another daughter of Mr. Largelamb's, was also an early contributor to Grosvenor's magazine. So was the late William Howard Taft, a second cousin of Grosvenor's, who produced *Geographic* articles upon such diverse subjects as Bermuda, the League of Nations, the Lincoln Memorial, the Philippines, and "Washington (D.C.): Its Beginning, Its Growth, and Its Future." Grosvenor has always paid a good deal of editorial attention to the capital; a couple of years ago, when the Society appeared before the Committee on the District of Columbia of the Senate in order to ask that its exemption from taxation as an educational institution, which the Board of Commissioners of the District of Columbia wanted to annul, be continued, it was able to point out that its magazine had published seventeen illustrated articles on the District of Columbia and that these articles had had a total distribution of more than sixteen million copies. The Society also pointed out that a weekly school bulletin on current geographical matters which it publishes went to over thirty thousand public-school teachers in the United States. Its request was granted.

Taft, who later became successively President of the United States and a trustee of the Society, was a considerable help to his young cousin in the early days of the *National Geographic*. He presented the Hubbard Medal to Shackleton in 1910, and he often turned up, and sometimes spoke, at the annual dinners which the Society gave in Washington. One of the things Grosvenor feels most strongly about, as an editor, is that paragraphs should be short, and his gratitude for Taft's influential and continuing support did not blind him to the fact that his kinsman, as a writer, was given to sensational violations of this principle. "Break this up into short paragraphs," he once instructed an associate who had brought him a piece of Taft copy. Grosvenor's subordinate called the Chief's attention to the fact that an editor had already broken up the manuscript into one-sentence paragraphs but that the ex-President's sentences were rather long. "Well, break up the sentences," said Grosvenor. "The Bible does it. That's why people read the Bible. And that's why they read the *National Geographic*."

When Gilbert Grosvenor first became an editor of the *National Geographic*, several of the trustees of the parent Society, which in those days was publishing the periodical at a loss, felt that it should be established as a commercial publication, available to anyone who wished to subscribe and not merely to Society members, and completely apart from the other activities of the Society, such as its lectures and its expeditions to remote parts of the world. Grosvenor argued for the chummy policy of selling memberships in the Society instead of selling subscriptions to the magazine. He wanted the magazine to be one of the perquisites of membership. He won out. In view of the magazine's current circulation, its continuing tax-free position as an educational institution, and its success in rolling up a reserve fund of some ten million dollars, Grosvenor's insistence upon the membership principle appears to have been sound. This principle not only makes the readers of the *Geographic* feel as though they belonged to a club but also has been a factor in bringing the Society unsolicited legacies which total more than $100,000. The first of these was bequeathed in 1911 by Miss Jane M. Smith of Pittsburgh, who left the Society a trust fund of $5,000 with the provision that "the net income thereof be used for the purpose of creating life members of the organization in cases where worthy and competent persons are not able to pay for such memberships." A life membership costs a hundred dollars, and Dr. Grosvenor, who has been the guiding force of the Society since 1903 and its president since

1920, is a man of gentle breeding who would just as soon push a lady into a puddle as ask someone whether he had an extra hundred dollars on him. Grosvenor's disinclination to inquire into people's finances has led the Society to bestow Jane M. Smith Life Memberships on a number of persons who perhaps did not strictly belong in the category outlined by their benefactor—among them Hiram Bingham, a Connecticut explorer and politician who was and still is well off; the late Cornelius A. Pugsley, a wealthy Peekskill congressman and bank president; the late Sir Wilfred Grenfell; the late André Citroën, the French automobile manufacturer; Gene Buck, a well-to-do songwriter; and King Leopold III of the Belgians, a well-to-do king at the time of his award (1936).

Most of the Smith life members, who now number sixty-four, have, however, been worthy scientists of moderate means. Dr. Grosvenor, a man who gets fussed only when he is introducing speakers at Society dinners, is not given to worrying over the rich men who have slipped scot free into his domain, any more than he is over the fact that his loose conception of geography as a science which covers practically everything is sometimes regarded with a fishy eye by other geographers, or over the occasional criticisms which come in to him from readers. In fact, he solicits criticism, and once a year the Society plies a few thousand members with questions, on a form headed "The Spirit of Constructive Coöperation," on which they are invited to criticize the magazine in a constructive, coöperative way. Grosvenor's secretary, Miss Sibyl P. Peck, who has been with him for thirty-two years, makes a digest of the filled-in forms, which are known in the office as Spirit-of-Constructive-Coöperation slips, and places it on Grosvenor's desk, an enormous piece of furniture that is generally overflowing with maps. A recent digest included these comments from readers:

Think you are slighting Florida.
I am sick of picturesque native costumes.
Did not care for the Cats.
Captions poor.
Text poor.
Reading matter not very interesting.
Europe, Asia, and Africa do not interest us.
Don't take us through any more Himalayas or over any more glaciers.
Don't care for North and South Pole articles.
Don't care for prehistoric bones, carvings, or figures.
Washington, D.C., too often given space.
————'s style of putting his stuff on paper gives me a headache.
Less tiresome discourse.
All articles sound as if written by same person.
Object to immature, Sunday style of articles.
Birds—less.
Authors are not all they should be.

Grosvenor, who also receives hundreds of letters a year telling him he is running the most wonderful magazine in the world, thinks that pictures are more important than words. He likes to point out that the *Geographic* was a pioneer in the use of flashlight photographs of wild animals and in the use of color photography, since it has published, among other scoops, the first autochrome photographs taken on the ocean bottom, the first natural-color photographs of the Arctic, the first natural-color photograph of an eclipse, and the first natural-color photograph taken in the stratosphere. He does not believe that his magazine's text and captions are poor or that his authors, of whom he is one, are not all they should be. *National Geographic* captions, called "legends" in the office, are composed by a staff working under the supervision of Grosvenor's son, Melville, but their tone was set long ago by Gilbert Grosvenor. The editor of the *Geographic* has not always been in sympathy with the odd characters whom he has helped to publicize, and a somewhat detached tone has occasionally crept into the captions under their photographs. A series of pictures, published in 1913, of religious maniacs in India produced such legends as:

In other countries incorrigible idlers degenerate into vagrants, who are often a danger to the community. In India they can pursue a more decorous course and become honored ascetics.

After a little practice, lying on one of these beds of spikes is by no means as uncomfortable as it looks.

The rogue in the picture pretends that both his legs are cut off.

Under a picture of a man buried alive up to his nose was the legend:

This is regarded as a feat of heroic sanctity and may always be relied on to produce abundant offerings from the admiring laity.

Again, in the course of an article on the head-hunters of northern Luzon, the *Geographic* ran two pictures, one of a decapitated corpse bound to a pole, the other of the same corpse tossed into a pit. The first was rather jauntily captioned:

An unlucky Ifugao head-hunter who lost his own head.

and the second:

To lose one's head is considered a terrible family disgrace, so that the burial of the offender is a most unceremonious affair.

As long ago as 1902, when he was attending one of the Society's Constitution Hall illustrated lectures, Grosvenor began to realize that the public should not be shielded from horror pictures. The subject of the talk was a volcanic explosion in Martinique, to which the Society had sent an expedition; Grosvenor had instructed the speaker to omit most of his photographs of dead bodies. "I sat next to a couple of young women of fine Washington families," Grosvenor later told a friend, with the air of a man who had made a useful professional discovery, "and they kept asking where the dead bodies were." Since then, Grosvenor has seen to it that his magazine does not altogether ignore the gruesome side of life, but he prefers friendly pictures and friendly text. "Although in time of war I think it's permissible to point out things you don't like about your enemies, we prefer to print only what is of a kindly nature," he has said, and this editorial friendliness has always applied to animals as well as to human beings. At one time or another, for instance, the *Geographic* has published contributions entitled "Guernsey, the Friendly Island," "Friendly Crows in Festive Panoply," "Friendly Journeys in Japan," "Friends of Our Forests," "Our Friend, the Frog," "Our Friends, the Bees," "Our Friends, the French," "The Crow, Bird Citizen of Every Land: A Feathered Rogue Who Has Many Fascinating Traits and Many Admirable Qualities Despite His Marauding Propensities," and "Potent Personalities—Wasps and Hornets: Though Often Painfully Stung, Mankind Profits Immeasurably from the Pest-Killing Activities of These Fiery Little Flyers."

The editor of the *Geographic* likes to feel that the countries and individuals described in his magazine are in good spirits. He once ran a piece called "Smiling, Happy Philippines," and a caption adorning a picture entitled "Some Jolly Sicilian Boys" had this to say:

Though they are all of them poorer than Job, they are as happy as the birds in May, and if a few pennies are forthcoming there is no repressing their high spirits.

A few years ago, in the course of an article of his own, Grosvenor remarked, under a picture labelled "Aw Come On In—The Water's Fine":

New York policemen develop bad eyesight in the vicinity of park fountains on hot days, and those young Americans who play such an important part in the publishing business, distributing hundreds of thousands of newspapers, realize the visual deficiencies of these guardians of law and order. The bluecoat saunters off to the farthest corner of his beat and the boys jump into the fountain.

Grosvenor likes to feel that the bluecoats in Washington are as friendly a lot as their New York colleagues. One morning, as he was being driven into town by his chauffeur, he was stopped by a cop for speeding. The president of the National Geographic Society leaned out of the window and beckoned to the officer. "I'm Dr. Gilbert Grosvenor," he said. The policeman waved him on.

Dr. Grosvenor is only rarely beset by a mild feeling of cynicism about life and geography, and he has never allowed it to gain the upper hand. His kindly outlook always prevails in the end. Some years ago he devoted an entire issue of the *Geographic* to an article of his own about the United States, entitled "The Land of the Best." One of his captions, which appeared under a picture called "Looking Down Upon a Forest of Skyscrapers: New York City," tells as much about the author, in a way, as it does about Manhattan:

Upon the top of one of these man-made mountains there is the same peaceful quiet as on any mountain top. No sound from the streets below comes up this distance. Men on the sidewalks are infinitesimal dots, darting hither and yon. Looking down upon them, one is inclined to reflect what puny beings humans are, and from this lofty point of view almost forgets his sympathy for their personal interests. Then comes the realization that this mountain was built by these puny beings from materials dug out of the earth in a crude state, purified, shaped, and fastened together in a manner that will make it stand practically for all time, and then a feeling of reverence for the human brain—that God-given boon which has made these things possible. Note the men on the tower in the foreground.

Grosvenor's piety and attention to detail are qualities which the twelve hundred thousand members of the National Geographic Society on the whole appreciate, and they do not object to his passion for the use of quotation marks, which he feels tend to breathe life into otherwise commonplace phrases. A typical *Geographic* caption, under a picture of a sow suckling its litter, reflects this editorial principle:

"Pigs is pigs," but after the first few days each has his own special place at the "table."

The *Geographic's* readers also seem to enjoy their magazine's fearless use of the cliché. Its captions are often rich mines for the student of common usage. For example:

Off to a Winter Morning's Work: The hardy New England farmer is up betimes of a winter morning when Nature slumbers beneath a blanket of snow, and an overcoat would be useless baggage to him as he fares forth to his labors.

Moreover, to judge from their letters, *Geographic* readers look with favor upon Grosvenor's policy of running a good many pictures of lightly clad young people, generally of the colored races in far-off lands. Grosvenor knows that the *Geographic* is read by a great many ladies, so, in addition to pictures of girls, he makes a point of running occasional photographs, or paintings, of handsome young men, some of whom, being natives of tropical regions, are dressed in next to nothing. "One of the Chief's hobbies in the magazine is to see that both sexes are well represented on looks," a Grosvenor associate once said.

In addition to Alexander Graham Bell and William Howard Taft, Grosvenor's all-time roster of authors includes Duke Adolphus Frederick of Mecklenburg, Roald Amundsen, Robert E. Peary, Captain Robert A. Bartlett, Admiral Richard E. Byrd; Dr. Frederick A. Cook, whose claim to discovery of the North Pole the National Geographic Society inspected and rejected; Generals Pershing and H. H. Arnold; William Beebe, Mabel Boardman, Evangeline Booth, Andrew Carnegie, Frank Chapman, Herbert Hoover, Calvin Coolidge, Josephus Daniels, Joseph Conrad, Edward Everett Hale, Sir Wilfred Grenfell, Anne and Charles Lindbergh, General Billy Mitchell, Theodore Roosevelt, Sir Ernest Shackleton, Vilhjalmur Stefansson, Charles M. Schwab, John D. Rockefeller, Jr., and Joseph C. Grew. Grew made only one contribution to the *Geographic,* an article entitled "Waimangu and the Hot-Spring Country of New Zealand: The World's Greatest Geyser Is One of Many Natural Wonders in a Land of Inferno and Vernal Paradise." He wrote the piece in 1903, when, a year out of Harvard and travelling abroad, he came upon Waimangu in a lively state of activity. Grosvenor bought the manuscript, stuck it in a desk drawer, and pulled it out a year or two later, only to be told by his staff that Waimangu had cooled off some time before. He put the article away. In 1906, Grew, by then third secretary in the American embassy in Mexico City, wrote him asking what had happened to it. Grew continued to prod Grosvenor about the piece from time to time for nearly twenty years with needling letters from American embassies and legations in St. Petersburg, Berlin, Vienna, Paris, Copenhagen, and Berne. In 1925, when Grew was Undersecretary of State, he brought the matter once more to Grosvenor's attention in a rather sharp note. Shortly afterward, Grosvenor read with some relief an Associated Press dispatch to the effect that Waimangu had again commenced to perform, and he ran the article in the

August issue, bringing the whole thing up to date in admirable fashion by a note, signed "The Editor," which read:

Members of the American Fleet, now enjoying the sights of Australia and New Zealand, will upon their return to the United States in September have wonderful stories to tell of the antipodes. They are especially fortunate in that Waimangu (Black Water), the world's greatest geyser, for many years quiescent, has resumed activity, but not on the magnificent scale observed by the author.

Although the time lag between preparation and publication in this instance was greater than usual, Grosvenor has little patience with contributors who try to rush him. He has three hundred and fifty thousand unpublished photographs on hand, and he estimates that they, along with a few thousand manuscripts he has picked up but never run, would enable him to put out the magazine for fifteen years without any further contributions. During the war, this reservoir of material was frequently consulted by the War and Navy Departments, which found it extremely useful for information about weather, food, bombing objectives, and sanitation and transportation conditions in distant military areas. Among other war jobs, the National Geographic Society prepared special maps of the war theatres for the Army Air Corps, presented some fifty thousand copies of its various maps to government agencies, and published ten thousand copies of a book on the South Pacific area for the Navy Department. It also gave seventy-five thousand copies of old *Geographics* to the Adjutant General's office for distribution in camps and foreign posts.

Despite its imposing roster of outside contributors, the *Geographic* has for some time been very largely staff-written. In 1919, Dr. La Gorce inaugurated a series of articles about the states of the Union, which the *Geographic* has been running occasionally ever since, with an essay about his own home state entitled "Industrial Titan of America: Pennsylvania, Once the Keystone of the Original Thirteen, Now the Keystone of Forty-eight Sovereign States." La Gorce's other contributions have included several articles about salt-water fishing, of which he is a devotee, and "The Fight at the Timber-Line," which begins with this passage:

Among all the stirring struggles that the forces of Nature stage in their wars over disputed territory . . . there is none more intense or unrelenting than that at the timber-line, where the advance guard of the Legions of the Forest engages in mortal combat the entrenched troops of King Frost.

One would have to wander far afield indeed to witness more brilliant tactics or to meet with such masterful strategy as the tree armies employ.

Dr. La Gorce's easy mastery of this style of writing stems from thirty-eight years' association with the magazine and possibly from the fact that his offices adjoin those of the Chief. La Gorce is a husky, modest, genial man of sixty-three with a winter-vacation place in Miami Beach, a close friendship with Gene Tunney, and a penchant for prize fights. He is also active on the business side of the *Geographic*, which he likes to refer to as the romance of the magazine world; he is a director of the Riggs National Bank; and he has turned down offers from advertising firms which would have paid him twice his present substantial salary. Grosvenor tempted La Gorce away from Washington newspaper work in 1905; he dangled before him the peculiar cachet which attaches to the Society, a future, and a decrease in pay of eighty dollars a month. La Gorce often tells people that the day he accepted this financial demotion was the most fortunate one of his life and that he and the Chief have never had a word of personal disagreement. The vice-president of the National Geographic Society is an authority on weapons, and the walls of his office are lined with everything of the sort from a primitive stone club to a Commando dagger. "As my wife doesn't share this interest, I keep the weapons here," he once explained. "When problems get tough, I handle the weapons. It helps clear my head."

Other notably productive writers on the *Geographic* staff are Jesse R. Hildebrand, a Washington newspaperman who came to the *Geographic* in 1919 and has been represented in its pages by articles ranging in subject matter from Budapest, Edinburgh, and Copenhagen to "Our Most Versatile Vegetable Product" (rubber) and "The Sources of Washington's Charm"; Maynard Owen Williams, another newspaperman, who also came to the *Geographic* in 1919 and since then has travelled all over the world in its behalf, taking photographs and writing; and Frederick Simpich, a former pulp-magazine writer, consul general in Guatemala, and State Department adviser, who began contributing to the *Geographic* in 1914 and joined its staff eleven years later. Simpich, who smokes inexpensive cigars by choice but thoughtfully carries more costly ones in his pocket for friends, was the first *Geographic* employee to smoke openly in the office. He pulled out a cigar the first day he was there, and a few days later Grosvenor, whose avoidance of tobacco had, in office hours, been followed by his associates as a matter of course, quietly placed ashtrays on the desks of his more important male assistants. Today most of the *Geographic* editors smoke pipes while they work, and they are grateful to Simpich for having broken the ice.

Simpich, an astonishingly youthful man of sixty-four who has led a number of expeditions for the Society and is still on the road about half the time, has an office littered with a collection of carved wooden animals he has picked up on his travels and a guitar which plays the same rôle in his life as La Gorce's weapons do in his. "When I get stuck on a paragraph, I play something by Brahms," Simpich says. Simpich is a more realistic reporter than certain other *Geographic* contributors, and he has on occasion mildly violated the magazine's speak-kindly-of-everything tenet. A few years ago, in an essay on Alabama, he observed that certain goats in that state were afflicted with a curious nervous disorder:

Slip stealthily up to where these goats are feeding or resting . . . jump suddenly out, and the timid animals . . . actually sink to the ground, stiff and trembling. Though they soon revive, their legs are for a few seconds so stiff that they can hardly walk. The malady has been diagnosed by State veterinarians as a form of epilepsy.

Several Alabama goat-fanciers took exception to these remarks and, not even waiting to receive Spirit-of-Constructive-Coöperation slips, wrote to the *Geographic* denouncing Simpich as an alarmist and a man with the wrong attitude toward goats. On the whole, however, Simpich is highly popular with the magazine's readers, who are delighted with such typical passages of his as:

World's Fair! What words to conjure with! . . . They expect 60,000,000 paid admissions to the Fair. What a crowd! Think of the lost children, and the aching feet!

New York! Man's incomparable feat! As incredible, almost, as that ants should have built the Andes! Colossal monument to that genius which creates new things faster than simple words can be found to define them!

The Mexican border! What a frequent phrase! How it hints at turmoil and intrigue, at wild night rides by cavalry patrols, at gun-runners and smugglers! How suggestive it is, too, of brown-faced, snappy-eyed girls in red shirts and *mantillas*, peddling *tamales* and *dulces*; of Mexican women washing clothes, babies, and dishes in irrigation ditches; of burros, hens, and pigs foraging about adobe doorways!

Bagdad! What a magic word to conjure with! How it hints at romance, adventure, intrigue! . . . But how many Americans know just where Bagdad really is or how important it has lately become?

Simpich's dramatic style, which he employs deliberately to lure Society members into reading articles that are usually crammed with facts, has found disciples in other *Geographic* contributors. In an article entitled "The Conquest of Antarctica by Air," Admiral Byrd wrote:

What a challenge to the explorer! Is it a continent? . . . How thick is the ice cap? How old? How is it fed? What of geology? Are there coal beds, minerals, fossils?

"Though he's over sixty, he's one of those men that are always improving," Grosvenor recently said of Simpich. He is also appreciative, in a rather affectionate and paternal way, of the other men who help make the *Geographic* what it is. Several of them, like Grosvenor, are members of the Cosmos and Chevy Chase Clubs, and Grosvenor sometimes fraternizes with them there or has them out to his place in Maryland for Sunday lunch after a round of golf. He is equally benevolent toward his twenty-three fellow-trustees of the Society. He presides at quarterly board meetings and discusses the Society's finances, and projected Society expeditions, with a self-perpetuating group that includes, in addition to Pershing, Hughes, and Fleming, General H. H. Arnold; Juan Trippe; Leroy A. Lincoln, president of the Metropolitan Life Insurance Company; and Walter S. Gifford and Lloyd B. Wilson, respectively presidents of the American Telephone & Telegraph and Chesapeake & Potomac Telephone Companies. Gifford's and Wilson's connection with the Society is a tribute to the fact that the editor of the *Geographic* is a son-in-law of the late Alexander Graham Bell. Grosvenor, in turn, is a director of the Chesapeake & Potomac.

Grosvenor's relationship with the Bell family has been an important factor throughout his adult life. Bell was a member of the board of regents of the Smithsonian Institution, founded in 1946 as the result of a legacy of $550,000 from an English chemist named James Smithson, who, though he had never been to America, had made the bequest because he thought that the pursuit of knowledge had a great future here. Smithson had been buried in Genoa, and in 1903, when his body was about to be exhumed because of quarrying operations, Bell went to Italy to bring the remains to Washington. Smithson was an illegitimate son of the Duke of Northumberland, and while Bell was returning from his mission on the Princess Irene, he began to worry about how enthusiastically the body would be received by this country. He cabled Grosvenor to arrange for suitable ceremonies, and Grosvenor, game but not quite sure about protocol, wrote Theodore Roosevelt, then in the White House, "It would seem appropriate that a Government vessel, a ship of war, a revenue cutter, or even a tug be detailed to meet the Princess Irene when she enters the harbor of New York and receive Smithson's remains." Roosevelt came through handsomely. He sent a warship and arranged for the body to be received at the Washington Navy Yard by an escort of fifty cavalrymen and an artillery caisson. The distinguished corpse was placed briefly in a cemetery and then transferred to a tomb just inside the main entrance of the Smithsonian. Bell gave Grosvenor the credit for the gratifying reception. Grosvenor's devotion to Bell has been constant, even since his father-in-law's death, in 1922. Four years ago, when Darryl Zanuck made the movie called "The Story of Alexander Graham Bell," Grosvenor and his wife went to Hollywood as advisers, serving without fee. Although Grosvenor's chief piece of advice, which was that Don Ameche, who played Bell, should wear a beard, since Bell had worn a beard, was disregarded, he had a thoroughly good time in Hollywood, where he met Shirley Temple, dined at Dave Chasen's restaurant, and generated a number of ideas for *Geographic* articles. Grosvenor's adjustment to Hollywood was subsequently commented upon, with some astonishment, by his college's graduate magazine, the *Amherst Graduates' Quarterly*:

Despite a marked innate dignity of manner and life, and with all his fineness of personality, Grosvenor does not lack versatility when it comes to enjoyment; in other words he is not too "highbrow" to have a good time. The month or so which he and Mrs. Grosvenor spent in Hollywood, aiding in the production of the movie which depicts the life of Mrs. Grosvenor's famous father, appears to have been thoroughly enjoyed by both.

The aura of Bell surrounds Grosvenor in both his leisure and working hours. The shelves of his office contain a hundred or more loose-leaf books, bound in black, full of family letters and memorabilia, marked "Mother to A. Graham Bell 1864— G.H.G.'s Copy," "A. Graham Bell to Mrs. A. G. Bell," "Letters from A. G. Bell to Mrs. Gilbert Grosvenor," "Anecdotes of A. G. Bell," "Unusually Fine Tributes to Mr. and Mrs. A. Graham Bell," and so on. Grosvenor's farmhouse in Maryland is a repository of Bell as well as Grosvenor relics. The collection includes great carved doors which Bell brought back from India, more chaste New England doors from houses owned by Grosvenor forebears in Massachusetts, early models of the telephone, and a number of family portraits.

Grosvenor is an enthusiastic family man. Five of his six children are married, and at Sunday lunches he and Mrs. Grosvenor preside over a long table of a dozen or more descendants. After lunch he plays bridge, supervises work on various family Victory gardens, or perhaps goes up to his bedroom and looks over old copies of the *Geographic*, of which he has complete bound files from 1888 on, both at home and in his office. The fact that two hundred thousand members of the National Geographic Society think enough of his magazine to have copies of it bound year after year makes him very happy. He is also pleased that, during the war, thirty-five thousand copies of the *Geographic* continued to go to members in England every month. His regret at the sinking of almost the entire shipment of the November, 1942, issue was somewhat mitigated by his receipt of the following letter, written on the letterhead of the Provident Clothing & Supply Co., Ltd.:

Mr. Cyril Waddilove,
Hazel Brae, Bank Crest,
Baildon, Shipley, Yorkshire, England.

DEAR SIR,

I am requested by the above mentioned to say that his November, 1942, copy of The National Geographic Magazine reached him absolutely saturated with water.

He has dried the magazine, but some of the colours have run, and the pages are not flat—in fact the magazine is completely ruined.

Mr. Waddilove makes a point of having all the magazines bound, and he would be obliged if you would let him have another copy of the November, 1942, issue, as he is very anxious that the sequence should not be broken.

Yours faithfully,
H. CHAPMAN,
Cashier

Grosvenor sent Mr. Waddilove another copy. Then he ordered the plates of the November issue back on the presses and had thirty-five thousand extra copies run off for the benefit of his other English readers.

September, 1943

Orchidologist

T<small>HIS</small> Friday, October 18th, Mr. Rodney Wilcox Jones, president of the American Orchid Society, sets off for Brazil, where, in the forests near São Paulo and Rio de Janeiro, he expects to gather many bagfuls of rare orchid plants to add to five thousand he already has, in nine greenhouses, at his New Rochelle estate. We confirmed this piece of news last week when we called on Mr. Jones at the Society's Madison Avenue headquarters. Ushered into his office past a room containing a collection of excellent prints, several vases of orchids, and a man sorting union suits on a long table, we found Mr. Jones at his desk, upright, dynamic, bespectacled, and clad in a belted herringbone suit. In front of him were a drinking glass with three large yellow orchids, and another, with half a dozen smaller, purple and yellow-and-brown spotted ones; back of him was an advertising poster showing a man in his underwear, shaving. "A Word to the Wives!" its legend ran, in part. "Your men-folks deserve JONES quality HAPS . . . they'll be happier and so will you! Just ONE piece to wash, no ironing . . ." Mr. Jones was listening on the telephone as we entered. He waved to us genially and said into the instrument, "You'd have twenty-cent cotton instead of forty," and shortly thereafter hung up. He then told us that the American Orchid Society has twenty-five hundred members and that he gets five hundred letters a week from orchid lovers all over the world. "It's a terrible thing," he said, "this orchid game. It gets under your skin. Orchids are like a narcotic. It's impossible to break away. There's nothing like orchids! Each plant is an individual." Mr. Jones indicated an individual, or part of an individual, on his desk. "Here's a fellow with loads of color," he said. "A very famous Vanda, but its petals are too short. I've crossed it with another for more style and color. Color! I think that's all there is in life." He pressed a small, perfect orchid, similar to one he was wearing in his buttonhole, upon us and said he got into the orchid game, purely non-commercially, fifteen years ago, when his wife presented him with a plant, and that during the four years he has been at the helm of the American Orchid Society, its membership has quintupled. He has made several orchid-hunting trips to Central and South America, and proselytizes both home and abroad. He has recently lectured on orchids at the Botanical Gardens, the Union League, and the National Arts Club.

We asked Mr. Jones how about the union suits, and he explained that the Society's headquarters are also the Manhattan H.Q. of the Augusta Knitting Corporation, a Utica underwear-manufacturing firm, of which he is also president. "I've invented many improvements in knitted fabrics," he said. "We're now promoting one-piece knitted underwear of varying lengths—keeps your legs warm in winter and doesn't turn your heart into a heating plant." Mr. Jones was born in Utica, got to love flowers by working in his mother's garden, and is the possessor of a summer home at Amagansett, two or three thousand varieties of orchids, an orchidological library comprising nearly everything published on the subject in English, and six children—three sons in business with him and one at the Wharton School of Finance, and two daughters at boarding school. "I deck all their friends out with orchids for proms," he said. "I have some flowers smaller than a pencil point. Bringing orchids up here, I dry out the plants and get them dormant. They plump up when I put them on moistened coke in my greenhouses. Some people think all orchids are parasites. Nonsense! As many grow on rocks as on trees. I've developed a number of new hybrids. Miss Richter!" A young woman entered the room and, on President Jones' instruction, dived into a large carved cabinet, which he told us he bought at the Arthur Curtiss James sale, and came up with a bound volume of the *American Orchid Society Bulletin*. This revealed that recent hybrids flowered and named by Jones include the Charlotte Jones (for one of his daughters), the Thomas J. Watson (for Thomas J. Watson), the Amagansett (for Amagansett), and the Edna Richter (for Miss Richter). "It takes a year for the pod to develop," said Mr. Jones, "then a year in a flask, then several years in a community pot, then repot into a single pot, and so on into larger and larger pots. I've had some plants for fifteen years that haven't flowered yet, but I can wait. You might describe me as an erect sixty." He winked, and pressed a union suit on us as we wished him a good trip.

The Great Aviculturist

J EAN DELACOUR, Technical Adviser to the New York Zoological Society, and one of the three or four men who operate the Bronx Zoo, is generally conceded to be the world's foremost aviculturist. Aviculture is the breeding and rearing of birds in captivity. In the course of the past fifty years, both in France, where he was born, and in this country, of which he is now a citizen, he has reared approximately forty thousand birds. Until the spring of 1918, he housed his pets on an estate his family owned at Villers-Bretonneux, in Picardy. Almost every building on the place was destroyed by the Germans during their last offensive of the first World War. In 1919 he bought an estate at Clères, near Rouen, and in the years that followed stocked it with three thousand exotic birds. This place was bombed by the Luftwaffe in the spring of 1940 and subsequently taken over by the German Army. Only a few of its birds survived the war; the rest were either killed in the bombing, starved to death, eaten, stolen, or allowed to fly away. Delacour, who served with the French Army in both wars, escaped to this country after the fall of France, and the Zoo snapped him up. Since then, except for a token roller canary that he keeps in his hotel apartment, his aviculture here has been confined to birds which belong to the public. His attitude toward them is proprietary, however, and on his frequent visits to them they greet him with noises of intimacy and respect.

Serious aviculturists like Delacour not only breed and rear their birds but go on to study dead birds, or skins, as well as living birds, from a zoological point of view, thus becoming ornithologists as well. Following this tradition, Delacour, an unflagging field worker on four continents, has collected over fifty thousand bird skins on behalf of museums in Paris and London, and he now studies skins, and writes about them, at the Museum of Natural History, where he is a Research Associate in the Department of Birds. He is not the world's foremost ornithologist, but he is ranked among the eight or ten best in America and among the best three or four American authorities on birds of the Far East. He is also a mammalogist of some stature. He has collected, on his expeditions, fifteen thousand mammal skins for the museums, and at Clères he maintained, in addition to his aviary, a small zoo of antelopes, wallabies, Chinese deer, and gibbons, the last a specialty of his. He has conducted seven expeditions to Indo-China, where gibbons abound, and is presumed to have acquired a more extensive first-hand knowledge of these apes than anyone else alive. He is not sure which he prefers, gibbons or birds. "One never tires of watching them," he has said of both. He has spent more time with birds, however, and they have brightened up his life to a remarkable degree.

For climatic reasons, American aviculture centers in California; for more complicated reasons, American devotees of the science are chiefly an unworldly bunch. European aviculture, on the other hand, especially in England, is a fairly stylish avocation. The roster of the Avicultural Society of America, an organization which has its headquarters in Los

Angeles and of which Delacour is a vice-president, contains few names that would ring a bell in the memory of a *Social Register* or *Who's Who* editor; the Avicultural Society of London, to which Delacour has belonged for thirty years, includes or has included among its members two Dukes of Bedford (one of them the author of "Parrots and Parrot-like Birds in Aviculture"), several Rothschilds, one Earl of Leicester, one Earl of Mansfield, one Marquess of Cholmondeley, one Duchess of Wellington, one Countess of Lovelace, one Lady Cecil, one Lord Percy, and one Mrs. Sebag-Montefiore. Its council of fifteen governors, on which Delacour has sat since 1921, is headed by Alfred Ezra, the son and husband of Sassoons and a big bird man. The Society's members are all more or less crazy about birds. Many of them write for the Society's *Avicultural Magazine*, swap birds, invite one another to their bird parks, and participate in a kind of avicultural freemasonry in which animated conversations about velvet scoters, short-billed minivets, ocellated turkeys, Chinese tragopans, African pygmy geese, Darwin's rheas, and Wagler's woodpeckers are carried on in an atmosphere of culture, refinement, opulence, and frequently real scientific knowledge.

Delacour has long been the acknowledged titan, and sparkplug, of this group. The Bedford collection at Woburn Abbey and the Ezra collection at Foxwarren Park are larger than those at Villers-Bretonneux and Clères, but Delacour's collection of waterfowl and pheasants was the most complete there has ever been, and in diversification of bird personnel, arrangement of aviaries and landscape, and consuming interest of his captives, he was, until the destruction of his establishment in 1940, unrivalled. Delacour is a bachelor, so he has been in a better position to give his complete attention to frequent, protracted, and far-flung bird-hunting jaunts, and to watching and ministering to his birds, than his colleagues, most of whom foolishly have got married and in some cases have even had children, thus surrounding themselves with extra-avicultural distractions. For the better part of thirty years, Delacour divided his time between either Villers or Clères; Paris, where he exchanged bird lore and specimens with the Paris Zoo people; England, where Ezra always kept a room waiting for him in both his London and his Surrey house; and expeditions to the West Indies, South and Central America, China, Indo-China, Africa, Madagascar, India, Japan, and California. He is or has been president of the International Committee for Bird Preservation of Europe, the Ligue Française pour la Protection des Oiseaux, the Syndicat des Chasses Coloniales Françaises, and the Ornamental Pheasant Society, another European organization; a vice-president of the Société Nationale d'Acclimatation de France; general secretary of the International Ornithological Committee; and a member of the Council of the Société Ornithologique et Mammalogique and the Société Zoologique de France. He is the only foreigner ever elected to the Council of the Zoological Society of London. He has a great liking for the mammal- and bird-loving classes of England and, before he came to America to live, he attended most of the monthly meetings of the Zoological Society, at which he was greeted with friendly quacks and growls by such fellow-councillors as Julian Huxley; Sydney A. Monckton Copeman, discoverer of glycerinated lymph for smallpox vaccination; Sir Hugh S. Gladstone, author of "The Birds of Dumfriesshire" and "Record Bags"; Martin A. C. Hinton, who, according to the British *Who's Who*, "has studied many hoaxes including the Loch Ness Monster"; Professor Robert T. Leiper, a leading Scotch helminthologist; the Right Honourable Sir Francis O. Lindley, a former British ambassador who is chairman of the Test and Itchen Trout Fishing Association; the eleventh Duke of Bedford; Major

Albert Pam, a J. Henry Schroder partner who has a notable bird collection; and Lord Horder, the King's physician. "I was considered as a native in England," Delacour says.

Delacour introduced to Europe—at his own bird parks, at those of other collectors, and at the London and Paris Zoos—a number of birds that had never before been seen alive there, and he has bred and raised many species that have never before lived, let alone reproduced, in captivity. His studies have made him an important figure in the field of ornithological taxonomy, or the classification of birds by families. The four-volume "Les Oiseaux de l'Indochine Française," which he wrote in 1931 in collaboration with Pierre Jabouille, a former government official in French Indo-China, is the standard work on the birds of that region. Last year, he and Dr. Ernst Mayr, curator of the Whitney-Rothschild Collection of skins at the Museum of Natural History, published a revolutionary monograph entitled "The Family Anatidae," which contained proposals for reclassification of the duck family and gave ornithological circles a jolt. Some of the more prominent members of the American Ornithologists Union (of which Delacour is an Honorary Fellow) and one faction in the Smithsonian Institution bird crowd are thought to be skeptical about certain of the Mayr-Delacour proposals. They have gone so far as to characterize them, off the record, as "challenging," but up to now no formal rebuttal has been forthcoming. Delacour is confident, and perhaps even dogmatic, in his opinions about birds, but as a man of the world he is inclined to be self-deprecatory in casual conversation. "This book is full of my rubbish," he once said of a volume containing many articles of his. Altogether, he estimates, he has discovered and written about over four hundred species and subspecies of birds and mammals, many of which he has named after friends. Conversely, a number of new varieties of birds, fish, insects, and animals have been named after him by scientific colleagues, usually because of leads he gave them on these creatures as the result of his journeyings. "I can't remember all the things that have been named after me," Delacour says, "or all the things I have named after other people. I was lucky to be able to go on so many expeditions. Of course, you never name anything after yourself." One of his favorite namesakes is a rather flashy monkey which Dr. Wilfred H. Osgood, former curator of zoology at the Field Museum in Chicago, christened *Trachypithecus delacouri*. "It has a crest and a beautiful white bottom," Delacour says, with satisfaction.

Delacour's interest in taxonomy has carried over to the field of genealogy, especially the genealogy of people who are fond of mammals and birds. The late Lord Moyne, British Resident Minister in the Middle East, who was assassinated in Cairo in 1944, took Delacour along on a bird-hunting cruise along the West African coast eight or nine years ago, in company with Lady Broughton and the late Lady Moyra Cavendish. "Moyne was a Guinness—very mild and nice," Delacour says. "Lady Moyra Cavendish, who was sixty-three at the time, was a great old girl; she carried my gun and cleaned all my bird cages for me. She was the third daughter of the tenth Duke of St. Albans and married the brother of the ninth Duke of Devonshire. One of her four daughters is Lady Cranborne; she married a Cecil. He will be the fifth Marquess of Salisbury. We left the yacht at Dakar and travelled over the Sudan, Senegal, and Sahara, where we came across many ostriches—*Struthio camelus*—large bustards—*Choriotis arabs*—the very rare Savile's bustard—*Lophotis savilei*—and thousands of guinea fowl." Delacour's appreciation of titles is well reflected in an obituary he wrote, many years ago, of Hubert D. Astley, president of the Avicultural

Society of London and his best friend. "Mr. Astley," he wrote, in part, "was born on 14th July, 1860; a cousin of the 21st Baron Hastings, he was the son of the late Francis Le Strange Astley."

Delacour has written more than a hundred and fifty contributions for the *Avicultural Magazine,* some of which he has signed simply with his last name, after the fashion of the British peerage. This habit and his lordly air have given a number of people the idea that he is some sort of baron himself, which he is not. He is a descendant of Racine and of a North of France family which, in Napoleonic times, made a fortune in textiles. He was born in Paris in 1890 and began bird fancying with a pet chicken when he was three. A really successful aviculturist is one who can both rear and breed birds in captivity. Delacour raised his chick to be a large, bearded white hen, which, domiciled on the six-thousand-acre country place then owned by Delacour's parents and several relatives at Villers-Bretonneux, became a wildly prolific matriarch. She developed a fondness for Delacour, and whenever he visited the farmyard, she would shoulder aside the other fowl, patter up, and cackle at him affectionately. Delacour wants his birds to like him. He particularly enjoyed an eight-year friendship with a certain parrot, and in 1942, twelve years after the bird's demise, described their relationship in an article entitled "In Memory of an Old Friend." While the parrot was in residence, Delacour spent most of his autumns and winters on expeditions abroad, and he was much gratified by the way this "very intelligent and most affectionate Red-headed Conure (*Aratinga rubrolarvata*)" greeted him on his return.

As soon as I landed from the car [Delacour wrote], he was there to welcome me home, showing extreme pleasure and excitement. He unhesitatingly picked me out of all people at Clères, following me everywhere I went, and settling on my shoulder as often as I permitted. He gave me every proof of his affection, warbling at my ear, gently picking at my neck, playing with my fingers, and even offering me food, the politest of all gestures in a Parrot. When I sat down, he would first play on my knees, then cuddle himself in my arms and go to sleep. There was no other reason but his own fancy for the Conure to act in this way. I never gave him anything special to eat, except a few bread crumbs when I fed other birds in the park, and his proper food was offered to him by keepers whom he never particularly noticed. But, of his own choice, he had taken to my person. One day, as I was walking in the park with friends, he alighted on the shoulder of Prince Paul Murat. At that time we were both much of the same build and the Conure mistook him for me. My friend started calling me and as soon as the bird heard his voice he bit the Prince on the neck as hard as he could, which stopped all jokes about the shifting of his affection!

Delacour went on to say that during his absences the parrot would chum up with Frank Fooks, an Englishman who was head keeper and manager of the Clères estate, but he intimated that this was simply a matter of making do, since upon Delacour's return the bird always showed a preference for him and practically snubbed Fooks. Murat is a good friend of Delacour's, and there is no one whom Delacour holds in higher esteem than Fooks, but aviculturists do not care for triangles, and Delacour still feels happy when he recalls the gratifying conduct of the Conure, which died, in a state of considerable agitation, while his master was off on a trip that took fourteen months instead of the customary seven or eight.

Delacour is a singularly attractive aviculturist, and it is small wonder that birds like to warble at his ear, pick at his neck, play with his fingers, and offer him meal worms. He is just under six feet tall and sturdily built, has the expression of an intelligent robin, and, unlike most robins, has his suits made in London. His manner is alert, sardonic, assured, and good-humored. He is accustomed to success, and the fact that his main accomplishments have been demolished by war has made him philosophical rather than glum. His early childhood, which was dominated by his passion for birds and plants, was spent about half in a Paris apartment and half at Villers. At Villers, he had the run of an eighteenth-century château and extensive woods, orchards, gardens, farms, and greenhouses. These last had been neglected for decades, but when Delacour was eight, a new head gardener began to grow orchids in one of them. One day he invited the boy to see what he had done. "I shall never forget the shock I felt," Delacour wrote many years later, "as a heavenly vision revealed to me, for the first time, the true splendor of nature. It was the astonishing Mexican orchid called *Stanhopea oculata*. . . . For a long time I remained speechless. I had never dreamt that such fantastic loveliness could exist." Jean began to invest his allowance in orchid plants and to help the gardener transform some of the greenhouses into small tropical jungles, which he equipped with pools, rocks, waterfalls, and reptiles and birds that he caught on the place or bought from animal dealers in Paris. It was at about this time that he commenced to take an interest in an old aviary on the place which had once housed pheasants. One of his two older brothers had filled the aviary with fancy Bantams. The future president of the Ornamental Pheasant Society told his father that this was a hell of a note, and Delacour *père*, who was a very sympathetic *père*, after ascertaining that his Bantam-fancying son had long before lost interest in this hobby, presented Jean with the aviary on his tenth birthday. Jean sent the Bantams off to the farms and filled the aviary with cardinals, troupials, parakeets, pheasants, and doves. He had always been educated at home, by governesses and tutors, but that fall he was sent to a Jesuit school in Paris. Delacour, horrified at the thought of having only four months a year in the country, quickly persuaded his father to let him visit Villers at Christmas, Easter,

Whitsuntide, and one weekend a month during the school term. Then and during the summers, he worked on his aviary, planting it, stocking it, and talking things over with its occupants. The rest of the time, he fretted at school, though he visited, as often as possible, the Paris Zoo and the Bois de Boulogne lakes, great places for waterfowl. He studied just hard enough to lead his class, his mother having bribed him with an extra allowance to buy birds and plants, and he feels that the education he got from his aviary compares favorably with the one the Jesuits gave him. Of his life at Villers, he has written:

The old aviary, together with the greenhouses, constituted for me the center of the universe. I could not imagine that anything more wonderful might possibly exist. I spent all the hours I could watching my birds. I knew every one of them—their history, their peculiarities, their temper, and their record. Their tragedies, comedies, dramas of love and jealousy filled my thoughts. Undoubtedly, the world was wonderful, but at the same time it abounded in evils and difficulties. This deplorable truth was first brought home to me by the birds. What a lesson Nature was giving me!

· Delacour's father, the late Theodore Delacour, a country gentleman who served on a few textile-company and railroad directorates and who occasionally allowed himself to be elected mayor of Villers-Bretonneux, died in 1905, leaving a good many stocks and bonds, as well as his share—fifteen hundred acres— of the Villers place and a three-hundred-and-fifty-acre farm at Radicatel, in trust to his wife for their three sons. Jean, who was only fifteen when his father died, already has assembled several hundred birds, including some rare ones. He graduated from school a couple of years later, with honors in science, literature, and philosophy. Being a conscientious capitalist as well as a natural aviculturist, he enrolled at the Sorbonne for courses in zoology, botany, economics, finance, and business management. His mother, who liked birds fairly well and her youngest son a great deal, turned out to be an indulgent trustee. She gave him an annual allowance of twenty-five thousand dollars, and this, which was doubled by a trust-fund income that he began to receive, under the will, when he was twenty-one, enabled him to transform the Villers estate into what the *Avicultural Magazine* called "a veritable ornithological park." He became even more well-to-do the next year, when one of his brothers died, leaving him approximately two hundred and fifty thousand dollars. During the six years before the first World War, he installed a hundred or so steel-framed aviary compartments; built a dozen paddocks for rheas, cranes, flamingos, storks, wild turkeys, emus, and other large birds; fenced in several acres and constructed a house for ostriches; dug a big lake for swans and ducks; and put up another birdhouse with seventy steam-heated compartments. Altogether, he spent over a hundred thousand dollars on making Villers a place that birds could be proud of and on stocking it with them. He has never ceased to be thankful for his silver spoon. "The necessity of making money, which has poisoned the lives of so many promising young men, did not exist in my case," he says. In 1914, when he was twenty-four, he owned thirteen hundred birds of nearly three hundred and fifty species, including samples of every variety of pheasant that so far had been able to exist in captivity. He studied them all closely, noting their incessant quarrels, and was not particularly surprised by Sarajevo and its aftermath. "I had been watching my birds," he said recently, "and I knew that storms were ahead."

Delacour, who had had the customary two years of compulsory military training, joined the French Army as a lieutenant when war broke out in the summer of 1914. He served first in the eastern part of France, near Verdun, and then in the north, as a liaison officer of a French mission attached to the British Army. In 1916, during the Battle of the Somme, his veritable ornithological park, which overlooked the valley of the Somme only ten miles from the German lines, was for several months General Foch's headquarters. During this period, Lieutenant Delacour made straight for his birds whenever he got leave. The first time he got home after the Army had taken it over, he was met at the Amiens station by a car sent by Foch. "That night, Foch and his generals invited me to dinner in my dining room," Delacour says. "The next night, I invited them. Of course, I placed Foch at my right. He was lively and brusque, but very well brought up and very nice, and took an interest in my birds." (Delacour is less enthusiastic about General Weygand, who was also quartered in his mother's house. "Weygand showed no interest in the birds," he says.) Foch won Delacour's heart one afternoon when the two of them went on a tour of the aviaries, which were being cared for by a few overage keepers. "When I'm dead," Foch said, "I want to come back as a bird in your aviaries." The Lieutenant nodded politely.

Delacour kept his scientific colleagues posted on his birds throughout most of the war, chiefly by bulletins he sent to French and English avicultural magazines. "I came to the conclusion that the close proximity of the battles had no bad effect upon my birds," one of these stated, early in 1917. It continued:

A much greater number of eggs were unfertile, a fact which is no doubt annoying, but not important on the whole. . . . The coming and going of aviators, their fights, and the appalling bombardment in the near neighborhood seemed to trouble the birds very little and to cause no damage amongst them.

A few months later, Delacour, writing from the front after a brief visit home, reported:

The war and the submarine campaign have hindered the importation of exotic animals into France, but they have not entirely stopped it. Thus it was that I was able to receive at the beginning of the year a very interesting package from the Gabun, in which was found a superb bird—the Great Touraco.

"I am particularly happy to be able to announce that a young 'Pigeon Hollandais' has been born and reared at Villers-Bretonneux," he wrote in the March, 1918, *Avicultural Magazine*. "I will report later when the young pigeon assumes its parents' plumage." Delacour never did report on this, for his aviaries, along with the pigeons Hollandais and the rest of the birds at Villers, were blown to bits by German shells that spring and summer. "By a misfortune without parallel in the history of aviculture," the *Avicultural Magazine* observed, in an editorial headed "Ave Atque Vale," "Lieutenant Delacour's collection . . . has been utterly destroyed." Delacour ran into Foch after the war, reminded him of his remark about the aviaries, and told him he hadn't picked a very good spot for his afterlife. Foch interpreted this as a reproof. "I did all I could to save them," he said.

Delacour came out of the war a captain, and he is still called Captain Delacour by most of his friends. His second brother was killed at Verdun in 1915, and from him Delacour inherited seven hundred and fifty thousand dollars. "My mother and I rebuilt our place at Villers," he says, "but it lost all the charm its eighteenth-century buildings used to give it. The château and the park, a mass of shattered bricks and stones and broken trees, were given to the municipality for public grounds, but for me Villers had ceased to exist. Whenever I visited it, I felt the painful impression that one has when seeing, ruined by age and injuries, an old woman one knew many years before, young and beautiful. Moreover, I wanted to build up a new collection of birds in a warmer part of the country." Delacour persuaded his mother to leave Villers, and Madame Delacour sold her share of it to her relatives, and in 1919 she helped him buy the place at Clères. It had a thirteenth-century château which had been restored in the sixteenth and nineteenth centuries, a brick-and-timber manor house, a lake, a half-mile of river, and six hundred acres of grounds. Despite the *Avicultural Magazine's* farewell, Delacour's collection had not been utterly destroyed; during the war he had sent several hundred of his rarer birds to the London and Paris Zoos, and to collectors in England, for safekeeping. Starting off with these remnants of his collection, he began to put together a new one. At Clères, he built fifty aviaries for small birds, several greenhouses for humming-birds, sunbirds, and other birds that like greenhouses, and enough other buildings to house the largest collection of game birds ever assembled. He also fixed up a dungeon for horned and snowy owls, and made it cozy for them by covering its entrance with wire netting on which he trained ivy. He fenced off forty acres with an eight-foot-high wire netting, and in this enclosure he kept, pinioned but uncaged, waterfowl, cranes, pheasants, parrots, and rheas. Soon Delacour was plunged into a state of postwar avicultural bliss. The Marquess of Tavistock, later the twelfth Duke of Bedford, presented him with some unusual parakeets; a Bordeaux bird dealer whom he had long patronized gave him a Colombian Wagler's woodpecker (*Mela-nerpes wagleri*, Salvin and Godman), which Delacour remem-bers was partial to sponge cake and "most attractive in his ways"; and he kept in his bedroom the only living long-tailed African roller in Europe. "The Roller possesses altogether the four most important qualities for a bird in captivity: beautiful plumage, tameness, sensibility, and rarity," he wrote, in what might be taken as a summation of his philosophy about birds. "When I come in, he flies to me, opens his wonderful blue wings in salute, uttering his loud crowlike call, and he takes the keenest interest in everybody and everything."

Between 1921 and 1940, Delacour spent nearly a third of his time on expeditions. Sometimes accompanied by his mother, whom he had trained to skin birds, and nearly always by one or two assistants, whose salaries and expenses he often shared with museums in Paris and London, the American Museum of Natural History, or collector friends, among them Alfred Ezra and John Spedan Lewis, a wealthy London department-store owner, he penetrated Africa, Asia, and South America and returned laden not only with living birds but with bird skins, insects, gibbons, bears, tiger cats, civets, squirrels, deer, and porcupines. As an *Associé* of the Museum d'Histoire Naturelle of Paris, a governmental outfit which runs the Paris Zoo much as the Smithsonian Institution runs the Washington Zoo, and a collector for this organization, he enjoyed an official status on these excursions, since he travelled as *chargé de mission* of the Ministère de l'Instruction Publique. His transportation expenses were often paid by countries he visited, and he was frequently the house guest of government officials. His mammal skins, and most of his mammals, went to the Museum d'Histoire Naturelle, the British Museum, or the London Zoo, but he kept a fair number of mammals for his own zoo. His bird skins went mostly to these museums, and occasionally to the Natural History Museum here. A few were snagged by the late Lord Rothschild, whose collection at Tring Park, the greatest private collection in the world, was sold in 1932 to the Natural History Museum. "The old boy was a fanatic," Delacour has said. "He would turn up at the British Museum, when my skins were being unpacked, wearing a morning coat with extra-sized pockets. 'I *wonder* if you could spare one for me,' he would whisper when he saw something he didn't have, and then put it in his pocket. I never kept skins myself because you never have enough—unless you're a Rothschild. I'd rather study them at museums."

According to Delacour, anyone with sufficient means, a knowledge of what he wants, and plenty of time can do pretty well on bird-collecting expeditions, since the details of catching are usually handled by natives. The trick is to bring the birds back alive, and in good shape, and this requires a lot of coddling, persuasion, patience, dietary background, and understanding. Hummingbirds, for example, are sometimes caught by being stunned while on the wing by pellets of soft earth shot through blowpipes. On Delacour's expeditions, the marksmen brought each victim to him unconscious. He would revive the bird by holding it in his hands and making encouraging remarks. At the first sign of returning consciousness, he plunged its beak into a fresh mixture of Mellen's Food, sugar, honey, and milk.

It usually begins to drink at once [Delacour has written]; but some were stubborn; they were conquered by putting their beaks into my mouth and breathing gently on them, then plunging them into the mixture again. Should this not succeed there was another [sic] infallible plan: to plunge the whole beak and nostrils into the liquid; the bird begins to suffocate, puts out its tongue, and having tasted the mixture, willy nilly begins to drink greedily. The effect of this food is immediate; one moment the bird is apparently lifeless; one swallow, and it flies joyously about; but it weakens quite as rapidly, and must be taken up again and fed every ten minutes until it is seen to feed itself. This usually happens in about four to six hours' time. Some must be forcibly fed for several days.

Food on a hummingbird's plumage generally kills it, so it is fed by means of a covered vessel with a small hole in the lid. "You often have to resort to tricks to make newly captured birds eat," Delacour says. "You see why they're not happy, and fix it; you must have a kind of understanding. Insect eaters, such as pittas, are the worst. You have to force-feed them, and then quit at just the right moment, when they begin to show an independent interest. Sometimes a dark cage, with light just on the water container and a nice live insect dropped in the water, will do the trick. I once brought back a blue pigeon from Madagascar which had never been brought alive before. I had to cram him with crushed bananas four or five times a day for four months before he would begin to eat himself. He was perfectly tame and polite, right from the beginning, but he lacked initiative."

Delacour is tolerant of timidity in birds, especially recently captured ones, but he likes them to have a certain style, and he gets impatient with them when he thinks they lack it. "All Tree Ducks look charming," he once wrote. "They have varied but always handsome plumages. They are elegant in shape, extremely attractive in their behavior, and often become absurdly tame. I dislike Spur-Wings intensely. I find them extremely ugly, with their huge, coarse feet and bill of a sickly purplish tint. All the males I ever possessed proved the savagest bullies one could imagine." Delacour's aesthetic approach to aviculture sometimes makes him brusque with more easygoing scientists. Once a youthful colleague told him that he was writing a paper on barbets. "Drab little things!" Delacour said. "Why bother with them?" He feels that birds not only should look pretty but should be well spoken, even in time of war. "Their characters are not attractive," he wrote in 1917 of three red-crowned pigeons he had visited at Villers on what had apparently been a disappointing leave. "I have never heard them coo."

Since coming to America to live, Delacour has joined five New York clubs. He appears to feel as much at home here as a member of the St. Nicholas Society. His ability to orient himself has probably been sharpened by the fact that he works in fields that have no national boundaries. While he was building up his collection at Clères, he not only conducted expeditions in Asia, Africa, and South America but carried on an immense avicultural and zoological correspondence with fellow-collectors in Paris, London, Rome, Berlin, New York, San Francisco, Moscow, and Tokyo. In the course of the nineteen-twenties, his passion for rare birds took him to Annam, where he captured, and subsequently brought to Europe, fourteen living, breathing Edwards' pheasants, birds previously familiar to Continental ornithologists only in inanimate form—four skins in the Paris Muséum d'Histoire Naturelle. In 1924, he electrified birdmen everywhere by bringing home from Indo-China a pair of dark blue pheasants of a variety no ornithologist had ever seen before, even stuffed. They had been snared in a remote section of northern Annam by a missionary, who brought them to Delacour. On his way home, Delacour suffered a severe shock when, as a ship he was on sailed up the Saïgon River in the port of Saïgon, the female of his unique pair broke out of their cage and off the boat. He watched, transfixed, as the bird flew several hundred yards up the river and into a warehouse. Delacour shouted, the warehouse doors were closed, and twenty minutes later, when he stepped ashore, he recaptured his prize. These unheard-of birds were his to name, and he christened the pair imperial pheasants. He later succeeded in breeding them in captivity, at Clères, and sold or gave some of the progeny to other collectors in Europe and this country. He has made several expeditions to Indo-China since 1924, but neither he nor anyone else has ever brought back another imperial pheasant. Even now, only ten or twelve examples of this bird exist in captivity. All are in California or Pennsylvania, and all, naturally, are descendants of Delacour's pair.

Other great rarities which Delacour brought into Europe

include several yellow-breasted cissas from Cochin China and
Renauld's ground cuckoos from Annam, the former the first
ones ever to reach Europe alive. Delacour, an open-handed
aviculturist, gave four of his cuckoos and three of his cissas to
Alfred Ezra. One of the cuckoos obligingly laid an egg, and
Ezra subsequently reported, in the September, 1927, issue of
the *Avicultural Magazine*, that he had presented this to "Lord
Rothschild, as I believe it is the first known egg of this bird."
One of the cissas also came across. "On the 16th April," Ezra
wrote in the December, 1927, *Avicultural Magazine*, "I found
one of the birds visiting the nest, and on the following day there
was one egg. As it was the first known egg of this bird, I removed
it and sent it to Lord Rothschild for his collection." Despite his
own friendship with Rothschild, Delacour feels that Ezra
might at least have tried first to hatch the cuckoo and cissa eggs
and that his failure to do so may have been the fruit of a rather
regrettable clannishness, since Ezra was a cousin of the late
Sir Philip Sassoon, whose mother was a Rothschild. As part of
the Rothschild Collection, the eggs are now in the Museum of
Natural History, where Delacour, who, as a Research Associate
in the Department of Birds, has the use of an office adjoining
the rooms in which the collection is displayed, sometimes gazes
at them reflectively.

Altogether, Delacour has written something like a million
words for avicultural and ornithological publications. His
articles have ranged from such purely avicultural topics as "My
Long-Tailed Roller" and "A Collection of Small Birds in New
Jersey" to such strictly ornithological matters as "Un Nouveau
Stade dans la Mutation *Tenebrosus* du Faisan Ordinaire" and
"Monographie des Veuves (Révision des Genres *Euplectes* et
Vidua)." In 1920, he singlehandedly founded an avicultural
magazine he called *L'Oiseau*, chiefly to provide himself with a
publication in which he could, without consulting the whims

of editors, hold forth on birds for the benefit of the French-speaking world. He filled it with costly color printing and made up its annual deficit of two or three thousand dollars. At first, *L'Oiseau* was concerned solely with aviculture, confining itself to the collecting and care of living birds, but in 1927 Delacour decided to cover ornithology as well. He turned *L'Oiseau* over to a friend in 1940, when he came here, and it is still being published. "For more than a decade, Jean ruled French ornithology with an iron hand," a European colleague of Delacour's recently said.

The Technical Adviser of the New York Zoological Society prefers the company of people who are wealthy, well connected, eccentric, scientifically inclined, or, if possible, all four. He used to spend several months a year in England, where his avicultural friends—some of whom thought nothing of writing four-thousand-word articles for magazines about pets called Owlikins and the cute bathing habits of their imported hummingbirds—tended to live up to these specifications. His own contributions to British bird magazines, reflecting his expeditions and the progress of his bird collection, also reflect the man:

In 1930 one [Darwin's rhea] hen laid six eggs on which the cock sat for weeks in the rain; the eggs were clear, and the poor bird became so exhausted that he died shortly after. Fortunately, the Duke of Bedford kindly replaced him.

My old Black-Necked Crane, the only one ever imported into Europe, died last summer [1932]. A great loss!

In the early months of 1932, my friend, M. R. Homberg, sent me two male Velvet Scoters (*Œdemia fusca*). One survived only a few months, while the other one lived at Clères just about six years. I have never yet seen another Velvet Scoter in confinement, nor heard of any having been kept in captivity for more than a few weeks.

I strongly advise [Avicultural Society] members to cut [meal worms] off entirely from the bill of fare of their Minivets, Fly-catchers, and other small insect-eaters. A good insectile mixture,

with a few flies, ant-cocoons, clean maggots, and other small insects is what they want.

I could not possibly do without Parrots and Parakeets, some
of the most beautiful, intelligent, and interesting of all feathered
creatures.

Contrary to what many may believe, Macaws and other large
Parrots are perfectly happy and do exceedingly well chained by one
leg to a perch, though naturally the ring and chain must be perfect.
After having tried many sorts of supports, I have adopted a long
fence made of concrete, imitating rough wood in a perfect way,
on which each bird is tied at intervals of about three feet. The
chain is long enough to allow the Macaw to reach his neighbor,
preen him and play with him, without getting entangled. The top
of the cement fence is hollow, and a piece of wood is fastened into
it, in such a way that the birds' feet rest on wood and not on
cold concrete. Suitable holes are made in the concrete and used as
feeders and drinkers, and the whole affair looks neat and nice.

Delacour's whole estate at Clères was so neat and nice that a
good many opportunistic French birds of no great rarity simply
settled in it of their own accord. The International Ornithological Congress held one of its quadrennial meetings at Rouen,
a few miles away, chiefly so that its three hundred delegates
could inspect Delacour's treasures. "Delacour's collection was
arranged with the best taste of any in Europe," one of them
afterward said. "His hummingbirds lived in greenhouses planted
with rare orchids, his flamingos and demoiselle cranes danced
on the lawn like a *corps de ballet*, against a background of
green pines, his wallabies chased his Australian emus in the
most dramatic manner imaginable." European and American
ornithologists were constantly visiting Clères, and from 1925
on the public was also admitted. Delacour decided upon this
move after he had added up the salaries of his thirty keepers
and gardeners and the cost of upkeep, buying new birds, and
so on, and figured out that, over and above living expenses, the
place was costing him around a hundred thousand dollars a

year. Thirty thousand dollars of this was taxes. Pondering what he had learned in a course in finance and business management at the Sorbonne some years before, he concluded that it was foolish for him to go on paying taxes on such a scale and thereupon incorporated the estate as the Parc Zoologique de Clères, issued five hundred shares of stock (he kept four hundred and ninety-three and gave the rest to a few friends), elected himself president, made his head keeper, Frank Fooks, director, and invited the public in to inspect the corporation's avicultural assets. Visitors paid five francs to see the birds weekdays and ten on Sundays; school children were admitted free. "We always lost money," Delacour says triumphantly. "We were fortunate enough to become virtually bankrupt. Clères became a non-profit business—indeed, a losing business—run for the benefit of the public, instead of a luxury, and I saved a lot of taxes." On summer Sundays, more than ten thousand people were likely to show up at Clères. Some came from as far away as Belgium and England. Their fees, the saving in taxes, and the sale of some duplicate birds to dealers and collectors enabled Delacour, who, with perfect legality, kept making wonderfully unsound loans to the corporation and deducting them in his income-tax computations, to run the place at an average cost to him of only fifty thousand a year. "Such crowds came on Sundays that I had to go away and visit friends or else hide in the house," he says, "but it was a small price to pay. They were taken around by the keepers and behaved perfectly well. No one ever went off the paths. It brought prosperity to the little town of Clères, and my neighbors were less inclined than before to shoot birds that escaped from my place to their orchards. They even asked me to run for mayor. Of course, I did nothing of the sort. It would have taken too much time from my birds, and as mayor I could hardly have spent six months of the year in Indo-China."

Delacour's last trip to Indo-China, in 1939, netted him, among other scarce items, a number of red-tailed laughing thrushes, and he gave some of them to Ezra, who was very much pleased; no such thrushes had ever laughed in England before. On his expeditions, Delacour has received some nasty pecks from maladjusted birds, and once he nearly died of amoebic dysentery in Tonkin, but he has no patience with people who get into trouble in the wilds. "Nothing bad happens to you unless you're a damn fool," he says. "Those miserable fools that get eaten by a tiger or trampled by an elephant—I don't know how they do it." Actually, Delacour feels sorry for people who get eaten up—or for their children, at any rate—but his conversation is deceptively astringent. "He was a low, middle-class Englishman," he once said of someone he liked rather well, "an old bachelor, very shabby and dirty. Poor old fool, he got blown up during the war by a mine, which was the best thing he could have done. He wasn't a bad soul, after all."

During his last several years at Clères, when Delacour lived on the estate with his elderly mother, he used to get up at five, slip a dilapidated pongee dressing gown over his pajamas, and visit some of his rarer caged birds. He then fed the greatest collection of waterfowl in the world and passed a few remarks with his gibbons. He fell in love with gibbons during an expedition to Indo-China in 1923, and two years later the Governor of Cochin China sent him four as a present. "Monkeys at Clères!" Delacour has written in an unpublished paper. "I shuddered at the idea. What could I do with them?" He decided just to let them loose. "Soon they were running along the Gothic balustrade of the terrace, which always remained the Gibbons' favorite promenade," he added, "up in the tall trees beyond, jumping and calling. It was a marvellous sight, which was to last fifteen years, and they looked very happy."

During those fifteen years, Delacour kept bringing back new gibbons with him from every visit to Indo-China. He named them Suzy, Didi, Siki, Nenette, and the like, played with them for hours, compensated his neighbors in the village for their occasional larcenies, and, since gibbons cannot swim, consigned one or two dangerous ones to an island in his lake. Of his favorite, Suzy, he wrote in his paper:

To her friends, she was touchingly affectionate. I was one of them. Suzy had an exceptionally pretty face and clever eyes. For several years she was the Queen of Clères. Unfortunately, she became too impatient of a number of people, including my mother, and very reluctantly I had to send her to the park of John Spedan Lewis. I often visited her there and she recognized me perfectly. She unfortunately died a few years later, just after having given birth to her first baby. I shall never forget Suzy, nor cease to regret her.

Around seven-thirty in the morning, Delacour would leave his gibbons, return to the château, breakfast, read his mail, go upstairs to say good morning to his mother, shave, and bathe. By eight-thirty, he was once more out, still in his dressing gown. He would spend several hours planting or transplanting shrubs and dosing ailing birds. Delacour likes to do things quickly, and he preferred to perform certain favorite chores—such as planting a tropical greenhouse—when his men were not around, so as not to be slowed up by their assistance. He used to traipse briskly through the village of Clères in his dressing gown, and was sometimes still wearing it when friends of his, or his mother's, arrived for lunch. Afternoons he generally devoted to writing letters, articles, or books about birds, and to reading something from his enormous ornithological library. Despite all these labors, he managed to spend two days a week in Paris, where he stayed at the Crillon, a hotel controlled by one of his cousins, and ten days a month in England, where he stayed with his friend Ezra, a multimillionaire controlled by a passion for birds.

This congenial routine was interrupted by the war, but even that did not take his mind completely off his birds, although he was by then a captain in the French Army, working as a liaison officer with the British. In the fall of 1939, he wrote in the *Avicultural Magazine*:

All our gardeners and four bird-keepers have joined up since the beginning of the war; another one is soon going. But Mr. Fooks is fortunately staying at Clères, and is able to carry on with a reduced staff. By the doubtful privilege of age, I am remaining in the district, though on military duty, so that I can see my birds at frequent intervals. We have eight excellent young Ostriches, hatched in an incubator in August. Ostrich chicks are extremely quaint and amusing, round in shape, and looking rather like hedgehogs in their rough down; they have curious short jelly-like legs and swollen nape the first day. They proved very tame and sensible.

Delacour went on to report that he had fed his ostrich chicks biscuit-meal mash and cut-up greens with plenty of grit, and that, because of the coal and manpower shortages, he had deposited his rarer plants at the Rouen Botanical Gardens and closed his greenhouses. As president of the Ornamental Pheasant Society, he called the attention of his fellow-phasianists to the fact that during the first World War such rare breeds of Chinese pheasants as Temminck's and Cabot's had practically died out in France. "The tragedy of the disappearance of these fine Tragopans must be avoided this time," he declared, and urged all owners of these birds, as well as the owners of Blyth's tragopans, koklass, imperial, Edwards', copper, Bulwer's, and Rheinart's, not to mention Palawan and bronze-tailed polyplectrons, to send them, in the event that it had become impossible to continue to care for them, to live with "others, more fortunate, who can endeavor to see them safely throughout the present war."

Delacour did not send any of his own polyplectrons or other pets away, thinking they were safe where they were, and when, in May, 1940, Clères was bombed by the Luftwaffe, about fifty of his birds and mammals were killed. Half of those that remained there were dead four years later, mostly at the hands of hungry, retreating Germans. Mr. Fooks escaped to England in 1940, just before the German Army overran the Delacour place; Mme. Delacour went into the Unoccupied Zone. "Though the President of the Ornamental Pheasant Society, Monsieur Jean Delacour, is for the moment cut off from his colleagues in England," the *Avicultural Magazine* said in that desperate summer, "there is no doubt that he will endeavor to get into communication with them at the earliest possible opportunity." Delacour was demobilized that July, in the Unoccupied Zone. He was advised by Vichy officials not to return to Clères, because it was in the Occupied Zone and his friendship with prominent Englishmen had made the Nazis suspect that he was a British agent. He gave a power of attorney as president of the Clères company to a neighbor, and this deputy later got permission from the Germans to move a few of the rarest Delacour birds to the Paris Zoo. Several hundred others were sold to the Louis Ruhe zoological store, in Hanover. Thus not many remained at Clères. James C. Greenway, one of the curators of the Museum of Comparative Zoology at Cambridge, Massachusetts, told the American immigration authorities that he would see to it that Delacour did not become a public charge, and Delacour decided to come here. He proceeded to New York via Marseille, Algiers, Casablanca, Rabat, Spanish Morocco, Tangier, and Lisbon.

Delacour arrived in Manhattan on Christmas Eve, 1940. He called up Fairfield Osborn, president of the New York Zoological Society, which runs the Bronx Zoo, and spent part of

Christmas Day with the Osborns. Osborn, an old ornamental-pheasant man himself, had visited Clères eighteen years before, and he had since kept up a correspondence with Delacour and had seen him whenever he came to his country. Osborn had never forgotten his visit to Clères. "I was met at the station by Jean's smart French car and chauffeur," he says, "and when we reached the château, there was his charming mother at the top of the stairs. A few days after he arrived here, I invited him to join us as Technical Adviser. He accepted, and brought to us an almost unique experience: he knows everyone in Europe; his position in his field is incomparable. We have no director. I'm administrative officer for the Bronx Park, and John Tee-Van is my right-hand administrative man. We operate through a planning committee, which consists of Tee-Van; Lee Crandall, general curator of mammals and birds; Delacour; and myself. The ball is being pitched by the team as a whole."

While helping pitch this zoological ball, Delacour has introduced a number of improvements in the bird house of the Bronx Zoo, among them a series of small, brightly lighted, glass-fronted hummingbird cages in a dark passageway, and—to replace a lot of old-fashioned parrot cages—five long "flights," or high-roofed "flying cages," for quetzals, buntings, barbets, mannikins, pittas, and so on. These cages, like some of those at Clères, have been provided with such amenities as, to quote the signs describing them, a "tropical American mountain stream," a "tropical rain forest," a "desert," and an "Indian-Malayan jungle." Delacour has also brightened up the Zoo's great outdoor flying cage, which is a hundred and fifty feet long, seventy-five wide, and fifty-five high. After forty years of service, it was in sorry shape when he arrived on the scene. On his recommendation, all its occupants—pelicans, ibises, herons, and gulls—were moved to a lake in the northern section of the Park. "Their heavy feet were crushing the shrubs," he

says, "and they were making the place filthy." The cage's concrete foundations were then concealed with mounds of rock,
an island put in its pool, and the enclosure planted with rho-
dodendrons, mountain laurel, andromedas, and barberries. He
then stocked the cage with egrets, ducks, spoonbills, and
pheasants, comparatively clean and light-footed birds. Delacour
often accompanies George Scott, the head bird keeper of the
Zoo, into the bird cages, where he plants or transplants shrubs,
moves rocks around so they will look prettier, and tries to
imagine what the Duke of Bedford would have to say about his
improvements.

Delacour's salary at the Zoo is six thousand dollars, and he is
the beneficiary of a somewhat larger, and tax-free, annuity,
which he had the forethought to buy in Canada years ago. Most
of the money he and his mother inherited is in France, in the
custody of the government. For a while after he came here, his
mood was one of philosophical gloom. He let himself go in
nostalgic articles in the *Avicultural Magazine*, such as "The
End of Clères" and "Geese I had at Clères." In the former, he
wrote:

With the passing of Clères went the last great private [bird]
collection in Continental Europe. It is not for me to say how fine
it was. I shall only mention that it was situated in a pretty, narrow
valley surrounded by picturesque hills. Today practically nothing
remains of what I spent the best years of my life in creating. It was
a dream come true, and then, at fifty, I suddenly find it vanished in
thin air, like a pinpricked bubble. It is very much to be doubted
that the world will ever again see another collection the like of
that at Clères. Perhaps my bitter experience may serve as an object
lesson to those who hold material possessions in too great esteem
and to remind others that nothing in this life should be regarded as
permanent.

After eight or ten months in the Bronx, Delacour began
to perk up. He made arrangements to bring his mother to

America; he helped arrange, on behalf of the New York Zoological Society, for an assistant to go to Colombia on an expedition, which produced the largest catch of tropical American
birds ever brought to this country, including twelve very rare
scarlet cocks of the rock; and in the fall of 1941 he accompanied Osborn on a tour of the West, during which he met bird
fanciers all over California, attended the annual meeting of the
American Ornithologists Union in Denver, and, as he has since
written, "in the nearby Rocky Mountains renewed my acquaintance with such delightful species as the Pygmy Nuthatch,
Clarke's Nutcracker, Canada Jays, Western and Mountain
Bluebirds, Sapsuckers, etc." Delacour thinks well of American
birds, and has sent favorable reports to his British colleagues.
"The truth is," he wrote in the *Avicultural Magazine* not long
after he came here to live, "that the North American avifauna
is richer and brighter than the European." He is, however, distressed by certain non-ornithological species, or subspecies, he
has detected in the Western Hemisphere. "Unfortunately,
Waterfowl breeding in the [Bronx] Park has many enemies,"
he wrote in the same report. "Horrible wild boys, unfortunately
too numerous in this part of New York City, destroy many
nests, in spite of the keepers' vigilance. Then we have, in North
America, a terrible pest unknown to Europe, the snapping
turtle. Some of them, in our Bronx waters, reach fifty pounds,
or even more . . . strong enough to kill any bird."

Delacour's admiration for the local avifauna and his meetings with nuthatches and nutcrackers have not altogether
reconciled him to the change in his circumstances. In an article
he wrote on "Tree Ducks (*Dendrocygna*)," he revealed something of his feelings about it. The veneration in which the only
man in the world who ever brought back an imperial pheasant
from Indo-China is held among bird-fanciers has perhaps never
been more splendidly expressed than by the fact that in the

summer of 1942, though the paper shortage had forced it to change from a monthly to a bi-monthly, the *Avicultural Magazine* published this article in its entirety. It commenced in this curiously roundabout fashion:

At 168 East 63rd Street, in a district of New York comparable to the Mayfair of London, I sit at my desk to write on Tree Ducks for the *Avicultural Magazine*. How many times before have I sat down to write for the *Avicultural Magazine?* I started more than twenty-five years ago at Villers-Bretonneux, and I have done it again and again, on innumerable occasions, mostly at Clères, and sometimes also at some dear friend's house: Brinsop, Foxwarren, or Wormley. . . . Today is Easter Sunday, a mild sunny day, and it is late in the afternoon. New York is just as nice a city to live in as Paris or London. But I always disliked cities. I look through my window and I see a row of small houses, not at all offensive, but just indifferent and disparate. A town street has always looked unlovely to me. When still a small boy I had loudly announced that I wanted always to live in the country, in the middle of a large park, where nothing ugly could offend one's view as far as one could see. It then seemed to be reasonable enough a wish and I have long pretty well succeeded in fulfilling it. But when my world goes to ruin it all seems so remote and fantastic! What now calls back to my memory the regret of a lost paradise is the sudden vision of Tree Ducks. Had I been sitting at my desk at Clères, in King Henry IV's room, only a very few years ago on the late afternoon of an Easter Sunday, I should undoubtedly have seen through the large mullioned windows dozens of Tree Ducks on the wing, calling shrilly high in the sky on their evening flight. Where are my flocks of full-winged Tree Ducks now, and all the countless bird treasures accumulated at Clères, and, further back in the years, at Villers? Gone with the wind. I fear that in this present dreary world, at least in our lifetime, there will be no opportunities for the restoration and the continuation of such activities as the keeping of large private collections. We shall have to be content with the care of public ones, and I feel fortunate in having been given the charge of those of the New York Zoological Park. From my new office at the Bronx I see only wild woods and water, and this is some consolation. . . .

But to come back to the Tree Ducks . . .

Delacour has since moved farther north in Mayfair, to the Stanhope, at Fifth Avenue and Eighty-first Street, where he lives with his mother, who is eighty-six. He spends three days a week at the Bronx Zoo and two or three at the Museum of Natural History. At the Museum, he likes to poke around in trays which contain seven hundred and fifty thousand bird skins, noting the relationships between various species. In collaboration with Dr. Ernst Mayr, Curator of the Whitney-Rothschild Collection of skins at the Museum, he has just finished a book on the birds of the Philippines and is now working on one about the birds of Malaysia and on a monograph on pheasants. On his Museum days, he gets to his office at nine, and pokes and writes until around one. He then lunches at the Century Club, or, if he feels in a mood for mental relaxation, at the Knickerbocker. Afternoons, he returns to the Museum for a few hours more of research and writing. He is a restless man and does not like to stay in the same place very long, and the fact that he has two widely separated offices gives him something like the feeling of change his old Clères-Paris-England routine once gave him. He is convinced that if he had to show up at the same place every day, he would go crazy.

Delacour has made several trips to the West since 1940, generally on behalf of the Fish and Wildlife Service, a branch of the Department of the Interior to which he is a consultant. In this capacity, he has made a determined effort to save the trumpeter swan, the biggest wild bird in North America, from following in the footsteps, or the wingbeats, of the passenger pigeon, the Carolina parakeet, the heath hen, the Labrador duck, and the great auk. In 1935, there were fewer than sixty trumpeter swans in the United States; in 1944, thanks to refuges in Yellowstone Park and Red Rock Lakes, Montana, which the Fish and Wildlife Service supplied with grain, there were nearly three hundred. During a visit to these lakes that summer, Delacour and a couple of colleagues sneaked about in a rowboat and captured twenty trumpeter cygnets, or over one-fifteenth of the United States trumpeter swan population. Delacour packed them in pairs in crates, and chaperoned them on a three-day, seven-hundred-mile trip by truck to the Malheur Lake Refuge in Oregon, where the Fish and Wildlife people have set up a breeding pen. In town, where he is a popular extra man, Delacour's closest friend is James Hazen Hyde, and his dinner-party companions are a fairly formal bunch of Tuckers, Vanderbilts, and Rothschilds, but on his Western tours he is the soul of democracy. According to Osborn, who has accompanied him on several, Delacour is known by his first name (but pronounced "Gene") in avicultural circles from western Missouri to the Pacific. "In San Francisco and Los Angeles," Mr. Osborn says, "all these homely, native, nice Californians up in the hills come in to see 'Gene.' They tell him about their little aviaries, and he'll go fifty or sixty miles to see these little collections, and hold long palavers in their back yards about the breeding of the sulphur-crested cockatoo. He's just one of the boys. He has an absolute brother love for anyone interested in birds." Delacour is, however, a trifle snobbish about birds. His passion for rarities is the dominant one, and he doesn't care much for tramping around fields merely to look at any old bird, as many ornithologists do. When he is in the company of other worldly bird fanciers, his sense of noblesse oblige becomes inoperative and he gives way to his true feelings. A few years ago he spent a weekend at the Connecticut country house of Dr. Dillon Ripley, a well-connected ornithologist. Delacour stared, but said nothing, when his host suggested that they get up early the next morning to inspect a flight of warblers. Ripley knocked doubtfully at Delacour's door at six. His guest presently came downstairs, in shirt and gray flannels, took a few steps outside the house, said, "I guess I won't go," and went back to bed. "Jean was trying to be polite because I was a new acquaintance," Dr. Ripley says, "but he just couldn't go through with it."

Soon after going to England following the bombing of Clères, Fooks, Delacour's head keeper and estate manager, was engaged to take charge of the aviaries of Major the Honourable Henry Broughton, an old friend of Delacour's and a grandson of H. H. Rogers, the American oil millionaire. The Germans, in their retreat from the Rouen-Dieppe area, abandoned Delacour's estate in August, 1944. Within a few days, a British service woman who is a niece of his friend Ezra happened to be in the neighborhood and had a look at the estate. "There are about sixty duck, three swans, two sarus cranes," she wrote him, "and Nenette is still there. The last hyacinth macaw was taken off by a German lieutenant." Delacour's spirits rose at news of Nenette, and they rose higher shortly before V-E Day, when another British Army friend, a lieutenant colonel who had just visited Clères while on duty nearby, wrote him that little serious damage had been done to the grounds. Mr. Fooks, who had gone to work for Delacour in 1920 and felt that, in spite of the job of caring for Major Broughton's birds, he had been marking time for five years, managed to get to Clères in July, 1945, to have a look at the situation. He reported that the neighbor to whom Delacour had given his power of attorney had kept three gardeners working on the place throughout the occupation and that most of the aviaries were in fair shape. "Far more damage has been done by Plichon's children than by bombs," he wrote; Plichon was one of the gardeners. Fooks has been living at Clères, building the bird collection up again on his own. He has been given access to some of the Delacour money still in France. Furthermore, the Paris Zoo has returned the survivors of the handful of Delacour birds it took for safe-keeping in 1940 and has been sending Fooks consignments of birds and eggs, on the understanding that the young will be shared between it and Clères. The London Zoo has helped out on the same basis. Many of Delacour's zoological friends, among them Ezra, Lewis, and the Duke of Bedford, have presented waterfowl, wallabies, and pheasants to the Parc Zoologique de Clères.

Next May, the Parc, which now contains more than four hundred birds and animals, representing fifty species or sub-species, will be opened to the public for the first time in seven years. This fall, Delacour will make a trip to France and England, and he expects to visit his place, but not to settle down there. He hopes that either the Paris Muséum d'Histoire Naturelle or the New York Zoological Society will accept it as a gift. "From anywhere in Clères, you could see nothing nasty," he told a friend recently. "The trees were planted at the right places, it was surrounded by low hills, and there was nothing that wasn't nice to look at. I suppose it can be fairly decent again—even now, the waterfowl collection is better than the Zoo's here—but I never want to stay there more than a few days. I've been very well received here, I'm a citizen, and it really makes no difference to me if I am in New York, in London, or in Paris—I see the same kind of people. I like to see people who are nice and sensible and with whom you can talk about something you like—birds, for instance, or gibbons. It is not amusing, after all, at fifty-five, to contemplate the pitiful remains of what you've taken so much trouble about. You can do without things altogether but you can't do with odds and ends."

Delacour's friend went away, however, with the feeling that

the New York Zoological Society's Technical Adviser might someday decide, after all, to stretch a visit to Clères to more than just a few days. Not long after this conversation, Delacour spent a pensive half hour reading a long letter from Fooks, in which the head keeper itemized his latest acquisitions, among them a consignment of parrots and parakeets from the Paris Zoo. "All are in splendid condition," he wrote, "and the Queen of Bavaria's Conure is a marvellous color: almost orange."

August, 1946

For Bird Fanciers Only

A ᴺ elderly troupial owner of our acquaintance has relayed to us, without comment, two editorials published, respectively, at the outset of the first and second World Wars in the *Avicultural Magazine* of London, a monthly periodical devoted to the interests of people who keep birds. The first one appeared in the issue of September, 1914:

It is calamitous and infamous that not only peace-loving nations should be forced into stupendous war, but also that thousands of Germans who must hate and loathe it should have to be involved and become our enemies. The Germans are great bird-lovers; everywhere in Germany there are signs of this in the numerous nesting-boxes for the benefit of the wild birds. . . . The vileness of the plots of the Prussian War Party, with the inflated vanity of the Kaiser to back it up, is completely outside our experiences of and dealings with German bird-lovers.

The second appeared in the October, 1939, issue:

A war has now broken upon us bringing untold misery and suffering—a war which no one wants and which we have done our utmost to avoid. It is not a war against a country, but a war against a system. . . . Though we are now inevitably cut off from the German aviculturists, I feel sure that I am voicing the opinion of the majority of their colleagues in other countries in saying that the friendly regard for them will remain unchanged, and if they ever read these words they will know that no bitterness is felt towards them.

Bird fanciers everywhere, it seems clear, are permanently in an anti-global-strife mood, which we applaud. Settle them, we say, in influential roosts—presidencies, premierships, cabinet posts, ambassadorships, U.N. delegateships—with plenty of light, air, water, and meal worms. Insist that the present occupants of high places *become* bird fanciers. Nesting-boxes in every chancellery, dancing cranes in the Kremlin and White House ballrooms, friendly chirps instead of gruff ultimatums; roll up the iron curtains and insert a piece of lettuce, thoughtfully seasoned with cut-up carrot. Just think what might have happened had Chamberlain flown to Berchtesgaden with an umbrella bird!

Boy Meets Bullfinch

D R. FRANK M. CHAPMAN, who has been Curator of Ornithology at the American Museum of Natural History
since 1908, has probably spent more time in the society of birds
than any other man of his generation. For over sixty years he
has patiently concealed himself in bushes and blinds all over
North and South America in order to study at close range the
habits of everything from the blue jay and the pelican to the
vulture and the dusky-tailed ant tanager. He has reported his
findings in some two hundred scientific papers, in *Bird-Lore*,
an ornithological magazine which he founded in 1899 and
edited for thirty-six years, and in fifteen books, which have sold,
all told, over a quarter of a million copies. His "Handbook of
Birds of Eastern North America" first published in 1895, still
sells around 800 copies a year. Since going to work at the
Museum in 1888, Dr. Chapman has helped build up its collection of bird specimens from about 10,000 to over 750,000 and
to make its bird department the best in the world.

With the exception of a few species which he dislikes, like
starlings and English sparrows, Chapman has a whole-souled

admiration for birds. His approach to his subject is aesthetic and social rather than physiological, and he is more concerned with a bird's appearance, song, and way of life than with its underlying bone structure. His book "The Warblers of North America," for example, carefully classifies warblers into such groups as Warblers Which Have Loud, Whistled Songs; Warblers Which Have Not Loud, Whistled Songs; Warblers Which Have Songs of the Wee-Chee or Cher-Wee Type, with a Whistled Quality; Warblers Whose Songs Possess Pebbly, Twittering Notes or Which Suggest a Song of the Chipping Sparrow or Junco Type; and Warblers in Whose Songs There Is a Pronounced Zee Quality. This book contains plenty of the sort of prose which has made Dr. Chapman the most influential man since Audubon in interesting people in birds, prose which in its way tells a good deal about Dr. Chapman himself:

All the sweetness and promise of spring seems stored in Parula's little sizzling gurgle; there is good cheer and sunshine in Yellow Warbler's lay; peace and rest in the quaint *zeeing* of the Black-throated Green. . . . If, however, you would see the [Yellow-Breasted] Chat satisfactorily, fight him with his own fire. Seat yourself in the thicket where as pursuer you are at the bird's mercy, and with pursed lips *squeak* gently but persistently. Soon there will be an answering *chut*, and with due patience and discretion you may induce this elusive creature to appear before you. I do not recall a more suspicious bird than the Chat. . . . The song of the Redstart can be readily recognized by those who know it but like so many Warblers' songs of what may be called the *weechy* type, loses all character when it is reduced to syllables.

Dr. Chapman's idea of a tremendous compliment is to compare a person to a bird, and he once said of the late Lord Grey, bird-loving statesman, "Grey was the most charming host and companion, just like a bird." Dr. Chapman likes to think that birds are fond of him, too, and enjoys telling friends of the time an English wild eider duck permitted him to stroke her as she sat on her eggs. "She turned and pecked my finger gently, almost caressingly, I thought," he says. A good many birds have come to tolerate Dr. Chapman during his long career, and this pleases him immensely. One winter in Florida he spent the better part of three days forty-five feet up in a cypress tree, in a blind consisting of a green umbrella and a lot of Spanish moss, in order to observe herons and egrets. The birds in the vicinity kept their distance for a while, but toward the end of the third afternoon a spoonbill and two snowy egrets came and roosted in the same tree with him. Dr. Chapman, then a young man, felt he had arrived. "Surely," he later wrote in the first of several autobiographical books, "Camps and Cruises of an Ornithologist," "this was an honor these rarest of American birds have accorded few ornithologists." He did not allow the experience to turn his head, however, and went on to report in a matter-of-fact way that the adult egret says "Cuk-cuk-cuk," while young egrets say "Kek-kek-kek."

For the last thirty-five years, Dr. Chapman, along with most North American birds, has migrated South in the winter, usually going to Florida, South America, or Panama. In the spring he comes North again with the first robin. He is able to reproduce the songs of any number of birds by whistling and likes nothing better than to fool a bird into thinking he is another bird. By answering their songs in the woods, he has astonished many varieties of birds, who have come up within a few feet of him and looked at him closely. Since some of them sing only to attract mates, Dr. Chapman's replies have led to a certain amount of disappointment, misunderstanding, and bad feeling among birds. He often used to imitate an owl's cry while walking in the country, in order to get a flock of crows, who despise owls, to fly up and caw at him. He once played this trick when a real owl was around. Crows flew up and attacked the owl, which was quietly taking a nap. The owl was amazed.

Dr. Chapman, who likes an owl as well as the next bird, has not done this since. He did, however, in the interests of science, play a rather elaborate trick not long ago on some blue jays. He wanted to see, at close range, the jays feed their young, and after spending several fruitless hours near a blue-jay nest, while concealed in a canvas affair painted to resemble tree bark and liberally draped with poison-ivy vines, he hit on the idea of wiring a mounted blue jay to a limb below the nest. He thought the parent jays, who were frightened away by his blind, would come back to evict the stranger loitering near their home. Instead, the mother at once returned and fed her young, apparently reassured by the mounted bird, whom she took for an old friend of the family's. Dr. Chapman next removed the dummy jay and replaced it with a mounted screech owl, which is a great enemy of the jay. The parent jays screamed in horror and attacked the owl, which they knocked over so that it hung upside down, still wired to the tree. Even in this position it continued to terrify the jays, and Dr. Chapman, who thought the thing had gone far enough, finally removed it.

Dr. Chapman has on several occasions occupied the nests of some of the larger birds himself. Some years ago, marooned by a storm on a small island in a Canadian lake, he moved three pelican eggs from one nest to another and climbed into the vacant nest, which was made of heaped-up sand and pebbles and was well above water level. He sat there in comparative snugness until the downpour was over, feeling exactly like a pelican. Another time, on a beach in the Bahamas, he passed several days in an unoccupied nest in the middle of a settlement of two thousand flamingos, making notes and taking photographs. The flamingos accepted Dr. Chapman as one of themselves and poked about right under his nose. "Seated on the deserted nest," he reported, "I myself seemed to have became a flamingo." For all this, Dr. Chapman realizes that he is actually neither a flamingo nor a pelican. He deplores the fact that there is no real communication between men and birds and that consequently he is unable to let certain birds know how much he enjoys their singing. "I often wish there were some way of assuring vireolanius that he is doing more than his duty," he once said.

Most of the time when he has not been directly fraternizing with birds, Dr. Chapman has spent classifying them, skinning them, writing about them, agitating to get them off women's hats, helping establish sanctuaries for them, and lecturing on them. He began to lecture in the eighteen-nineties in order to supplement the modest salary he was then getting as associate curator of the Museum's Department of Ornithology and Mammalogy. He made his first talk at the Ogontz School, a girls' institution near Philadelphia. Dr. Chapman, who in those days felt more at home in a cypress tree than on a lecture platform, pretended to himself that he was talking to a group of birds, and everything went smoothly. He soon became known as the most articulate ornithologist in the country and was invited to give lecture courses at places ranging all the way from the University of Indiana to the Lowell Institute in Boston. In 1901 he got a letter from the New York Farmers, an organization he had never heard of, asking him to speak on farm birds at their annual dinner. Dr. Chapman, then a rising young ornithologist of thirty-seven, was reluctant to waste an evening before a group of agriculturists and rather offhandedly recommended another speaker, pleading a prior engagement. The next year the Farmers invited him again. Not wishing to be rude, he accepted and found himself at a dinner at the Metropolitan Club, surrounded by such farmers as J. P. Morgan, George F. Baker, Cleveland H. Dodge, and Adrian Iselin. The New York Farmers turned out to be a group of part-time country gentlemen who met once a year to eat

an enormous meal and discuss the problems of Long Island and
Westchester estates. The private dining room where Dr. Chapman addressed them was embellished with moss, plants, a small
log cabin, and dozens of mounted birds. Dr. Chapman was
torn between pleasure at the company and dismay at the
arrangement of the stuffed birds. "Without regard to haunt
or habit, 100 or more of these specimens were distributed where
they could be most easily attached or seemed to produce the
best effect," he wrote in his autobiography. "It was a Habitat
group such as never was seen before or since. There were Terns
in the evergreens and Swallows on the forest floor, while birds
of the Temperate and Tropic Zones met in a hitherto unheard-
of association."

In recent years, Dr. Chapman, who is seventy-five, has had to
give up lecturing, but he still likes to talk about birds by the
hour to friends and visitors at the Museum, and he is writing
his sixteenth book about the subject with which he has been
in love all his life. He was born in 1864 on his family's forty-
acre farm in Englewood, N.J. The place was full of birds and
he was conscious of the songs of wrens, bluebirds, and red-
winged blackbirds from the start. He was the first birdman in
the Chapman line. His father, a lawyer associated with Joseph
H. Choate's firm, paid no particular attention to birds. Frank
thinks he may have inherited from his grandfather the patience
which has enabled him to set down long, detailed classifications
of birds. His grandfather was Lebbeus Chapman, a banker who
between July 1, 1846, and May 25, 1847, copied the entire
Bible in longhand, averaging four hours a day at this work.
    Dr. Chapman recalls seeing his first cardinal at the age of
eight while visiting his grandparents in Georgia. This visit also
brought him into contact with a European bullfinch, owned
by a neighbor of his grandparents, which made a deep impres-

sion on him. He memorized the song of this bird and still whistles it occasionally. It takes twenty-three seconds, which is long for a birdcall. An uncle to whom he whistled the bullfinch song was so favorably affected that he gave Frank his first book about birds, Johnson's "Natural History," and later sent him some pelican feathers. These became the nucleus of a rather large accumulation of feathers. Frank got his mother's cook to give him wings of prairie hens, then common in butcher shops, and enlarged his collection of feathers by shooting robins, blue jays, Carolina parakeets, and cedar waxwings, and by trapping bobolinks. Today he wouldn't think of trapping a bobolink. He has followed the bobolink to its winter quarters in the Argentine and has pronounced it his favorite American bird. "I like it for its sweet song," he wrote in one of his books, "for its high character, for its habits, and for its extraordinary migrations." He feels different about ducks, and has been an active duck-shooter most of his life, pursuing this sport somewhat surreptitiously in later years out of deference to an anti-duck-shooting bloc in the Audubon Society.

Dr. Chapman graduated from Englewood Academy in 1880 and then went to work for the American Exchange National Bank in New York. He had an independent income of around $2,000 a year, left to him by his father, and although he had no particular desire for more money, he thought he should find some sort of conventional career. He commuted every day and on the train fell in with a couple of Hackensack bird-lovers, who lent him ornithological books, showed him their collections of mounted birds, and introduced him to other birdmen. Dr. Chapman toiled faithfully at the bank, but his heart was in the woods and he frequently stimulated his colleagues by whistling bird songs as he worked. He became a faithful reader of *Forest & Stream* and in 1884 answered an appeal in this publication, issued by Dr. C. Hart Merriman, chairman of the committee on

bird migration of the recently organized American Ornithologists' Union, calling for volunteers to observe and report on the
seasonal movements of birds. In the line of duty, Dr. Chapman rose at dawn every morning from March 10th through
May 23rd and went into the woods to shoot birds. He followed
a route which got him to the West Englewood station at 7:30,
where he checked the birds, changed from rough clothes to a
double-breasted blue suit, and boarded the 7:39 train to business. In the evening he would pick up the birds at the station
and usually shoot more specimens before dinner. After dinner
he skinned the day's haul and took notes. During this period
he turned up at the bank every day except May 15th, when he
got so excited after getting a Brewster's warbler that he took
the day off. His report was pronounced the best in the Atlantic
Division and he was invited to join the Linnæan Society of
New York, a natural-history group which specializes in birds.
Through this organization he got to meet still more birdmen. In 1885 he was elected an associate member of the Ornithologists' Union. His passion for birds made him dissatis-
fied with his work at the bank but didn't interfere with his
business progress, and in the fall of 1886 he was placed in
charge of the city collecting department. He saw ahead long
years of steady advancement and this discouraged him. He
resigned at once. He had decided to become a full-time birdman.

He spent the next year studying water birds in Florida
and helping Dr. J. A. Allen, Curator of Ornithology and
Mammalogy at the American Museum of Natural History,
assort, catalogue, label, and arrange a collection of 8,000 birds
which had been given to the Museum. Dr. Chapman claims
his previous experience in sorting checks at the bank was good
training for this. He worked at first as a volunteer, living on
his small income, but in the winter of 1888 Dr. Allen took

him on as an assistant at $50 a month. Dr. Allen was more concerned with research than exhibition, and Dr. Chapman concentrated on building up ornithological showcases. One of the first things he did was to arrange a collection of all birds found nesting within fifty miles of City Hall. He later enlarged this to include migratory birds, which he placed on view at the time they were passing through the metropolitan district. Boys would come in from the Park to identify birds they had seen and Dr. Chapman's office became a centre for informal ornithological discussion.

During the eighteen-nineties, Dr. Chapman became recognized as one of the country's leading birdmen. His famous "Handbook" came out in 1895. Around this time he wrote a popular series on the birds of Central Park for the *Evening Post*, was selected president of the Linnæan Society, served on the council and committee on bird protection of the American Ornithologists' Union, and helped edit the Union's official magazine, the *Auk*. He wrote original papers on subjects like the origin of Bahaman bird life and the habits of grackles. He once tried to get permission to shoot a grackle in Central Park, but the Parks Department politely discouraged him. In 1897 he arranged the first meeting of the New York Audubon Society. Morris K. Jesup, president of the Society and of the Museum, spoke on bird conservation. "The audience . . . was doubtless the largest that had ever gathered in this country to urge recognition of Citizen Bird," Dr. Chapman wrote of the meeting. A few years later he was asked for his opinion of the eagles on the new $10 and $20 gold pieces designed by Augustus St. Gaudens. Dr. Chapman said the eagles were incorrect in pose and structure, but approved of the coins on aesthetic grounds.

Dr. Chapman's formal education stopped with high school. He owes his title of Doctor to an honorary scientific degree which Brown awarded him in 1913. He holds evolutionary theories which most scientists today feel are old-fashioned and incorrect, to the effect that environment can cause germinal changes. Younger curators on his staff, like Ernst Mayr, James P. Chapin, and Robert Cushman Murphy, have a command of morphology which Dr. Chapman lacks, but these men admire Dr. Chapman for making ornithology, once an almost esoteric affair, an enormously popular subject and for creating a good will which has been worth millions to the Museum. When Dr. Chapman first came to the Museum, the bird department consisted of a single room on the top floor of the original Museum building on Seventy-seventh Street. Today it has a $1,500,000 wing of its own, presented jointly by the late Harry Payne Whitney and the city of New York. The department overflows onto three additional floors, one of which is devoted to the Rothschild collection of 280,000 birds. Mrs. Whitney bought the Rothschild specimens for the Museum a few years ago from the late Lord Rothschild. Like ninety-nine per cent of the Museum's birds, they constitute a study collection and are not on public view. The skins, unmounted, repose in filing cabinets, where students may inspect them. The publicity which accompanied this gift brought hundreds of people to the Museum, who were indignant at not being able to see the birds. Some of them angrily told Dr. Chapman that they would report him to the Mayor. The British Museum was indignant, too, because Lord Rothschild, although a trustee, had never even offered to sell it his collection. Dr. Chapman has mollified the London Museum by giving it a lot of British birds which are of greater interest in England than here.

Dr. Chapman's greatest contribution to museology has been the introduction of the habitat idea in exhibitions. Fifty years ago an American museum's concept of a bird exhibit consisted of a lot of stuffed specimens arranged in a manner reminiscent of the grill of a college club. Around 1900, John L. Cadwalader, an early patron of the Museum, gave Dr. Chapman $1,200 and asked him to get up a bird group with a background that would make sense. Dr. Chapman produced a Cobb's Island, Virginia, group which contained black skimmers and other indigenous birds against a setting of beach composed of actual sand and artificial seaweed, which merged with a painted background of ocean, sky, and birds. Nesting birds were placed on the beach. A good many of the people in the Museum thought this was too informal and that the painted background verged on the sensational, but President Jesup proclaimed it beautiful and the Cobb's Island group, which is still there, is now part of a gallery of habitat groups of North American birds. The habitat idea has been applied to all the other departments in the Museum and has been taken up by museums all over the world.

In getting material for habitat groups, Dr. Chapman has travelled extensively in this country, Canada, the West Indies, and Central and South America. In order to facilitate expeditions through oil or mining territory that is closed to foreigners, he fortifies himself with letters from Museum trustees, which he does up with gold ribbon and calls his dago-dazzlers. He is inclined to minimize the occasional hardships of these trips and in his autobiography refers to being "interrupted" on one excursion when actually he had developed a fever two weeks from the nearest railhead and was blind for ten days. He is a pioneer photographer of wild life, never going on a trip without half a dozen cameras, and his pictures of tropical birds were the first photographs the *Century Magazine* ever published. He has written two 700-page volumes on the distribution of bird life in Colombia and Ecuador and has had a number of South American birds named after him—among them what was thought to be a new genus of parrots. A Brazilian naturalist named it Chapmania. Dr. Chapman is a little disparaging about Chapmania. "It wasn't really a separable genus," he says.

About fifteen years ago Dr. Chapman made his first visit to Barro Colorado Island, which is in Gatun Lake, a part of the Panama Canal. The island, once a mountain top, is a complete faunal unit, which means it has all the birds and animals it ought to have, with no depredations at the hands of man. Dr. Chapman built a house on Barro Colorado and has spent eight or nine winters there, surrounded by over 230 species of birds, including guans, parrots, wood hewers, purple gallinules, crested tinamous, wood quails, and short-keeled toucans. He has installed a Barro Colorado habitat case in the Museum, and he has also observed and taken flashlight pictures of ocelots, tapirs, peccaries, agoutis, crocodiles, and pumas. Most of these photographs were taken at night by camera traps sprung by trip wires, which set off the flash when an animal touched them. Dr. Chapman is the last man in the world to hurt the feelings of a peccary or a puma and has refused to install a second camera to get the animal's reaction to the flashlight of the first. "It is bad enough to give an animal the scare of its life," he says. "To photograph its uncontrollable response to the impulse of fear is adding insult to injury." Dr. Chapman has often lured animals to the trap by tying a ripe banana to the wire. The first time he got a tapir this way, he left a banana, unwired, as a gift the next day. While at Barro Colorado he got to like four-footed animals almost as much as birds. "Indeed, there were moments," he writes, "when I felt that I *was* an agouti."

After fifty years in the same office, Dr. Chapman moved to the new Whitney wing a year ago, but he still keeps his old rolltop desk. He seems to be more sensitive to electricity than most people and to keep from getting shocks he wears crêpe-soled shoes and has had his doorknobs covered with rubber. He used to encourage pigeons to come into his office, feeding them lavishly with seeds, but the Museum eventually discouraged this. He lunches with the other curators in a special room off the main restaurant in the Museum and at mealtimes he and Dr. Chapin often exchange whistling sounds, challenging each other to identify the bird whose song is being imitated. "It's near the genus Myiagra" is the kind of thing they say to each other on these occasions. Dr. Frank Lutz, the Museum's Curator of Entomology, sits opposite Dr. Chapman at lunch and the two men bandy remarks about the merits of their respective departments. New insect species turn up much more often than new birds, so Dr. Chapman is at a disadvantage in this respect, but his department naturally occupies more space than Dr. Lutz's, and Dr. Chapman is gratified by Lutz's charges that the Museum houses far too many birds. Everyone envies Dr. Barnum Brown, who is in charge of dinosaurs.

Forty-one years ago, Dr. Chapman married Mrs. Fannie Bates Embury, who had divorced her first husband, a lawyer. Dr. Chapman was delighted to find that his wife was a competent bird-skinner. He tried her out on their honeymoon in Florida with a long-billed marsh wren that had been badly shot, and she did so well that he next gave her a dusky seaside sparrow, a bird so rare, he says, that "I handle it myself with caution." Dr. Chapman has a son, Frank, Jr., who is married to Gladys Swarthout, the singer. Frank, Jr., is a singer, too, and attributes his vocal prowess to the wind power he developed blowing up air mattresses on early bird expeditions with his father in the Andes, where the 7,000- to 13,000-foot altitudes make blowing up mattresses very taxing. The senior Chapmans, who live on Fifth Avenue, have a dining room full of paintings of birds, and like to give musical parties at which Dr. Chapman whistles birdcalls he has brought back from South America.

When thinking back over his long career, Dr. Chapman takes especial pride in the fact that in 1899 he started the Christmas Bird Census, which today inspires several thousand bird-lovers all over the country to send reports to the Audubon Society of birds seen on Christmas Day walks. He is also proud of his conservation work. He got into a bitter conservational row several years ago with the late Dr. William T. Hornaday, director of the Bronx Zoo. Dr. Hornaday, whose eyesight was failing, got the idea that American birds were rapidly disappearing and declined to be reassured by Dr. Chapman, who said there were plenty of birds around. Dr. Hornaday said the entire avifauna of the continent was dying out and talked and wrote sarcastically of Dr. Chapman's beautiful faith in the future of birds. His attack was pronounced unfair by the scientific world. Dr. Chapman's position was strengthened by the fact that it was he who started the whole system of bird sanctuaries in this country by persuading Theodore Roosevelt to declare Pelican Island in Florida a bird reservation in 1903. At first the pelicans failed to appreciate this, owing to the circumstance that the Audubon Society erected an enormous white sign on Pelican Island with "No Trespass" on it in black letters. This frightened the pelicans so that they went to other islands, but after the sign was removed the next year, they came back. Dr. Chapman corresponded about birds with Roosevelt over a period of twenty years. He was a frequent visitor at the White House during the Roosevelt administration and was, with several other scientists, dining with the President at Sagamore Hill in 1910 when Roosevelt was called to the telephone to be informed of Taft's first public attack on him. Dr. Chapman recalls with admiration that when the President returned to the table, his first words were "Now, where did you say the Hudsonian form intergraded with the Alaskan?"

March, 1939

Why I Give the
Postman Five Dollars
Every Christmas
III

My Unrequited Passion

Most people, it seems to me, have prodigious memories enabling them to recall Beatrice Lillie's first songs in this country, plots of novels read months before, and just what their mothers said about them, or to them, a few minutes after their birth. For some reason which I would not care to have a psychoanalyst explain, it is difficult for me at any given moment to put my finger on anything that has happened to me more than a week before. I have no idea what I was doing on the night of March 6th last, or where I spent my vacation in the summer of 1931, and the precise recollection of people on the witness stand, or at dinner parties, in matters of this sort frequently astonishes me.

Two recollections of my early youth still stand out, however. One is of the time I was given a Luna moth for my insect collection. The other is of sitting in the subway with my sister's governess, whom I occasionally borrowed for the day, a copy of the old New York *Globe* spread out in my lap, wondering why in the devil there was no afternoon paper of convenient size, untrammelled by advertising, without political affiliations but with strong feelings for or against this or that candidate in local, state, and national elections, against racial intolerance, and costing five cents a copy instead of two. "Governess," I said, after having mentioned these qualifications, "why is there no paper of this kind, with pages eleven and a fraction inches by fourteen and a fraction in size, printed on special-grade, dull-finish, full-fibred stock, its pages stapled together on the press for the reader's convenience, so that they do not fall apart?"

"*Tiens, le petit gosse,*" Governess replied, gluing together the pages of her Petit Larousse with a pot of glue which she always carried along for this purpose.

"What I should like to see," I pursued, "is a paper with columns thirty-six per cent wider than is now standard for newspapers, all stories printed in full in one place, edited, from the point of continuity, as if no other newspaper were being published, with so large a department devoted to Radio that it could not be compared to any existing treatment, and containing a Beauty department whose only preoccupation would be enhancing the good looks of the paper's readers in the most scientific way, at the lowest possible cost, and with the least trouble."

This conversation took place over twenty-five years ago, but it returned vividly to my mind late this April when I received in the mail a fifteen-page mimeographed prospectus marked "Confidential Memorandum From: Ralph Ingersoll To: The Staff of *PM*." Announcing the publication of a new daily newspaper, *PM*, the first number of which was scheduled to appear June 18th, the enclosure described the coming periodical as having no advertising, stapled pages eleven and a fraction inches by fourteen and a fraction in size, a policy of no political affiliations but strong feelings for or against this or that candidate in local, state, and national elections, a price of five cents a copy—and, in fact, all the other physical and editorial features which had occurred to me in the subway. Scarcely glancing at the accompanying letter urging me to subscribe, I filled out a subscription blank, according to which, as a Charter

Subscriber, I would receive *PM* from the very first issue.

A few weeks later, as I was waiting impatiently for June 18th to arrive, trying to calm myself with various odd tasks about the house, such as trying to open the living-room windows, I received another Confidential Memorandum, identical with the first one except that it was printed instead of mimeographed, had a red border, and was headed by a statement, in black capital letters, to the effect that it had been sent to me at the suggestion of John L. Loeb. Mr. Loeb is an acquaintance of many years' standing, a partner in the brokerage firm of Carl M. Loeb, Rhoades & Co., and a man who patronizes the same barber shop that I do; I felt that his implied recommendation was a good sign, and I became more impatient than ever for June 18th. I did not, however, fill out the second subscription card, which accompanied the memorandum, feeling that this would only confuse *PM's* circulation department, which had already sent me a letter confirming the fact that I was a Charter Subscriber.

On Saturday, June 15th, I received a preview copy of *PM*, marked Vol. 1, No. 0, and dated Friday, June 14th. "This special limited edition is being sent to you as one of *PM's* Charter Subscribers," read a statement on the first page. ". . . the staff asks you to withhold judgment until the actors have learned their lines." The pages were stapled together and did not fall apart; they were approximately eleven by fourteen inches in size and contained neither advertising nor any manifestation of racial intolerance. My boyhood dream seemed to have come true.

There really would be nothing more to say, except that this was the only copy of *PM* I ever got. June 18th came and went, with nothing to show but a copy of the *Times*, falling apart at every other page and full of the most undisguised advertising you ever saw. The story has been the same every day since then

—no *PM*, no strong feelings for or against this or that candidate in local, state, and national elections, no scientific enhancing of my good looks. As a Charter Subscriber, I feel as though I had joined a club whose doorman refused to let me in. I do not know Ralph Ingersoll—although I once knew a Ralph *McAllister* Ingersoll, a mining engineer who wrote a book called "In and Under Mexico"—so it cannot be anything personal. For a while I thought my rebuff might have been caused by my failure to fill out the *second* subscription card, but in that case why did *PM* send me the preview copy? It might have been just to tantalize me, of course, but somehow *PM* doesn't sound like that sort of paper. The experience has given an ugly twist to one of my few childhood recollections, and it is only a partial consolation to know that I still have the Luna moth, slightly damaged with the years but neatly stapled together, of convenient size, free of advertising, and without political affiliations.

How's Your Backhand?

M Y tennis backhand is terrible, so when I saw an envelope
marked "Donald Budge and Sidney Wood" in my
incoming mail the other day, I opened it with alacrity. Word
of my backhand has got to Budge and Wood, I thought, and
those two friendly tennis players are sending me a tip, perhaps
even a full set of instructions. Not at all. Budge and Wood, it
seems, are in the fur-storage, fur-cleaning, rug-, carpet-,
drapery-, tapestry-, upholstered-furniture-, pillow-, table-throw-,
and slipcover-cleaning, de-mothing, and laundry business, and
their communication to me consisted of three pieces of literature outlining the virtues of their services. "Your home deserves
. . . de-mothing," one of them read, and went on to say that
Budge-Wood's "trained workmen, under a supervising expert,"
would dust-clean my carpets "with specially designed non-beating vacuum cleaners that extract dirt *imbedded* in the fibres,
then gently but thoroughly shampoo them until the true colors
reappear in all their *original* brightness and lustre." As for
upholstered furniture, "each piece is first carefully vacuumed,
reaching every tiny crevice, then *hand* dry cleaned by our
skilled chemists . . . not only over the entire surface, but all
the way *through*."

I was about to apply for these services when I took a look at
the picture accompanying the text. This showed the living room
and bedroom of my house, all right, with six Budge-Wood
trained workmen de-mothing and dust- and dry-cleaning like
nobody's business—except, possibly, Budge-Wood's. Two men
were rolling up the living-room carpet, their hands deep in

moth pupae and larvae; another was scraping moths off a window curtain; a fourth, undoubtedly a skilled chemist (I think Dr. Harold C. Urey), was hand-dry-cleaning the back of an upholstered chair. In the bedroom, a fifth and sixth were busily at work—one vacuum-cleaning the carpet with a non-beating vacuum cleaner, the other removing a suit from my closet, doubtless preparatory to a thorough shampoo. The reason I decided against turning this fantasy into reality was that nowhere in the Budge-Wood panorama did I see the supervising expert. The supervising expert is, I suspect, a union fixture and I feared these reconverted tennis players were probably inviting trouble when they left him out. I know what this sort of negligence leads to—buffalo moths planted by union operatives in every sofa, table throw, and slip-cover; cigar beetles in the humidor; beds pied—and I want no part of it.

I turned next to a folder that showed four colored laundresses playing badminton over a net strung with drying towels and underclothing (the winning, irrelevant, associational touch: a Budge-Wood-laundered brassière whisks the owner to the wonderful Budge-Wood world of sport). The text read:

For "that personal touch" you've despaired of finding, try Budge-Wood this summer. Try us at our risk. Let us launder one full week's wash. Examine it carefully. See if it meets your most exacting requirements. Then, if in any way it does not come up to your expectations, you are under no obligation to pay. Try us on baby's best bib and tucker; on fragile summer frocks . . . fine monogrammed towels . . . bath mats, heavy-duty household linens.

On the back of the folder, headed "On Our Roster of Customers" and printed on a bright pink background, was a list of several dozen breath-taking names—among them, the Metropolitan, Harvard, and Racquet & Tennis Clubs; Miss Norma Shearer, Miss Lili Damita, Miss Marlene Dietrich, Miss Ruth Gordon, Mrs. Robert Sherwood, Mrs. Paul Gallico,

Michael Strange, Mrs. H. C. Brokaw, Mrs. Barklie Henry, Mrs. Courtlandt D. Barnes, Mrs. Grafton Pyne, Mrs. William Burton, Mrs. Sheldon Prentice, Mrs. Winthrop Aldrich, Mrs. W. K. Vanderbilt, Mrs. John Schiff, Mrs. Gerald Warburg, Mrs. Sam Lewisohn, Princess Windisch-Graetz, Deems Taylor, Joseph P. Kennedy, Count Igor Cassini, Sammy Kaye, Leo Durocher, and "Mr. Anthony." These clubs and people are all famous for keeping themselves spotless, and I had already peeled off my shirt and packed it up, along with a personal note to Budge, when a disquieting thought occurred to me. Had the most exacting requirements of these customers been met? Or, perchance, had Mrs. Burton found her Budge-Wood-laundered baby's best bib and tucker not quite up to scratch? Had Miss Damita discovered her table throw, fresh from Budge-Wood, not up to her expectations? Was the Racquet Club disappointed by the condition of its fragile summer frocks? Was "Mr. Anthony" troubled by iron burns in his heavy-duty household linens? In short, were or were not the customers listed by Budge-Wood repeaters? At least one of them, Baroness R. Rothschild, has been dead for some time. The inaccurate documentation which led to the inclusion of this name made me wonder whether the whole list wasn't just a bunch of one-full-week's-wash experimental patrons and no more, saddened beneficiaries of an unsatisfactory free ride. Was Budge-Wood a hive of unpaid bills, returned in anger and disfigured with such scrawls as "Most exacting requirements not met. Spot on bib. Mrs. W. K. Vanderbilt"; "Not up to expectations. Tear in tucker. Marlene Dietrich"; "On behalf of our client, Sammy Kaye, beg to state his socks have shrunk and he is under no obligation to pay. (Signed) Davis, Polk, Wardwell, Sunderland & Kiendl"? Probably not, but you can't take chances with a shirt these days, and before I send that package off, I think I'll give Joe Kennedy a ring and ask him how he came out.

Meanwhile, I am indebted to Donald and Sidney for a new conception of social and celebrity reporting, which I pass along to the society editors of the metropolitan press and to all Broadway and Hollywood columnists. I think the following sample item will make the idea clear:

"Mrs. H. McK. Twombly, accompanied by Leo Durocher, showed up at the Hickory Room last night arm in arm. Mrs. Twombly's blouse was freshly laundered by the Budge-Wood service. Mr. Durocher received congratulations on his faultlessly moth-proofed woollen suit from a group that included Miss Gertrude Lawrence, Mrs. Albert Spalding, and David Selznick. 'Fellow-customers,' he said, 'I owe it all to Flo Twombly. She put me up for Budge-Wood, got the Harvard Club to second me, and I was elected after a wait of only six months, during which I did all my own laundry. Dr. Alexander Hamilton Rice did his best to have me blackballed, but now that I'm in, we greet one another cordially enough in the taproom.'

"Standing on a hand-dry-cleaned rug, Mrs. Twombly and Mr. Durocher greeted guests until a late hour. Among those present were such striking Budge-Wood customers as Mrs. A. F. Schermerhorn, Mrs. Albert Lasker, and Leland Hayward. Cries of 'No moths on me!' mingled festively with the tinkling of swizzle sticks. Mrs. Amos R. E. Pinchot, immaculate in a dust-cleaned slipcover, announced that she is giving a tea for Hattie Carnegie customers at the Colony Club next Wednesday, and *on dit* that a Brooks Brothers-clientele smoker is being planned by several of the town's heavy-duty cotillion leaders."

Do Your Bones Keep Things In,
and If So, What?

GILBERT COLGATE lives at Lloyd Neck, Long Island, in the summer and at 55 East Eighty-sixth Street during the winter. Ensign Orson Munn, Jr., is with the Naval Reserve. Major General Fred Osborn was a recent lecturer at Town Hall. Lieutenant Commander John D. Rockefeller III got out of the Navy last October. Ken Straus is out of the service and married. Lieutenant Commander William E. D. Stokes, Jr., unable to find a house in New York, has settled down contentedly at Lenox, Massachusetts.

I am able to report these facts, and a whole lot more, without fear of successful contradiction thanks to a news-letter sent to my home recently by the Browning School, the alma mater of the aforementioned individuals. I opened the letter without noticing the superscription, and found it to be a printed report from Browning. I didn't recall having gone to Browning, and the nature of the enclosure sent me back to the envelope, which, I discovered, was addressed to Mr. Gouverneur Morris Helfenstein, at my home street and number. I have long thought of changing my name to Gouverneur Morris Helfenstein, having been advised by a numerologist in 1928 that I had better do this, but I kept postponing my decision, because I wanted to use up all my monogrammed handkerchiefs first and thus be in a position to consider the matter dispassionately. When I read the name on the envelope, I assumed that Browning knew my thoughts, and had, indeed, jumped the gun on them.

I turned again to the letter and read "Dear Alumnus." For an instant I suspected that someone who had gone to Browning had got ahead of me in changing his name to Gouverneur Morris Helfenstein and was perhaps living somewhere in my house. I cursed myself for a dilatory fool and an unobservant householder, but was reassured by the letter's opening sentence, which ran, "This letter is so overwhelmingly of and for Browning Alumni, I'm sure the few others who read it will forgive the dedicatory title." The letter was signed, "Lyman B. Tobin, Alumni Secretary." The logic of Mr. Tobin's initial statement puzzled me, but I concluded that he could scarcely be apologizing to persons for whom the letter was not intended and that I must be one of the "few others" to whom it was directed—doubtless a select group, chosen because of their interest in educational affairs. "Forgive and forget," I said to myself, and went on to read:

We can't resist "going to town" with the alumni. . . . Almost every mail brings from far-away places some revival of the "good old days." . . . How fine that we all share so many happy memories! Memories of Mr. Browning getting the hardboiled egg into the milk bottle or out of it again without breaking it, memories of "the white-haired gentlemen who taught us to make Sturdy Bones to Keep Things In," of the old Browning Buzzer, of Bronx Park picnics, Travers' Island track meets, of Yule Log processions, of public speaking contests and amateur theatricals, of the Rapid Addition Board, of Dr. Roberts' Divergings, of Dr. Downing's "Zero!" ringing out in the crisp winter air, of that hard-fought basketball game, of old Fifty-fifth Street, of the Browning dinners, of the pride we felt when some Browning boy made good,—and plenty have made good.

This passage touched so many responsive chords that for a few moments I thought perhaps I *was* an old Browning boy after all. My sturdy bones certainly seem to keep things in; I remember public-speaking contests, amateur theatricals, etc.;

I *think* we had an old Browning buzzer in the dining room; and I remember old Fifty-fifth Street because I was walking on it just the other day. I didn't recall the business of Mr. Browning and the hardboiled egg, but even as a boy my attention wandered during this sort of thing, and I decided that I might easily have missed it. However, the reference to the Rapid Addition Board finally convinced me I hadn't gone to Browning. The school I attended had a Halting Addition Board; I remember this because I was chairman of the board. Having arrived at this conviction, I read on, on the chance that I might find out why Mr. Tobin had written to me. "We hope you'll take this as the personal thing it's meant to be," he wrote. "Think of it as someone from the old school reaching out a hand to say 'hello.'" The idea of a letter being a person with a hand that could say "hello" made me dizzy, and I turned the page in the hope of regaining my balance.

It was then that I came across the information about Gilbert Colgate and the others, along with the following additional items, among many:

Edward Martin Degener, '38, of Wilton, Conn., who was Petty Officer, 3rd class, in the Coast Guard, has been honorably discharged and has resumed his studies preparatory to entering Williams. (Remember the day we got the 9 lb. pickerel, Ned?)

"M. Hartley Dodge, 120 Broadway,"—do come in some time and say hello!

Hello, George Graves, Jr., where are you and how's the dry fly fishing?

Col. George Hill, Jr., '26, of the A.A.F., lives on Rockrimmon Road, Stamford, Conn. (It seems only yesterday that we were fishing together at the breakwater!)

Congratulations, Emmet Van A. Murray, because you're D.K.E. at Brown! (I'll be able to say, "Yours-in-the-bonds, L.B.T., Alpha Alpha of D.K.E.")

We take off our hat to Miss Hirt's Luncheon Club, a most delightful and well-mannered organization.

Mr. Jones is about to ask all friends of Browning . . . for contributions to a much-needed Teachers' Retirement Fund. . . . Browning teachers have hitherto been ignominiously sloughed off at the end of their time into the sad obscurity of an almost penniless old age. . . . Of course you know, don't you, that, because of an $802.50 "tax saving," a person with, say, a $50,000 "Surtax Net Income" could contribute $1,000 at an actual cost of $197.50?

Of course I do! Hats off, I say, and pants pockets out, to "Hartley Dodge" and John D. Rockefeller III, and all other Browning boys in the $50,000 surtax bracket; hats off to Miss Hirt's Luncheon Club and to all other delightful and well-mannered organizations, wherever they may be; and three cheers and a locomotive for Mr. Lyman B. Tobin, a loyal Deke with a penchant for pickerel, parentheses, and saying "hello," and a man who writes, in closing:

By the way, if you haven't sent in some word of yourself, won't you do so? You're important to some of us even if you aren't to yourself. . . . Up Now! Let's hear from you!

Well, I *am* important to myself, and ordinarily I might resent this insinuation, but nothing softens me up more than an intimation that a $1,000 gift to charity would cost me only $197.50, so, alley-oop, L.B.T.! Here goes!

Last time I went fishing was during the summer of 1938, up in the Adirondacks. I was trolling by myself, and had the rod tied to my left foot with an old Rogers Peet tie for fear a strike might bounce it out of the boat before I could stop rowing and grab it. A strike came, and after three-quarters of an hour I worked the fish up near the boat, where I could see what it was—a 12 lb. walleyed pike! It gave me a walleyed look, shouted "Zero!," and broke the line, tearing off with a valuable triple-hook wooden minnow. I burst into tears and haven't fished since. In fact, I haven't done anything since but mope. I'm afraid I haven't made good, and I'm not sure that the pike made good either, since, unless it managed to worry the wooden minnow out of its jaw, it must have starved to death. I'm down at the breakwater right now, moping, but I see from the phone book that Lyman B. Tobin is located on East Fortieth Street, and I'll drop in on him just as soon as I can get my right hand to say "hello." So far, all it will do is twist people's arms behind their backs, the recalcitrant little beggar!

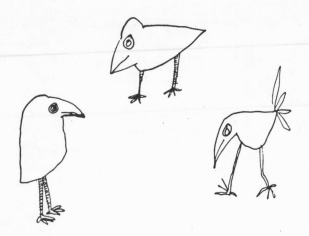

Mother Taft's Chickens

QUITE a few people have told me, and I have often seen it in print, that the main object of formal education is not so much to inculcate certain facts and dates as to teach you where to go to find out things you want to know. I can find out practically anything I want to know by calling up the *Times*, the Public Library's information desk, the British Library of Information, the French Information Center, or by asking my sister, and I have never precisely understood the connection between this easy ability of mine and the years I spent on algebra, geometry, geology, corrective posture, and Greek. Several months ago I asked the Public Library's information people just what they supposed the connection was, and they said they had no idea offhand but would call me back. I haven't heard from them yet.

My suspicion that the dissection of a frog teaches you, at best, how to dissect a frog, and not a thing more, received a regrettable boost the other day when I came across a printed list, headed "Lost Alumni," sent out by the Taft School, of Watertown, Connecticut, to several hundred of its graduates and ex-students. Taft, as anyone up on educational affairs knows, is one of the best-regarded prep schools in the country, with a student body recruited largely from thoughtful, substantial families and with an admirably low college-entrance-examination mortality record. Its annual algebra contests with Hotchkiss, discontinued a few years ago because of the terrible feeling they engendered, were at one time a lively feature of the Eastern scholastic scene. The list of lost Taft alumni which I have been studying contains four hundred and eleven names, ranging from William Tatlock, class of 1891, to John Ordway, of the class of 1939, who seems to have dropped out of sight like a plummet. The list is accompanied by a statement which reads in part, "You will help us by sending in addresses of any of those listed on the enclosure."

Well, I have every sympathy with Taft's inability to put its finger on Linson E. Tsao, 1914, and I don't suppose that John L. Lewis, 1907, can be the man I keep reading about in the papers, but some of the other lost characters strike me as being surprisingly accessible. Lawrence H. Nott, 1923, for example, is living at 108 East Eighty-second Street, New York, New York; Frederick B. Gleason, Jr., 1927, is at 315 East Sixty-eighth Street; and Alexis C. Coudert, 1931, is at 103 East Eighty-sixth Street. Horace H. Work, Jr., 1936, has an office at 535 Fifth Avenue, and I imagine that the whereabouts of Manfred W. Ehrich, Jr., one of the fifteen missing members of the class of 1933, could be ascertained by sending a postcard to his father at 20 Exchange Place. I am in a position to give this information about Taft's stormy petrels as a result of having spent a few minutes with the New York telephone book, without stirring from my desk.

Comparatively few Taft men come from New York, and perhaps for this reason a number of alumni have managed to conceal themselves right on Park Avenue. Thus, William H. Symington, 1908, listed as lost, is at 1021 Park, while Stockton Green and William S. Begg, Taft 1925 and Yale 1929 both of them, are living with their families at 1120 and 1192 Park, respectively. Leonard Cox, 1911, in what seems a more likely effort to throw the school off his trail, is hiding out in the Village, at 63 East Eleventh Street. Richard C. Plater, Jr., a Watertown classmate of Mr. Green and Mr. Begg and similarly listed as lost, is at 301 Nehoiden Avenue, Needham, Massachusetts, and at least two missing alumni are safe and sound in Connecticut—Warner Bishop, 1912, at 301 Park Place, Bridgeport, and John H. Lynch, Jr., 1921, at his place, Mountain Greenery, in Ridgefield. Another 1921 man-wanted, Mark H. Haight, is at 179-58 Selover Road, St. Albans, Long Island. I can't keep this up much longer, as J. Edgar Hoover is waiting in the reception room to take me out to lunch, but as an indication that my powers of raising the lost aren't confined to Greater New York and New England, I would like to reveal that William H. Woodin, son of the late Secretary of the Treasury and one of twenty missing members of the Taft class of 1919, is at Wilmot Road, Tucson, Arizona, while Spelman Prentice, 1929, a grandson of the late John D. Rockefeller whom Taft is unable to locate, is receiving mail, if not his class notices, at Wolf Pen Road, Prospect, Kentucky. The addresses of Messrs. Woodin and Prentice, and those of all the other lost alumni listed in this paragraph, appear in the current issue of the New York *Social Register*, a copy of which, along with the telephone book, is surely available in Watertown.

I haven't looked up Ambrose Bierce, but if he isn't in one of them, it's only because he didn't go to Taft.

The Ladies' Magazines
IV

The Very Latest in Tete-à-Tétes

Last Wednesday morning, upon awakening, I addressed myself to my feet. "Feet," I said, "I want you to dedicate yourselves to health and beauty. You might start out by rolling your toes over some glass marbles, which you will find under the bureau, and then have them clasp a pencil I have thoughtfully placed on the carpet. This will strengthen your tendons and enable you to tap impatiently at a moment's delay, rush swiftly to get places on time, or, for that matter, twirl beribboned on the dance floor, nakedly at home."

I got the novel idea of talking to my feet not from visiting a bunch of mental hospitals but from reading a last winter's issue of *Harper's Bazaar* (I had put it in the deep freeze, and it was good as new) which, under the title "Today's Feet," said, in part:

Now they lead a life alluringly, publicly their own. As expressively as hands, as tattletale as eyes, as mysteriously wrought as mind and heart and soul, they tap impatiently at a moment's delay; rush swiftly to get there just on time; fly gaily, uninhibitedly over long sun-baked beaches; twirl beribboned on the dance floor, nakedly at home. Feet speak, but they tell no lies. Dedicate your feet to health and beauty. . . . Roll your toes over glass marbles. Train your toes to clasp a pencil. . . . Feel the pencil strengthen the tendons. . . . Love your feet—they love you.

If feet could speak, I reasoned—and I had this on the authority of an influential arm of the Hearst organization, which is not given to whimsy—they could also understand, and I was not surprised when my right foot, after a brief powwow with the left, replied to my suggestions. I was rather taken aback by the nature of its reply, however. "No, it won't," my right foot said, "and we won't either. This marble-rolling and pencil-clasping business just wears us out, and we'll be goddamned if we'll do any such thing. On the contrary, we propose to take it easy, and we'll thank you to take your weight off us. That hike along the Palisades last Sunday was no joke, and we've been meaning to bring it up. We hurt." My left foot nodded.

I told them both to cut out the insubordination, and the left one piped up, "We're tattletales, remember? Another unwelcome peep out of you and we'll tell Carmel Snow where we were the other afternoon, twirling nakedly in you-know-whose apartment. How would you like *that* spread over the pages of *Harper's Bazaar?*" The two big things sneered expressively, like a couple of malevolent hands.

"Feet," I said imploringly, "don't you love me?"

"Yes," they chorused, tapping impatiently. "We love you all right, but we've been reading the memoirs of Madame Récamier's feet, a pair well in advance of their times, and we know what's good for us. Back to bed, big boy. We want the rest of the month off, and the union says we can have it. After that, a little cruise, two weeks on a sun-baked beach, and then we'll see about the office. Perhaps, if you'll take a taxi every day, and have lunch sent in . . ."

I stuffed some cotton in my ears and haven't dared leave my room since. I can feel my toes leering at me, and I can't help wondering whether we weren't all better off in the days when feet just carried you around in a lovely pedal silence, broken only by a noncommittal aside from an occasional squeaky shoe.

Confessions of An Opium Rubber

THE fact that Mrs. Edward Warburg and Mrs. Edward
Reeves wash themselves with camomile tea may mean less
than nothing to you, but knowledge of this, and of the bathroom and dressing-room habits of Mrs. John C. Wilson, Mrs.
Alexander Forbes, Mrs. Edwin Earl, Mrs. Julien Chaqueneau,
Mrs. McAdoo Taylor, and Miss Brenda Frazier—all of which I
have learned from Vogue—has done a good deal toward changing the entire course of my life. The truth is that for years I
have been washing my face with a mixture of scrambled eggs,
bacon, and buttered toast on weekdays, and with a cheese
omelet on Sundays and holidays, and because of some ridiculous reticence, I had been unable to get myself to tell people
about this. "How do you manage to keep your complexion?"
my friends would ask, or "What's that piece of bacon doing
under your left eye?" On these occasions I would change the
subject uneasily, gaining a reputation for inattention, rudeness,
uneasiness, and inability to eat bacon neatly.

My mental state was becoming pitiable when, last Tuesday,
I picked up a copy of the November 1st Vogue and turned to an
article entitled "Confessions of a Beauty Spy." "Confess all,"
this began. "Tell us how you keep those Good Looks, that lily-
white skin—we asked a number of beauties," and proceeded to
tell not only about the tea-dunking technique of Mmes. Warburg and Reeves but that Mrs. Wilson "washes her lovely face
twice a day in tepid milk," Mrs. Chaqueneau "swears by fresh
cream on the face," Mrs. Taylor applies her makeup on a
foundation of raw cucumber lotion, and Mrs. Forbes rinses

her hair with camomile tea and washes it with raw egg yolks. Miss Frazier, on the other hand, is a white-of-egg girl (she applies this part of the egg to her face, allows it to dry, and then rubs her face with ice), while Mrs. Earl according to *Vogue's* spy, retains her radiance by bathing in a solution of Epsom salts.

Well, I have obviously been a neurotic fool to conceal what I have been doing toward preserving my Good Looks, or, as I prefer to call them, my Looks, all these years. If Mrs. Warburg can wash and tell, so can I. At eight every morning, I rise from my Shredded Wheat mattress and plunge into a hot malted-milk shower, after which I rinse my hair out with a mixture of buckwheat cakes, maple syrup, and Ovaltine. I finish off with a cold *vichyssoise*, which comes out of a special tap installed for me by Facial Soups, Inc., a subsidiary of the American Radiator Company, and designed by Norman Bel Geddes. Next, I rub my face with a gritty composition consisting of one part opium, one part ground paper clips, and two parts Dunhill's Tobacco Mixture No. A9160, and then wash it with the scrambled eggs, etc. This makes it impossible, or at least inadvisable, to detect impurities in my complexion, and is also a considerable boost to industry, keeping, as it does, a good many people busy growing poppies, tobacco, hens, roosters, paper clips, and so on. I then shave with minestrone, dab my cheeks with marmalade, snatch a breakfast of Palm Olive soap and cold cream, and dash over to Brenda Frazier's to pick up her discarded egg yolks before Mrs. Forbes beats me to it. I rub these into my scalp, along with some old Willkie buttons, and by the time I get to my office, my looks are the envy of all.

My April Fools' Day Party

A LOT of people don't like to talk about their failures, I know, but there is a lesson in my April Fools' Day party fiasco and I have decided to tell all about it, or at least a good deal about it. The lesson is don't do everything *Harper's Bazaar* and *Your Life, The Popular Guide to Desirable Living* advise you to do. Early in March I read an article called "The Baroness d'Erlanger Proposes a Party" in *Harper's Bazaar* and decided to give a party before the month was out. By one of those retroactive coincidences that keep cropping up, retroactively, in my crowded life, I had met the Baroness a couple of weeks before at an open-air night club near Havana called Sans Souci. The indignation with which she repelled a suggestion from the headwaiter that she sit at a table behind a large tree made me realize she was a woman of the world, and when I received, through *Harper's Bazaar*, her proposal for a party, I felt it would be churlish not to follow it. "The table . . . ," I read, "is ingenious. Its base, of white Prince of Wales feathers, supports a reversible marbleized top, pink on one side, green on the other, so you may vary the foundation on which to build your ideas."

I wrote the Duke of Windsor for a few of his old feathers, bought a reversible two-color marble table top, began piling my ideas on the pink side, and picked up the Baroness's article again. "The festive wrought-iron chairs, lacquered in white, have slab seats covered in silks of different colors," it ran. "As your guests arrive, each is presented with a card naming the color he or she is to sit upon—an amusing idea instead of place cards, and a good way to start the meal with laughter."

An ordinary place card is usually enough to set me into gales of giggling, but I followed the Baroness's instructions and was about to invite my guests for the twenty-eighth of March when I came across a piece entitled "The Life of the Party," by Ruth Ann Douglas, in the Charm department of *Your Life, The Popular Guide to Desirable Living*, setting forth suggestions for an April Fools' party. This decided me to entertain on April 1st instead, and to incorporate in my party the best ideas of both Baroness d'Erlanger and Miss Douglas. "Decorations . . . can be amusingly ingenious," the latter wrote. "Place a Christmas wreath in one window, a Jack-o'-lantern in another, Fourth of July bunting on the wall, pictures turned upside down, rugs wrong side up, and so on. You might hook up a dry cell to the doorbell to administer a mild electric shock, and when the guest enters you slip an ice cube into his palm as you shake hands (of course you're smart enough to wear gloves). Have dunce caps handy for all guests as they arrive. Sprinkle a little sneezing powder around now and then, but keep out of range."

Well, I had no sooner made these various arrangements than my first guest, Mrs. Caresse Crosby, arrived. I'm afraid I had hooked up a rather powerful cell, for when I opened the door —I had turned my butler upside down and hung him next to an Utrillo as an extra bit of fun—there she was, lying unconscious on the stoop. I brought her to with the ice cube and some sneezing powder, and while she was boxing my ears in came a whole group of guests, among them Condé Nast, Cole Porter, the Reed Vreelands, the Duke di Verdura, Nicky de Gunzburg, and Herbert Bayard Swope. I clapped dunce caps on them all, handed them place cards marked "Red," "Green," etc., and waited for them to start laughing. Nothing much happened, so, following a suggestion made by Miss Douglas in her article, I propounded a question to break the ice. "If twenty-six cents will buy a pound of butter, how much butter will a cent and a quarter buy?" I asked, adding that special dunce caps would be awarded for failure to answer the question correctly. "Twenty-six cents won't buy a pound of butter," Mrs. Vreeland said—rather shortly, I fancied. I finally had to give the answer (which is one pound) myself, and stuck a *second* dunce cap on everybody except Mr. Swope, who cuffed me severely when I tried to approach him.

I realized that my guests hadn't quite entered into the spirit of the occasion, but I felt sure that the sandwiches, which, according to Miss Douglas's instructions, I served with the cocktails, would bring them around. "Get some rubber slices of ham at a novelty counter and mix them in with genuine sandwiches on the tray," Miss D. had written. "A round slice cut from a red inner tube will give a fair imitation of a piece of ham when placed between two slices of bread." My neighborhood novelty counter was all out of rubber ham, following a big Elsa Maxwell party the night before, and I had to cut up an inner tube from one of my automobile tires. I was therefore particularly nettled, when Mr. Swope, after taking a bite out of one of the sandwiches, yelled "I'll teach you a lesson!" and began turning my pictures and rugs right side up.

I saw that my whole party was going to be botched and, excusing myself for a moment, started rereading "The Life of the Party," for hints on how to save the situation. "Get two husky guests to hold a heavy book or piece of board between them, two or three inches above the floor," I read. "Then pick out one of the guests and tell him or her that the two men are going to lift him into the air as he stands on the book. Blindfold the victim, help him onto the book, then stand in front of him so that his hands can rest on your shoulders for support. Now, slowly, bend your knees, at the same time encouraging appropriate comment as to how high the guest is being lifted. The illusion of the victim is that he is being raised aloft, and he will sway unsteadily and utterly refuse to jump to the floor— and will his face be red when the blindfold is removed and he sees that he has never been more than three inches above the carpet!" I got Cole Porter and the Duke di Verdura to hold Simon & Schuster's "A Treasury of Art Masterpieces" in the fashion described. Next I persuaded Alfred de Liagre, Jr., the theatrical producer, to step onto the book blindfolded. I then proceeded as Miss Douglas advised, and I must say my butler was a great help, shrieking "How's the air up there? Look out! He's going to fall!" as, with Mr. de Liagre's hands on my shoulders, I slowly bent my knees. The only trouble was that Mr. de Liagre, far from swaying, stood firm as a rock, and when asked to jump, immediately jumped.

Mr. de Liagre's failure to cooperate in this joke, and Mr. Swope's hasty departure after swallowing some cork croutons I had put in his soup, seemed to me to put a damper on the party, and I again turned for help to *Y.L.,T.P.G.t.D.L.* This time I found another article in the Charm section—"How to Enjoy Your Own Parties," by Margery Wilson, the lady who sold a mail-order lesson on charm to the late Queen Marie of Rumania. In a paragraph designed to assist the host "who is not always successful in getting his guests to merge into a comfortable unity," Miss Wilson wrote, "Gather the newcomers together, possibly standing by a table where 'you are going to show them a little book,' but where you really stand and read some pithy excerpt, not more than a page long. The subject is not important. Your enthusiastic assumption that it is of interest will be all that is necessary. . . . You give the impression that you must be very sure of yourself, very comfortable mentally to read something aloud to them. . . ." I stood by my reversible marbleized pink-and-green table and confidently picked up a volume of the report of the New York Chamber of Commerce for 1891–92. "I am going to show you a little book," I said enthusiastically. "It couldn't be more fascinating." I began to read:

"The stock of cheese in store in New York on January 1st, 1891, was stated at 99,600 boxes against 128,621 boxes on same date in 1890, and the visible stocks at all points, including Canada, London, and Liverpool, were 887,100 boxes, against 923,471 boxes the previous year. The position of the market was a strong one. Jobbers had for some time been buying from hand to mouth, and were carrying little stock, and the foreign markets were showing signs of improvement, awakening a little more attention on the part of export buyers. The published accounts of stock at the principal distributing points indicated a lighter aggregate supply than usual for the season, giving holders much confidence, and after opening at nine and three-quarter cents fancy State factory immediately began a gradual advance, which continued, quite steadily, until early in April, when twelve and one-half cents was touched. During this period, trade was fairly active and satisfactory."

When I put the book down and looked around, I discovered that everyone had left but Mrs. Crosby, who was swinging from the Christmas wreath, sneezing steadily and picking bits of inner tube from her teeth with her free hand. I don't think either of us has had a moment of mental comfort since.

Flash! Mrs. Fairfax Potter Plaits Her Hair
with a Silk Handkerchief and
Winds It High

WHEN I was a young man hankering to become a reporter, the stock reply of a publisher or an editor of a Manhattan paper to a candidate for a job was the suggestion that he attend a school of journalism first, or else spend a couple of years gaining experience on a small-town newspaper. I recall Arthur Hays Sulzberger saying exactly that to me in 1928, when I besought him for a job on the *Times*. "Go to a school of journalism first," he said, "or else work on a newspaper in a small town for a couple of years, and then come back and see me." I have never thought much of this type of advice, and it is therefore with particular enthusiasm that I recommend the partial perusal of a recent issue of *Harper's Bazaar* as a shortcut journalistic apprenticeship, one calculated to accomplish in two minutes what used to take two years. "Go read pages sixty-eight and sixty-nine of the August, 1942, issue of *Harper's Bazaar*," Mr. Sulzberger will counsel aspiring young men in the future, unless I miss my guess. "Learn what really constitutes news, and report here tomorrow morning at a starting salary of a hundred and fifty dollars a week."

Under a picture of a fashionable matron, and also under the headlines "Mrs. Potter Dines Out. Over the Dress She Wears a Tie-Silk Jacket; Plaits Her Hair with a Silk Handkerchief and Winds It High" and "The Décolleté Dress Comes Back with a Short Skirt," *Harper's Bazaar* writes, on the first page of its two-page object lesson in crack reporting:

This is news. This is distinction. This is a fashion to be launched by a woman who has natural elegance and a feeling in her bones for clothes. It's a dining dress, a very personal dress . . . as décolleté as a ball dress of the First Empire, as circumspect, narrow, and brief as a 1942 street dress under the WPB regulations. Mrs. Fairfax Potter designed it herself, for herself, in stiff black tie silk; as an adjunct, a little black tie-silk jacket. We consider it big news, because it's creative, and because it's the right move out of a contemporary stalemate. In our effort to avoid the dressiness inappropriate in wartime we have gone out to dinner mournfully underdressed, or repeated last year's dinner dress season after season since 1939. Here is the dress that's been missing—an evening dress with grace for our time.

The second page of *Harper's Bazaar's* scoop consists of a full-page photograph of Mrs. Potter standing before a cosmetics table in a panelled, high-ceilinged room, her right hand resting lightly on a pile of paper-backed books, a basket of peonies on the floor. "Mrs. Potter dines at home," the accompanying caption reads, "or at the house of a friend in the very new, very personal, black tie-silk evening dress that she designed herself. It's narrow, it's short, it's décolleté."

In the interest of students who may wish to use this article as a stepping-stone to a journalistic career, I have attempted to reconstruct the scene in the *Harper's Bazaar* office when the story broke: (*Scene: The office of Mrs. Carmel Snow, editor of "Harper's Bazaar." Mrs. Snow is conferring with Mrs. T. Reed Vreeland, the magazine's fashion editor. The telephone rings.*)

Mrs. Snow: Hello?

Voice: This is Mrs. Fairfax Potter. Got a pencil?

Mrs. Snow (*to Mrs. Vreeland*): Get me a pencil. (*To Mrs. Potter*) Yes, just a minute. (*She sharpens a pencil.*)

MRS. POTTER: I want you to be the first to know. I'm dining out!

MRS. SNOW: No!

MRS. POTTER: Yes! At the house of a friend! And I'm wearing a very new, very personal, black tie-silk evening dress!

MRS. VREELAND (*to Mrs. Snow*): News?

MRS. SNOW: Big news!

(*Mrs. Vreeland grabs for the phone, and Mrs. Snow cuffs her smartly.*)

MRS. SNOW (*to Mrs. Vreeland*): I'll handle this myself. (*To Mrs. Potter*): What's the dress look like?

MRS. POTTER: Well, it's circumspect—

MRS. SNOW: It it narrow?

MRS. POTTER: Yes.

MRS. SNOW: Is it brief?

MRS. POTTER: It's as brief as a 1942 street dress under the WPB regulations. It's as décolleté as a ball dress of the First Empire. It's an evening dress with grace for our time! It's the right move out of a contemporary stalemate!

MRS. SNOW (*scribbling furiously*): Not so fast. Who designed it?

MRS. POTTER: I designed it myself, for myself!

MRS. SNOW (*to Mrs. Vreeland*): Hold the presses! (*To Mrs. Potter*): You wear anything over the dress? Any sort of adjunct?

MRS. POTTER: Over my dress I'm wearing, as an adjunct, a little black tie-silk jacket. Furthermore, I plait my hair with a silk handkerchief and wind it high!

MRS. SNOW (*to Mrs. Vreeland*): Get out the 240-point type. (*to Mrs. Potter*): We'll want an exclusive on this. I hope you aren't going to tip off any of the other publications.

MRS. POTTER: I'm a woman who has natural elegance and a feeling in her bones for clothes! Put that in and I'll keep mum.

MRS. SNOW: Okay, dearie, and we'll throw in a subscription

at the office rate. Our photographer will be around in fifteen minutes. You were sweet to call.

(*She and Mrs. Vreeland commence to set type furiously. Enter Arthur Hays Sulzberger.*)

MR. SULZBERGER (*sizing up the situation at a glance*): Good grief! Scooped again! Drat those schools of journalism! (*He exits moodily, the germ of the big new idea plainly in his mind.*)

Mrs. Edna Woolman Chase Please Notice

Mrs. Lowell Dillingham, of Honolulu, a well-bronzed strawberry blonde, likes to go barelegged in a thirty-dollar milky beige rayon crêpe Bendel dress and six-dollar, natural saddle-leather Altman sandals. In Old Westbury, Mrs. George Whitney, Jr., lounges around in tapered black slacks calculated to make her look taller than she is, plays golf in a creamy rayon fawnskin Wragge shirt, and spruces up for Sunday lunch in a gray flannel suit and sleeveless chenille sweater. She got these last two items at Stern's for a total of thirty-nine dollars. Here in town, Miss Ilka Chase is wont to address her typewriter in a ruffly white rayon crêpe shirt and black rayon taffeta shorts, and to relax of an evening in a flowery crêpe blouse and piqué skirt. These getups came from Bonwit Teller and Bendel, respectively, and cost around fifty dollars apiece. I have obtained this information not, as you might suppose, by collaring these ladies and examining the labels in their clothes or by combing their dressing-room wastebaskets for discarded price tags but by thumbing my way through a recent issue of *Vogue* (I was looking for a four-leaf clover I had pressed in its pages, and got sidetracked). "Flags it with a brilliant orange silk handkerchief," this publication's text says of Mrs. Whitney and her Sunday suit; the price of the handkerchief isn't given and, I judge, was modest, since in an accompanying water color a good deal of its dye is shown to have come off on Mrs. Whitney's skirt.

Other ladies whose clothes—and, in some instances, other hobbies—are described in this issue are Mrs. Cornelius Vanderbilt Whitney ("wears a Sherlock Holmes cape-coat, beautifully, blatantly checked"), Mrs. H. Gates Lloyd ("likes tweeds, abstract art, tennis, and anthropology"), and the Honourable Mrs. Pamela Churchill ("has the British talent for wearing evening clothes superbly"). "Nothing that slithers, dithers, dangles, and above all, nothing that teeters," *Vogue* states, summing up the wardrobe philosophy of these worthy characters and a few others. "Everything that's down to earth, up to the sun, on the level and right as rain."

Vogue is, of course, a girls' magazine, undoubtedly on the level and, as a rule, right as rain. Nevertheless, it seems to me unfair, and perhaps even wrong as hail, that in an issue which, like the aforementioned one, also features photographs and characterizations of a number of males, not a word is devoted to the color, texture, price, or origin of *their* clothes.

The reader's mood, relentlessly induced by the prevailing editorial slant, gets to transcend sex, and after seventeen pages of loving and specific sartorial prose and pictures dealing with the Mesdames Whitney *et al.*, it was with a feeling of acutely unsatisfied curiosity that I gazed at a full-page portrait of Bing Crosby tagged with a niggardly caption which simply observes that he is "rehearsing for a recording." Rehearsing in *what?* It looks like a gray flannel seventy-five-dollar Rogers Peet suit and a dollar-fifty Saks-Fifth Avenue polka-dot bow tie, but the suit might conceivably be a two-hundred-dollar fawn-colored number from Twyeffort, the tie might or might not be on an elastic band, and, all in all, there is a real likelihood that a grave injustice may be done to Mr. Crosby in the reader's mind.

Doubts sickened me when I came to this Crosby page, my imagination still on fire with the "flowering valentine of a bonnet" of Mrs. Sydney Wood, Jr., and Mrs. Churchill's "black chiffon dinner pyjamas with a billowing pink taffeta overskirt," and I felt even worse when, a little further on, I ran into a gallery of likenesses of Paul Klee, E. B. White, Johnny Mercer, Senator J. William Fulbright, Kenneth Delmar (Senator Claghorn), Billy Wilder, Charles Brackett, Molière, Ciano, and John van Druten, *not one of whose garments is mentioned.* White is certainly wearing a bold herringbone tweed, and his expression is that of a man tolerant toward abstract art, but has he flagged his coat or not, and if so, with what? His handkerchief pocket has been cut out of the photograph, clearly an evasion of the issue by *Vogue.* And are Brackett's French cuffs sewn onto a ready-made or a custom shirt? And where did Molière dig up that wig and what did he pay for it?

I hate purely destructive criticism and, by way of a creative journalistic object lesson, hereby report that as, like Miss Chase in one of *Vogue's* three sketches of her, I sit at my typewriter, I am wearing an April 8, 1942, one-hundred-and-sixty-five-dollar double-breasted slate-blue Whitaker suit flagged with a Partagas cigar; a seven-year-old blue-and-red Tremlett tie which, with the duty, cost around three dollars; a ready-made pair of brown down-to-earth Peal shoes which I bought at Brooks Brothers so long ago that I forgot the price; no bonnet;

and a misty-white Charles Dillon shirt, suitable for tennis and anthropology and ruffly as all hell. I'm afraid that the shirt dithers just a trifle and that my suit, in which I have detected a decided teeter, wouldn't fetch more at a thrift shop today than the price of Mrs. Dillingham's sandals.

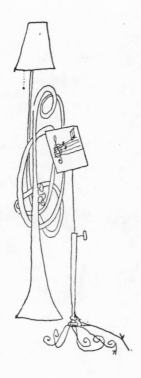

The Rich Have
Many Consolations—Plato
V

How Much Money Do You Make?

I<small>T</small> is an open secret, I believe, that when it comes to revealing the more intimate aspects of people, vegetables, animals, minerals, and so on, private conversation is more rewarding than a perusal, however diligent, of the newspapers, the *World Almanac*, or *Who's Who*. I know of only one subject in the field of special, personal information that is more widely aired in the papers than in conversation—how much money people make. Because of an inhibition that may have something to do with income-tax returns but, I believe, predates the income tax, this is seldom discussed in any specific way even by the oldest and most garrulous of friends.

If I had been playing poker, charades, or The Game every Friday night for forty years with, say, Thomas J. Watson, president of International Business Machines Corporation; Eugene

G. Grace, president of Bethlehem Steel; Nicholas M. Schenck, president of Loew's, Inc.; Robert Montgomery, Frank Capra, Louis B. Mayer, Harvey D. Gibson, Joan Crawford, Ginger Rogers, Fred Astaire, and Ben Hecht, I doubt whether, with the liveliest curiosity in the world, I could ever bring myself to ask, "How much dough did you boys and girls make during your last fiscal year?" I doubt still more strongly whether, if I did, I would receive anything more than evasive replies and chilling glances. Yet I can pick up the July 1, 1940, issue of the *Sun* and, with a simple flick of the wrist, find the answer, right on the financial page, next to the stock quotations—$453,440, $394,976, $275,673, $209,750, $294,166, $147,250, $133,725, $305,384, $208,767, $266,837, and $159,996, respectively.

I suppose that a lifelong frustration in this department of conversation is more than anything else responsible for the fact that I have recently been making an exhaustive study of Treasury reports on salaries and company reports filed with the SEC and released by the Stock Exchange to the papers. Be that as it may, my research in this field has led me to conclude that the day of the round-figure breadwinner making $15,000 or more a year is practically over. By round-figure breadwinner I mean a man, woman, child, or barrel-organ monkey whose salary, computed in one of three ways, can be correctly stated in round figures—specifically, in terms of $1,000 units for a yearly salary, or $100 units for a monthly salary, or $10 units for a weekly salary. I have, with one exception, confined my investigation to those making at least $15,000, because that seems to be the low for SEC salary reports and because I would have expected persons in this category to draw salaries no more irregular than, say, $230,000 a year, or, say, $11,100 a month, or (say!) $3,200 a week. Unless my memory is at fault, there was a time when most of our substantial earners were sensibly placed in one or another of these categories, generally the annual one.

Fifty thousand dollars a year was considered a good mark to shoot at when I was a boy, and the fact that this sum also represents $4,166.66⅔ a month, or $961.53^{11}⁄₁₃ a week, does not, of course, keep it from being a rational round-figure salary, easy to roll on the tongue and enter on the income-tax report. Today, apparently, men of affairs do not shoot at $50,000, or even $75,000 or $100,000. They shoot at $54,290, $65,630, $67,960, $105,620, or $138,410. According to the SEC reports, these are the precise salaries earned in recent twelve-month periods by, respectively, P. B. Sawyer, president of the National Power & Light Company; Sosthenes Behn, president of the International Telephone & Telegraph Corporation; Louis Bloch, chairman of the board of the Crown Zellerbach Corporation; Edward R. Stettinius, Jr., former chairman of the United States Steel Corporation; and Benjamin F. Fairless, president of U.S. Steel. These figures do not come out any rounder when computed on a monthly or a weekly basis. Mr. Sawyer made $4,524.16⅔ a month, or $1,044.03^{11}⁄₁₃ a week; Mr. Behn, $5,469.16⅔, or $1,262.11^{7}⁄₁₃; Mr. Bloch, $5,663.33⅓, or $1,306.92^{4}⁄₁₃; Mr. Stettinius, $8,801.66⅔, or $2,031.15^{5}⁄₁₃; and Mr. Fairless, $11,534.16⅔, or $2,661.73^{1}⁄₁₃. I know that when Mr. Stettinius resigned from the Steel Corporation to join President Roosevelt's Defence Advisory Commission, newspaper editorials referred to the salary he was giving up as $100,000 a year, but $105,620 is the official SEC figure for his 1938 salary, and I am inclined to believe it. I also know about Mr. Wendell Willkie and the $75,000 a year he got from Commonwealth & Southern; this was a hangover from the old round-figure days, and the fact that Willkie has seen fit to resign from C. & S. is simply an indication of how difficult it is for a man to stick to the old order and keep his place in the business world. A $100 cut to $74,900, and Mr. Willkie would still be sitting pretty.

There may be some explanation of the jagged figure, or fractional-unit, salary which the editors of the *Wall Street Journal* could supply, but don't tell me it is just a matter of bonuses, incentive compensation, directors' fees, or expense accounts. I have taken scrupulous care to select only figures which, according to the *Sun*, relate specifically to salaries. "R. F. Bessinger, president of Brunswicke-Balke-Colender Company," the *Sun* stated in June, "was paid $28,810 in salary, by the parent company, in 1939. J. O. Matteson, vice-president, received $25,303." R. F. *Bensinger*, president of the *Brunswick-Balke-Collender* Company, is what the paper meant, of course, but I cannot believe it mistakenly said $28,810 for $28,000 or $25,303 for $25,000. Nor do I think there can be any error about such other 1939 salaries as $22,895 for G. W. Vaughan, president of the Wright Aeronautical Corporation; $23,314 for William S. Menden, president of the New York Rapid Transit Corporation; $40,040 for Arthur O'Keefe, president of First National Stores; $138,919 for J. Spencer Love, president of the Burlington Mills Corporation; and $549,999 for C. J. Symington, president of the Symington-Gould Corporation. Mr. Symington was perhaps deliberately avoiding setting himself up as a $550,000-a-year man, on the theory that such an income might nowadays be considered ostentatious; it is nice to think of him coming home some evening in a period when retrenchment is less fashionable than it is today and saying to his wife, "Darling, just think! The stockholders have voted me a ten-per-cent raise, and you know what *that* means—$54,999.90 more a year, $4,583.32½ more every month, and $1,057.69½₆ extra each week—before I pay my taxes, of course."

In closing, I regret to state that the Woolworth Company, an outfit which runs a number of stores on a sensible system of prices, is no better than any other corporation when it comes to rewarding its high-priced help. Last year its Mr. R. W. Weber, assistant treasurer and director, received a salary of $33,821, or 650.40\frac{5}{13}$ a week. Mr. Weber also got a $48,367 bonus, but he could hardly count on this until the end of the year, and I like to reflect on his state of mind as he embarks on a two-week vacation, a check for $1,300.80$\frac{10}{13}$ in his jeans. Suppose, like any thoughtful assistant treasurer, he has a budget which provides that one-fourth of his salary go toward rent. Does he enter a summer hotel and ask for rooms for his family costing 23.24\frac{3}{13}$ a day? The position of Mr. R. H. Strongman, Woolworth executive-office representative and one of the few round-figure men I found, is even more perplexing, or was in 1939. In that year, Mr. Strongman received a salary of $1 and an $80,617 bonus. The fix of a man with a salary of one and twelve-thirteenths cents a week who cannot know what his bonus is going to be is not one I care to contemplate. Mr. Strongman may have some sort of regular income from a trust fund or a stationery shop which he owns on the side, but this is hardly any of Woolworth's business. In the interest of employee peace of mind, I think, the least his company could do would be to raise him to two cents a week, or $1.04 a year, thus putting him in the same kind of irregular annual-salary class as the big shots, bolstering up his ego, and making it possible for his wife to know where she stands when she goes out to do the marketing.

Department of Finance & Personal Thrift

W<small>E</small> curled up with the May issue of the monthly letter of the National City Bank the other evening, and this is what we read, in part:

The state of trade shows that consumers are spending a greater proportion, and saving less, out of their incomes. This had been expected. They want things they have been deprived of; they have larger savings than ever before and derive feelings of security from them.

If consumers—or people, as we sometimes call them—derive feelings of security from savings, why are they now saving less? The National City Bank's argument would seem to be that at some unspecified high-water mark of personal thrift— ten dollars? twenty? three hundred and fifty thousand?—a feeling of security comes over a man: he examines his wallet, safety-deposit box, or custody-account statement, slaps his thigh, and goes off, the future well taken care of, the present pure self-indulgence, to buy a hand-painted tie. In our opinion, this deduction is faulty. The desire for security is insatiable and the feeling of security chimerical. Any man who entertains them at all sticks to his old printed tie. The consumers the National City is talking about are a temperamentally care-free lot, with an average portfolio of seventeen-fifty, the wardrobe of a plush horse, and not an irrevocable trust between them.

Major George Fielding Eliot and
The Aqua Velva Club

THE war, my more gregarious friends tell me, has been raising Ned with the majority of men's clubs in this country;
memberships have been hit both by resignations and a
decreasing supply of candidates; former resident members of
social outfits in New York, Chicago, San Francisco and elsewhere have been moving in clouds, specially chartered by the
Government, to Washington, to take up their duties with
the O.F.F., the O.C.I.A.A., the O.C.I., etc., thus evolving
(despite their new affiliations with such Districts of Columbia
organizations as the Cosmos, the Metropolitan, and the
National Press) into *non*-resident members of the bulk of
their clubs, with a consequent diminution in dues; an even
greater number have joined the armed forces, enabling them,
in the case of most clubs, to retain their membership on either
a non-dues or lower-rate-dues basis. In Manhattan, the instal-
lation of ladies' annexes, a contemporary feature of nearly

all the college clubs as well as the Metropolitan and the Union League, and the inauguration of special Ladies' Days or mixed evenings, now prevalent in the Knickerbocker, Union, Racquet, and University, have resulted in a financial benefit incommensurate with the masculine distress they have occasioned; the general picture I get—and one doubtless typical of other cities as well—is one of deserted lounges, closed grilles, glassy swimming pools, cigars rotting in their humidors, billiard rooms that are mere shells, and a dwindling patter of feet in the squash courts.

As the possessor of a collection of silver linings second only to that of the Nizam of Hyderabad, I have recently been making a study of the Aqua Velva After-Shave Club, an organization studded with distinguished names which has, by prudent management and sensible attention to the current trend of world affairs, so adapted itself to the times as to flourish increasingly without resorting to dinner dances, powder rooms, or special assessments. The very location of the Club's quarters is, like those of the Motor Car Touring Society, of which Albert Eugene Gallatin is president, a secret; for all I know it may meet, like the Dutch Treat, in a hotel; or, like the Badminton, in an armory. During the two years or so of its existence, its progress has been recorded exclusively in the advertising pages of several national magazines; and while my records are not complete, since I usually give my old copies of national magazines to the elevator man, they are sufficient to make me believe that the Aqua Velva, like the Athenaeum in London, is no flash in the pan, and in any case begins with an A.

The Aqua Velva was founded in March, 1940, with Richard D. Morgan, Norman Rockwell, Lucius Beebe, Brock Pemberton, the Duke di Verdura, Burgess Meredith, and Francis Grover Cleveland as charter members. A hint as to qualifications for membership was given by the J. B. Williams Soap Company, which as parent organization to the Club stands in approximately the same relationship to the Aqua Velva as that of the Union to The Brook, in a series of advertisements it ran just prior to the establishment of the Club. "Your true gentle-man," these ran in part, "takes scrupulous care of the details of his dress and personal grooming. Attention to these fastidious details is the hallmark of business and social leaders." One of the first men to ally himself with the original group was Prince Paul Chavchavadze, "successful shipping man and international sportsman . . . of New York and Cape Cod, related by marriage to the late Czar"; he was followed by John Erskine and George Biddle, "artist, author, and scion of the famed Biddle family of Philadelphia." "Nothing I've tried leaves my face more refreshed than Aqua Velva," Biddle was quoted as saying as, adjusting his tie, he entered the lounge for the first time; it is a moot question in club circles as to whether he was referring to the Club or the shaving lotion, and oldsters around Piping Rock may be seen arguing the point to this day.

An early change in the Club's policy, indicative of its grow-ing standing, was effected in April, when the word "Mr.," hitherto absent in Club announcements, was affixed before the names of members. Two or three months later, its lists swelled with Mr. Ralph Guldahl, the golf champion; Mr. Lauritz Melchior, the singer; Mr. Boake Carter, the radio com-mentator; and Mr. Denis Conan Doyle, "noted world traveler, lecturer, and writer," the Club began to publish pictures of the members' roster: the various names followed each other in different sequences in different pictures, the signers apparently taking such relish in writing their names that they filled a number of books with them.

Eighteen months before Pearl Harbor, the Aqua Velva's

Admissions Committee, with an almost prescient appreciation of the coming importance of the military, elected Major George Fielding Eliot, the distinguished military expert and staff writer for *Life* Magazine and the New York *Herald Tribune*. With the help of Lucius Beebe, a newspaper colleague of his, the Major, encouraged by the Board of Governors, quietly began to revamp the Club. During the next year or so, he proposed or seconded countless soldiers, sailors, and aviators; their identity was naturally kept a military secret, and the first public sign of what had been going on occurred a little over a year ago, when the Aqua Velva printed a picture of four Army officers, members every one, standing around a globe of the world.

Two weeks later this same quartet was shown watching a polo game, doubtless an interclub affair with Meadow Brook. Last June, the sense of the close relationship between the civil and the military which has kept the Aqua Velva a going concern was illustrated in a picture of four members, two in uniform and two in sack suits, looking narrowly at the skies, presumably at a bomber squadron. As the summer brought us closer to war, at a time when other clubs were still innocently promoting bridge tournaments, hobby shows, the lectures on deep-sea fishing, Aqua Velva members, many of them Army or Navy men, were shown knowingly examining airplanes, battleships, and gun emplacements. A brief ivory-tower period set in early in September, while the Major was out of town: two members, whom I take to be Prince Chavchavadze and Louis Calhern, the actor (elected the month before), were depicted playing billiards in white ties while George Biddle, in a dinnercoat, and Boake Carter, in tails, looked on. This unfortunate impression was counterbalanced—and Chavchavadze and Calhern suspended for two weeks—later in the month by a picture of a naval officer, complete in gold braid, dressing for a Club dinner. The names accompanying this picture—Doyle, Guldahl, Rockwell, Beebe, Pemberton, and Eliot —obviously do not include that of the officer, whose identity will be made known when the war is over.

Since September, no picture of the Aqua Velva's activities has failed to include at least one man in uniform—a captain of infantry beating a civilian at chess, an officer in the Air Force exhibiting a giant searchlight or plane detector to a couple of fellow members, a member of the Coast Artillery scrutinizing a piece of coast artillery. Last March the Club released a picture of a tank; the background had, of course, been blacked out, but I assume it was the lounge. Below the machine appeared the signatures of Pemberton, Erskine, Cleveland, Carter, Rockwell, and Beebe, who were perhaps inside; the tank itself appeared to be manned by Burgess Meredith, while Melchior, Verdura, and Major Eliot, the last in uniform, looked on admiringly. No sign of a ladies' annex defaced this scene, or any of the preceding ones; and I suggest that every men's club in the country introduce a Flying Fortress in its locker room, watch its squash courts fill up, and reestablish its roof, in so many cases now a mere adjunct to the Ladies Dining Room, as a place where the older civilian members can sit these mild summer evenings, a stirrup-pump at their elbows, keeping a sharp eye out for incendiary bombs.

The Coordinator's Cufflinks

A FEW days before last Christmas, my incoming basket in the government war agency for which I work was brightened by a mimeographed interoffice memorandum which has given me considerable pause. Since the burden of its message is simply an extract from the law of the land, I feel at liberty to reproduce it:

In view of the approaching Christmas holidays, the attention of all employees is invited to the following paragraph of law regarding gifts to an official superior:

"No officer, clerk, or employee in the United States Government employ shall at any time solicit contributions from other officers, clerks, or employees in the Government service for a gift or present to those in a superior official position; nor shall any such officials or clerical superiors receive any gift or present offered or presented to them as a contribution from persons in Government employ receiving a less salary than themselves; nor shall any officer or clerk make any donations as a gift or present to any official superior. Every person who violates this section shall be summarily discharged from the Government employ (16 Stat. 63, Feb. 1, 1870; section 1784 of the Revised Statutes; 5 U.S.C. 113)."

No sooner had I read this than I picked up a costly Venetian vase I had bought as a Christmas present for the chief of the division in which I work, and took it into his office. "How much money you make?" I asked. "More than I do?" "Well, I suppose so," my official superior replied, nervously fingering his Tremlett tie. I threw the vase on the floor and it shattered into a thousand iridescent pieces. "I was going to give you this for Christmas," I explained. "Terribly sorry. Section 1784 of the Revised Statues, you know." "My God!" said my boss. "I'd almost forgotten about that. I might have accepted it, and we'd both have been in the soup." He got up and shook my hand warmly. "It's O.K. for you to give me a present," I said, "I'd sort of like a vicuna muffler."

New employees, unfamiliar with the ropes, are joining the various federal agencies every day. In an effort to spare them the rather extravagant near-mistake I made, or worse, I have attempted to reconstruct a relevant and instructive scene which took place in Washington a few weeks ago:

(*Scene: The suite of Paul V. McNutt, Chairman of the War Manpower Commission, in the Shoreham Hotel. It is Christmas afternoon, and Mr. McNutt is giving a reception. The butler ushers in a number of guests, all of whom are carrying gaily wrapped packages.*)

BUTLER: The Secretary of War and Mrs. Henry L. Stimson. The Under Secretary of State and Mrs. Sumner Welles. The Assistant Secretary of State and Mrs. Adolf Berle. The Administrator of Lend-Lease and Mrs. Edward R. Stettinius, Jr. The President of the Export & Import Bank and Mrs. Warren Lee Pierson. The Archivist of the United States and Mrs. Solon J. Buck. The Representative in Congress of the Seventeenth District of the State of New York and Mrs. Joseph Clark Baldwin.

MR. STIMSON: Merry Christmas, Paul. What's your salary?

MR. McNUTT: I don't recall exactly. I think it's around ten thousand.

MR. STIMSON: Mine's fifteen. Here you are. Best wishes. (*He hands his host a package.*)

MR. McNUTT (*opening it*): Toy civilians! Just what I wanted! Thank you, Henry.

MR. WELLES (*aside*): I get ten thousand. Guess I'll take a chance. (*He gives Mr. McNutt a present.*)

MR. MCNUTT: Peanut brittle! Aren't you nice, Sumner!

(*Mr. Berle is about to give Mr. McNutt his package when Mrs. Berle restrains him.*)

MRS. BERLE: Adolf! You know you only make nine thousand!

(*Mr. Berle hastily stuffs his package into his pocket. Several more guests come in.*)

BUTLER: The Secretary of the Treasury and Mrs. Henry Morgenthau, Jr. The Secretary of the Interior and Mrs. Harold L. Ickes. The Special Assistant to President Roosevelt and Mrs. Harry L. Hopkins. The Director of Foreign Relief and Rehabilitation Operations of the United States and Mrs. Herbert H. Lehman. Mr. George T. Summerlin, the Chief of the Division of Protocol of the Department of State. The Chief of the Division of Current Information of the Department of State and Mrs. Michael J. McDermott.

MR. BERLE (*pulling his package out of his pocket and addressing Mr. Summerlin*): How much money you make, George?

MR. SUMMERLIN: Ninety-six hundred.

MR. BERLE (*to Mr. Lehman*): Herbert?

MR. LEHMAN: I think it's ten thousand.

MR. BERLE (*to Mr. Baldwin*): Joe?

MR. BALDWIN: Ten thousand from Congress, then I have a public-relations business on the side.

MR. BERLE (*to Mr. Hopkins*): Harry?

MR. HOPKINS: Ten thousand and keep.

MR. BERLE (*to Mr. Morgenthau*): Henry?

MR. MORGENTHEAU: Fifteen thousand before taxes. Cabinet officer, you know.

MR. BERLE (*despairingly*): Any of you fellows get under nine thousand?

MR. McDERMOTT: Yes.

(*Mr. Berle gives his present to Mr. McDermott with a sigh of relief. Messrs. Stimson, Morgenthau and Ickes give presents to all the other guests. In general, a selective exchange of gifts goes on all over the room, preceded in each case by inquiries as to the salaries of potential donors and recipients. All rise as the President enters, heading another group of guests.*)

BUTLER: The President of the United States and Mrs. Franklin D. Roosevelt. The Solicitor General of the Department of Justice and Mrs. Francis Biddle. The Assistant Attorney General and Mrs. Thurman Arnold. The Coordinator of Inter-American Affairs and Mrs. Nelson Rockefeller. The Assistant Coordinator of Inter-American Affairs and Mrs. Wallace K. Harrison.

CHORUS: Merry Christmas, Mr. President.

THE PRESIDENT: Merry Christmas, all of you. (*He hands around presents to the men, while Mrs. Roosevelt showers gifts on the ladies. Everyone thanks them and begins to unwrap his or hers except Mr. Stettinius, whose wife draws him aside.*)

MRS. STETTINIUS: Ed! Aren't you still getting over $75,000 from the Steel Company?

MR. STETTINIUS: Gosh, I'll have to look that up. I better not take a chance. (*He hands his present back to Mr. Roosevelt with a wry smile.*) Sorry, Mr. President, but I have no choice. 16 Stat. 63, Feb. 1, 1870, you know; section 1784 of the Revised Statutes; 5 U.S.C. 113.

(*The President nods understandingly, and Mr. Stettinius hurriedly leaves the room.*)

MRS. ROOSEVELT: Mercy, Franklin, you might have been impeached. That thing works both ways, you know.

(*The ladies all give presents to Mrs. Roosevelt.*)

CHORUS OF MEN: Thank you, Mr. President. We wish we could give you something besides our best wishes, but you know how things are.

(*Mr. Roosevelt smiles a law-abiding smile. Re-enter Mr. Stettinius, clutching a package.*)

MR. STETTINIUS (*to the President*): A small token of my esteem, sir.

THE PRESIDENT: Thank you, Ed. (*Mrs. Roosevelt looks at him sharply.*) Perhaps I'd better not open it, though, until you've checked on your steel salary. (*He hands the box to Mrs. Roosevelt.*)

MR. STETTINIUS: First thing in the morning. Quite understand.

MR. ROCKEFELLER (*to Mr. Harrison*): You're a remarkably good Assistant Coordinator, Wally. Here's a little something for you, with my best. (*He hands Mr. Harrison a pair of cufflinks. The latter thanks him heartily.*)

MR. ARNOLD: Hold on, you two. What salary do you get, Mr. Harrison? (*Mr. Harrison names a figure in four digits.*) And what's yours, Mr. Rockefeller?

MR. ROCKEFELLER: I'm a dollar-a-year man.

MR. ARNOLD: Well (*reading*): "No officer, clerk, or employee in the United States Government employ . . . shall receive any gift or present . . . from persons in Government employ receiving a less salary than themselves. . . . Every person who violates this section shall be summarily discharged from the Government employ." You've both violated this section, or I'm not Thurman Arnold.

MR. ROCKEFELLER: Well, I think I have some sort of expense account, a sort of *per diem* arrangement—

MR. ARNOLD: It says *salary*. (*Turning to Mr. Biddle*): What you say, Francis?

MR. ROCKEFELLER (*beseechingly*): I have a few stocks, bonds and—

MR. BIDDLE: I'm afraid Thurman is right, Nelson.

(*Mr. Harrison returns the cufflinks to Mr. Rockefeller. The latter turns to the butler.*)

MR. ROCKEFELLER: Are you in the employ of the United States Government?

(*The butler shakes his head, and the Coordinator hands him the cufflinks.*)

BUTLER: Thank you very much, sir.

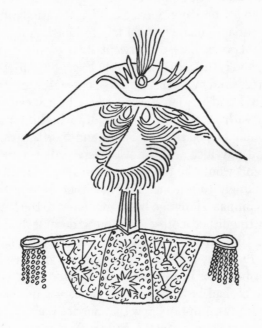

Whooping It Up

THE fact that Robert W. Service, author of nearly three hundred published poems, including "The Shooting of Dan McGrew," is alive, rather than dead, has been a source of pleasurable astonishment to a growing number of people on this continent during the past few years. They owe this surprise to the late Adolf Hitler and to Mr. Frank C. Dodd, head of Dodd, Mead & Company. Service was born in England in 1874, raised in Scotland, made his first trip to North America at the age of twenty-one, has spent twenty-two of his seventy-two years here, and is still a British citizen. Except for brief sojourns in California and Vancouver, he spent most of the years between 1912 and 1940 in France, where he associated almost exclusively with people who had no idea who he was. He also made a couple of side trips to Tahiti and North Africa, where *no one* had any idea who he was. Service has a hunger for obscurity and would be the last man in the world to identify himself willingly to anyone. The fact that his literary career reached its pinnacle long ago has contributed to the legend that he is a distinguished corpse. His most durable ballads were written in the Yukon territory, in northwest Canada, forty years ago. By 1921, he had had two novels and five books of verse published. For nearly two decades after that his poetical output, which had brought him his fame, was nil, and during those years the assumption grew that Service was dead, possibly as the result of a brawl in the Yukon. In the early twenties, Service wrote four novels, all of which escaped general notice, and in 1928 a health book entitled "Why Not Grow Young?

Or, Living for Longevity." Embellished with an orange jacket characterizing it as "the book every middle-aged man should read," this volume, in which Service pointed out that he ate twenty-two thousand potatoes a year, was read by few men of any age. Service, who would rather take it easy than do anything else he can think of, then lapsed contentedly into a twelve-year literary silence, during which he ate two hundred and sixty-four thousand potatoes. He divided his time between a house he owns in Brittany and apartments in Paris, Nice, and Monte Carlo. On the Riviera he swam, took long walks, read, played the piano accordion, sang, did setting-up exercises designed to woo longevity, and conversed easily in French with his neighbors, who rightly regarded him as a wealthy eccentric with a taste for simplicity, informal café life, and long spells of solitude.

He was living in his Breton house when, on June 17, 1940, he learned that the Germans had bombed Rennes, a nearby town, killing four thousand people. Service, who has a French wife and a grownup daughter, decided to get himself and his family out of there. Taking back roads in order to avoid the main highways, which were clogged with refugees, he drove his family to St. Malo, where he left his car, a Lancia, on a pier. Thanks to some British officers, the Services managed to squeeze onto a Weymouth-bound collier crammed with ammunition and wounded British troops, a number of whom died during the thirty hours it took to cross the Channel. According to Service, this was the last boat to get out of St. Malo before the British abandoned the port. The Services proceeded to London, in time for the first bombings of that city, and in September they sailed for Montreal, along with a thousand English children. By December they had journeyed on, via Toronto, Ottawa, and Vancouver, to Hollywood. "Oh, the huge Christmas trees lining the boulevards, the marvellous illumination after the blackout," Service said to a friend, "the sugar on the table, the wonderful markets, the abundance of everything—that's what struck us most." He took a bungalow in Hollywood and settled down. "Robert Service! My God, I thought you were dead!" scores of Californians were soon saying to him, and he realized, with a sinking feeling, that the sugar, the lights, and the abundance also meant the shattering of his dream of obscurity.

Frank Dodd, whose firm has been Service's chief American publisher for thirty years, then stepped in to do his part in the shattering of the Service dream. A year or so after the author's arrival, Dodd asked him to write his autobiography. Service refused, on the ground that it might bring his continuing existence to more general notice, but as he ran into more and more people who greeted him with "Robert Service! My God, I thought you were dead!," he saw that the game was up and set to work on his memoirs. He neglected to inform Mr. Dodd of this change of heart, so the publisher was agreeably surprised, late in 1944, when the postman brought him a one-hundred-and-fifty-thousand-word autobiography, complete to 1912. Dodd, Mead published this as "Ploughman of the Moon," a title Service took from a couplet by Verlaine:

> Pedlar of dream-stuff, piping an empty tune;
> Fisher of shadows, Ploughman of the Moon.

This book has cut down considerably on the number of people who think Service is dead. Even as an autobiographer, however, Service has a certain reticence; his recollections, for example, do not contain a single date, and it is impossible to find out from them even when the author was born. He concentrates on moods and impressions rather than on names, places, facts, and figures. Thus a reader of the autobiography with no knowledge of Service might easily suppose that he was perusing the vague memoirs of a literary vagabond who had hit a modest jackpot once or twice between moonlight walks and skating parties in the Far North instead of those of an author whose ballads have netted him a substantial fortune and have for nearly forty years been as familiar as Shakespeare to millions of people.

Service's long struggle against fame was an uphill one. His early Yukon ballads, which did not receive enough critical attention to be mentioned in any issues of the *Book Review Digest*, a monthly digest of American and English book reviews, began to catch on around 1910. For the next twenty years, Service was, with the possible exception of Edgar Guest, the most popular living poet in the English-speaking world. As recently as 1938, the New York *Times* stated firmly, "There can be no question that the author of 'Dan McGrew' and Edgar A. Guest are the two leading American [sic] folk poets of our time." In 1941, Simeon Strunsky, writing in the same paper, paid an emphatic, if left-handed, tribute to Service's renown:

But if we are to go in for the lighter literature, one wonders if among Canadian [sic] verse writers there ought not to be at least brief mention of Robert W. Service, if only by way of segregating him from true literature. The trouble that beset Dan McGrew in the Malamute saloon is now part of our folklore south of the 49th parallel.

The main motivation of Service's zeal for obscurity is his passion to be master of his own time. Until 1907, when he was thirty-three, Service, who worked at various times as a truck loader, dishwasher, gardener, and so on, and whose only real vocation was that of bank clerk, was afflicted with severe poverty. His resentment of this state, because it prevented him from doing just what he wanted to do, was continuous and intense. That year his first book of verse, "Songs of a Sour-dough," later reissued as "The Spell of the Yukon," was published. It was written on location. It has sold more than a million and a half copies. The ballad which gave it its final title begins:

> I wanted the gold, and I sought it;
>   I scrabbled and mucked like a slave.
> Was it famine or scurvy—I fought it;
>   I hurled my youth into a grave.
> I wanted the gold, and I got it—
>   Came out with a fortune last fall—
> Yet somehow life's not what I thought it,
>   And somehow the gold isn't all.

Many verses in this strain have identified Service, who never mucked for gold himself, as firmly with Canadian prospecting as Kipling, whom Service admiringly emulated, is identified with the Empire. In 1934, for example, the New York *Times* heralded a Canadian mining convention as follows:

Time was when one heard the cry that "there's gold in them thar hills" there immediately came to one's mind the rush of prospectors—men with whiskers, hobnailed boots, chewing tobacco, hardy and sturdy men inured to the hardships of the craft. Such men as these were immortalized by the Klondike poet Robert W. Service, whose poems have stirred the declamatory instincts of many a youth. But like so many other things, the picturesque, tobacco-spitting prospector has passed even as the gold he extracted from the soil has passed away. In his place will be seen a keen-eyed, well-spoken man, mostly rather young, who is indistinguishable from the mining engineer, metallurgist, and geologist with whom he mingles. This fact will be brought out clearly in Quebec in April at the annual meeting of the Canadian Institute of Mining and Metallurgy.

A couple of years after "The Spell of the Yukon" appeared, Service turned out a volume called "Ballads of a Cheechako," which introduced to the public such characters as the Sailor Swede, the Dago Kid, Claw-Fingered Kitty and Windy Ike ("bad as the worst were they"), Pious Pete (who "tried to refine that neighbor of mine, honest to God, I did"), Blasphemous Bill MacKie ("a dainty kind of cuss"), One-Eyed Mike, Hard-Luck Henry, Muckluck Mag ("there's concentrated honey in her smile"), Gum-Boot Ben, Clancy of the Mounted Police, and the Last Recorder (God). This book was also a big success. Then Service, having ten thousand dollars in royalties put away in the bank, decided, with joy and amazement, that he no longer had to be any man's slave. He had worked himself up to nine hundred dollars a year as teller in the Canadian Bank of Commerce, in Dawson, the capital of Yukon territory, but the job, in the light of his extracurricular success, hardly seemed worth the effort, so he retired, with a cat and a Siberian bearhound, one of which unfortunately ate the other up, to a nearby mountain cabin. There he lived alone, wrote, sang, and played the guitar, occasionally mushing to town for a moose steak and a romp with the girls. "With what joy I arranged my cabin!" he recalls in his up-to-1912 recollections. "I was keyed up to such a pitch of happiness that I brimmed over in dance and song."

Service's ecstasy was short-lived. His royalties kept increasing, and within a year he was sobered by the suspicion that he was on his way to becoming rich and famous. Ever since then he has been trying to duck what he considers the hazards of wealth and fame. He has done this first by forgetting who he is, thus causing a number of other people to lose track of him, so his fan mail and aren't-you-the-man-who conversational problems have, on the whole, been negligible. He also has adopted a very casual manner of handling his finances, involving himself in almost none of the fretting and fussing with financial advisers and investment portfolios other men worth several hundred thousand dollars like to go in for. "My books have sold between two and three million copies, I guess, and I'll be goddammed if I understand why," he told a friend when he was last in New York, on his way back to France, some weeks ago. "It's kind of staggering when I think of it, but I don't often think of it. I've never kept much track of my finances since I saved my first ten thousand dollars, nearly forty years ago. I keep my money in cash or life annuities and I never know within thirty or forty thousand dollars what I have in the bank." Service took a rather sophisticated flyer in arbitrage in the nineteen-twenties and worked his way up to over a million dollars before the 1929 crash demoted him to the six-figure class. Since then, he has been strictly a cash-and-annuity man.

In 1912, when it began to look as though his renown as the Kipling of the Klondike might get troublesome, Service, after bringing out his third book of verses, "Rhymes of a Rolling Stone," left North America, where he was better known than he was on any other continent, and went to Europe. After a few months in the Balkans as a war correspondent for the Toronto *Star*, he settled in France. He shrewdly foresaw that there the danger of his name's becoming a household word was greatly lessened by the difficulty of Gallicizing such passages as:

A bunch of the boys were whooping it up in the Malamute saloon;
The kid that handles the music box was hitting a jag-time tune;
Back of the bar, in a solo game, sat Dangerous Dan McGrew,
And watching his luck was his light-o'-love, the lady that's known
     as Lou.

Service's campaign to drop out of sight *qua* Service and to avoid the trappings, and traps, of wealth was so adroitly executed that in 1913 he was able to marry an otherwise well-informed Parisian girl without her having more than a vague idea of who he was. Service met the lady, Mlle. Germaine Bourgoin, the daughter of a *petit-bourgeois* family, one day when he rescued her and her younger sister from a crowd milling about two streetcars that had been in a spectacular collision. After being properly introduced to the young lady's mother, he began a courtship under the pretense of wishing to learn French from a girl who really knew the language. He posed as an obscure writer of small means through his period of wooing and right on into matrimony. Mrs. Service knew only that her husband was a poet whose verse, which was entirely incomprehensible to her, enabled them to live pleasantly in a small apartment on the Boulevard Montparnasse and maintain a budget that provided for good food and good wine. She had no idea, in the fuzzy days of early married life, that his poetry had brought him over a hundred thousand dollars or that during his courtship he had been living on a mere tenth of his income. Her innocence of Service's circumstances was a great help when, on a bicycle trip through Brittany, the honeymooning couple developed a crush on a house in Lancieux, on the coast. The mayor of the town, who owned it, was willing to sell it for twenty-five thousand francs. Service and his wife wheeled to the mayor's office. Service was wearing old clothes and assumed the attitude of a man in a modest financial condition. He removed the bicycle clips from his pants, and offered the mayor seventeen thousand francs, adding that he would pay seven thousand down, which he agreed to forfeit if he couldn't raise the remaining ten thousand within four weeks. *"O mon Dieu!"* said Mrs. Service apprehensively. The mayor, heartened by Mrs. Service's authentic alarm, took the offer up eagerly and a few days later smiled a wry Gallic smile when he received Service's check for ten thousand francs.

Service has never attempted to deny that he has been influenced by the works of Kipling. In his autobiography, he says that when, as a young man, he was an amateur recitalist "Gunga Din" was one of his favorite items, and in one of the "Rhymes of a Rolling Stone" there are the lines:

I'm dreaming to-night in the fire-glow, alone in my study tower,
My books battalioned around me, my Kipling flat on my knee.

It is just possible that Kipling had his Service flat on *his* knee when, in his autobiography, "Something of Myself," he wrote, "And, if it be in your power, bear serenely with imitators." Service's challenge to Kipling's serenity was remarked upon in the Boston *Transcript's* review of the "Rolling Stone" ballads:

Philosophy, mood, and meter have as strong and savory a flavor of Kipling as ever, revealing an unchanged and singlehearted discipleship on the part of their author.

During the first World War, Service, who was living in France when it broke out, became an ambulance driver for the American Red Cross and then, after an illness had forced him to give up the work, an intelligence officer in the Canadian Army. During that illness he wrote "Rhymes of a Red Cross Man," a collection of war poems. This was by far the most popular book of poetry about the war published in this country. It headed the non-fiction best-seller lists in 1917 and 1918, and is caused Service to be bracketed eulogistically with Kipling on at least two occasions. Reviewing it in the *Dial*, Witter Bynner, the poet, observed:

Robert W. Service has been a poetic phenomenon. More or less ignored by the critics, he has won a vast following. And it seems to me time for a fellow-craftsman to protest that in this case the public is right. . . . We have been inquiring for the poetry of the war. In my judgment, here it is.

In 1921, the *Texas Review,* a literary quarterly, expressed the same sentiment in an article entitled "Kipling Influence in the Verse of Robert W. Service," by William A. Whatley, of the University of Texas history department. Whatley felt that Service was an enthusiastic follower rather than a mere imitator of Kipling and that he had poetic genius in his own right. "Kipling failed utterly to contribute anything of poetic value to the literary output of the period of the Great War," Whatley remarked severely, "and it was left to Service, hitherto a simple follower of the elder poet, to sing the saga of the trenches, the hospital, and the camp." Part of "Rhymes of a Red Cross Man" was translated into Norwegian by Carl J. Hambro, a Norwegian journalist who later became President of the League of Nations Assembly. In the June, 1918, issue of *Litteraturen,* a Norwegian literary monthly, Mr. Hambro pointed out irritably that nothing of Service's had been included in a collection of war poems translated into Norwegian by one Valdemar Rørdam, and added:

This in spite of the fact that the note is one of the most unusual and the voice one of the most masculine in the entire orchestra of war. . . . There was in Rørdam's book . . . nothing as great as this, nothing which made it immortal. . . . His [Service's] earliest war poem . . . is an overture with an utterly different chime and strength than usually written in those days. A grasp on the strings so mighty that they could hardly be strained further.

Service, who had for some time been mildly nettled by the refusal of most critics to take him seriously, was gratified by these tributes. He was less gratified by the reception of his next book, "Ballads of a Bohemian," a collection of verses he wrote in Paris after the war and which, in a way, had everything. It abounded in apaches, grisettes, cocottes, gendarmes, absinthe drinkers, cocaine sniffers, tuberculous shopgirls, cigar-smoking boulevardiers, and selfless prostitutes. It even had a poem called "It Is Later Than You Think," which read in part:

> There's the wretched rent to pay,
> Yet I glower at pen and ink:
> Oh, inspire me, Muse, I pray,
> *It is later than you think!*

"Despite the occasional excellent poems . . . 'Ballads of a Bohemian' is a far cry from the vigor of Mr. Service's early work," the Boston *Transcript* wrote, and went on to make what is probably the most concise critical evaluation of Service ever attempted, "In those days Mr. Service was—Mr. Service." The *New Republic* also detected a retrogression: "One does not, of course, expect poetry from Mr. Service. But the present volume must seem a little flat even to those who felt so strongly moved by the red-blooded virility of the versifier's earlier works." These two notices appeared in May of 1921. Three months later, Service was rather puzzled by another journalistic attention— a parody of his Yukon style published in *Vanity Fair* under the title "The Ballad of Yukon Jake." Its author, Edward E. Paramore, Jr., had graduated from the Sheffield Engineering School at Yale in 1917, when Service's vogue was terrific. Paramore's class had voted Tennyson its Favorite Poet, with thirty-four votes, and Service the runner-up, with thirty-three. (Students of Yale undergraduate psychology feel that this tabulation represented the same kind of lip service to culture that impels so many Yale College courses to name Phi Beta Kappa, rather than Skull & Bones, as the Honor Most Desired, and that a number of the Tennyson men would have voted for Service had they been sure that Billy Phelps wasn't looking over their shoulders.) The Paramore parody, which chronicled the hair-raising activities of Jacob Kaime, the Hermit of Shark Tooth Shoal, aroused such enthusiasm that *Vanity Fair*

reprinted it twice, in 1926 and 1934. Condé Nast, publishers
of the magazine, have also distributed three thousand photo-
stats of it and still fill three and four requests a month. "Yukon
Jake," which, according to some critics, bears the same relation
to Service as Service does to Kipling, was even published as a
book by Coward-McCann in 1928. It won its author, who lives
in Beverly Hills, an invitation to join the Los Angeles Adven-
turers Club, the club having assumed that Paramore must have
been an old explorer of the Yukon.

Service, who has been reprinted in many anthologies, has
undoubtedly been not only parodied more often, but declaimed
in or at schools, colleges, clubs, bars, soldiers' camps, conven-
tions, smokers, and office parties more often, than any other
living author. "Is there . . . a doughboy that has not heard
(for the seventeenth time) 'The Shooting of Dan McGrew'?"
Louis Untermeyer wrote in the *Bookman* in 1922. Mr. Untermeyer, generally considered an authority on verse, thinks that
Service's immense popularity derived largely from the mascu-
linity of his subject matter and treatment. "Like Burns, he took
the curse off effeminacy in poetry; he cashed in on the reaction
against the 'sissy' writing of Tennyson and Wordsworth,"
Untermeyer said recently. "Kipling did it first and did it better,
but Service was the American answer." Untermeyer once
parodied Service (and Kipling) in "Rudyard Kipling and
Robert W. Service Collaborate on a New Red-Blooded Ballad,"
which commenced, "Now there was a man of the Sassenach
clan and he was a garrulous *goy*." This appeared in Untermeyer's "Collected Parodies" in 1926 and brought its author
several letters from Service fans who said it wasn't cricket to
attack a man who was no longer alive to defend himself.

After the first World War, Service became distressed by the
growing volume of his fan mail and the demands it might

eventually make on his time, and he was delighted by an authoritative indication that his obscurity was at least safe in his native land. "The London *Times* ran an article called 'Heritors of Unfulfilled Renown,'" he said not long ago. "It was about writers and artists killed in the war, in which they included me. I never contradicted it. I rather liked the idea. I'm amused that so many people in America think I'm dead. As a matter of fact, most of the people I used to know are dead. I'm one of the few people I used to know who *aren't* dead."

Service is again living in Monte Carlo, where he is working on a 1912-to-date autobiography. The day before he left this country, Frank Case, owner of the Algonquin Hotel, where Service was staying, took him to lunch at the Dutch Treat Club, where he was encouraged to recite a few of his verses. At the end, Service was admiringly surrounded by members of the club, a supposedly knowing bunch of publishers and writers. "Bob Service!" several of them said. "My God, I thought you were dead!" Service beamed at this professional tribute to his obscurity. His pleasure at the supposition that he is dead has its limits, however. He was rather miffed last year when, autographing copies of "Ploughman of the Moon" in a Los Angeles department store, he was confronted by a woman who said, "I thought you were dead for *years*." That was going too far.

Service is a clean-shaven, short, handsome, ruddy-faced man with bushy gray hair and a slight Scotch burr. He often wears a sweater under his coat. He is polite, modest, gentle in manner, and rather formal in conversation. He is proud of his youthful appearance, and this, as well as his tendency toward vagueness, often makes him misstate his age. Sometimes he pretends to be younger than he is, because this makes him feel younger; sometimes he pretends to be older, in the hope, frequently realized, that this will cause people to exclaim, "My goodness, you look

young for your age!" He was born—in Preston, England—on
January 16, 1874, the son of a bank teller who, without a bit of
hesitation, retired when Service's mother, around 1880,
inherited a legacy that brought her an income of two hundred
pounds a year. The Services moved to Glasgow, where Robert
was brought up with a crowd of younger brothers and sisters
which he thinks numbered nine at its peak. "I forget how many
there were," he has written in "Ploughman of the Moon." He
knows that one of them, Albert, was killed in the first World
War, and he thinks that three are still living, all in Canada—
Stanley, a doctor in Ottawa, and, in Vancouver, Alexander and
Peter, a retired electrical engineer and a second-hand-bookshop
proprietor, respectively. Service thinks this because, when he
made a trip to Canada a few months ago, three men representing themselves as his brothers greeted him affectionately in
three different hotel lobbies, saying they had seen his picture
in the papers. "My God, Bob," two of them said, "I thought
you were dead!" Stanley, the brother who didn't say "My God,
Bob!," is, as it happens, a faithful reader of the British *Who's
Who*, in which Service is listed, and was not surprised to find
Bob, whom he had not seen for twenty-four years, alive.

Service, though largely an expatriate, is still a British citizen.
He attended school in Glasgow until he was fourteen, and then
became a bank clerk, at twenty pounds a year. He quickly
evolved a philosophy about work which in the fifty-eight years
since then he has never seen reason to modify. He has set it
down in writing thus:

The great thing was that the work was easy. I always had a prej-
udice against hard work, or indeed any work. I would rather do little for poor pay than strain myself for a big salary. . . . Curse this
business of making a living! I have always regarded it as a necessary
evil. Although I was in the banking business for fourteen years, I
never discovered what it was all about. . . . And though my work

was easy, I tried to make it still easier. I dawdled over my daily errands and dreamed over my ledger. I made rhymes as I cast up columns of figures. It was so pleasant, with a big fire warming the spine. I crooked over my desk. Through the plate-glass window I could watch the cold grey street, where sailors and longshoremen met and wrangled. There were all sorts of Dickens-like characters meandering from pub to pub and an atmosphere of picturesque squalor that charmed me. I would gaze pensively from my high stool till a customer aroused me from my torpor.

In his teens, between fits of torpor, Service wrote verse that appeared in the Glasgow weeklies—the *Herald, Scottish Nights, People's Friend,* and so on. Whenever he felt that there was any danger of his getting ahead in the bank too fast, he read Thoreau to slow himself up. This worked for a while, but at the age of twenty he was promoted to a job paying an annual salary of seventy pounds, an emolument he feared might tempt him to strain himself. He resigned almost at once and lit out on a tramp steamer for Canada, where he had heard it was possible to do little for poor pay. There he got a fifteen-dollar-a-month job on a farm near Duncan, British Columbia, a town about thirty miles north of Victoria. He saved a hundred dollars in ten months and quit. He spent most of the next few years in and around San Francisco, Los Angeles, and San Diego, working as a dishwasher, a sandwich man, an orange picker, and a gardener at a rural bordello. These activities, and others of a similarly modest nature, were relieved by periods of relaxation, during which he simply bummed around the country, walking barefoot to save shoe leather, sleeping on beaches to save mattresses, playing a guitar and singing for his supper at farms. One day in 1901, sitting in a public square in Los Angeles, he suffered a severe reaction against his way of life. "I had reached the depths," he told a newspaper interviewer years later, "the depths a gentleman could reach." He thought longingly of the time when he had been worth a hundred dollars. He returned to Duncan, got his old job back, and three years later, when he had saved two hundred dollars, quit again. But his banking blood reasserted itself; he went to Victoria and became a clerk in the Canadian Bank of Commerce. He got this post by exhibiting a testimonial from his Glasgow bank which he had been carrying around for ten years. The Victoria bank offered him fifty dollars a month. Acting on his poor-pay-rather-than-strain-yourself-for-a-big-salary theory, Service tried to beat the bank down to twenty-five, but it stood firm. After a few months, he was transferred to a branch of the bank in Kamloops, a British Columbia inland town, and in 1905 to another branch, in White Horse, in the Yukon territory, in northwest Canada.

The Gold Rush of 1898 had brought to the Yukon a frenzied life. By the time Service got there, it had begun to taper off, but it was still fairly lively. White Horse was the northern terminus of the seaboard railway the prospectors came inland on; from there they proceeded four hundred and sixty miles by river boat to the Klondike gold fields. The town held thousands of excited transients during the summer but dwindled to less than a thousand residents during the eight-month cold spell, when, as Service has written, "the real life of the Yukon began." Possibly because the weather was so cold, the real life of the Yukon had an immediate and extraordinarily exhilarating effect on Service. His bank closed at four, and he then took a three-hour walk through the snowy woods, generally accompanied by a dog. Evenings he spent more sociably, skating, tobogganing, dancing, or just whooping it up. He had written almost nothing since his teens, but he began contributing verse to the town paper, the *Star*. One dull winter day the *Star*'s editor asked him to compose a local-atmosphere poem to be recited at a church concert. Service took his usual three-hour stroll with a congenial Malamute, dined at a saloon, returned to his teller's cage, and picked up a pencil. By five in the morning he had written "The Shooting of Dan McGrew." After looking it over, he decided it wasn't precisely the thing for church, and when he got home, which was then a room above the bank, he stuck it in a bureau drawer. A month later, at a party, he heard a man from Dawson tell a story about a miner who, far from any undertaker, had resourcefully cremated a defunct associate. Service went off on a reflective six-hour stroll. As he tramped through the snow in the moonlight, he thought out the four-teen stanzas of "The Cremation of Sam McGee," a poetic obit-uary notable for rhyming "frozen chum" with "crematorium" and for utilizing an old joke about cremating a man who had long complained that he was never warm enough. He wrote this ballad out the next day and put it, too, in the bureau. On his hikes during the next two months, he composed ballads at the rate of about one a walk. Then his inspiration suddenly ceased. The manuscripts got under some shirts and remained there for a year, until Service, running low on haberdashery, uncovered them. He reread them with interest and decided to invest a hundred-dollar Christmas bonus he had received from the bank in having a few copies printed up and bound, to give to friends. Their reaction was noncommittal.

Service thought a while, then sent his verses and a hundred-dollar check to his father, who had emigrated a few years before to Toronto, asking him to see whether a more professional printing job could be done on them. Service, Sr., went to William Briggs, a firm that specialized in Methodist hymn-books but also did jobwork. Briggs agreed to take on the assign-ment. The firm soon returned Service's hundred dollars to him, along with a letter informing him that a bug-eyed man in the office, after reading the galley proofs, had shown them around in local bookshops and received advance orders for seventeen hundred copies. Although it was not in the company's line,

Briggs offered to bring the book out at a dollar a copy at the firm's own risk and to pay him a ten-per-cent royalty. Service accepted. "Songs of a Sourdough," later brought out as "The Spell of the Yukon" in the United States by Edward Stern & Company, a Philadelphia firm, was published in the spring of 1907. That summer nearly every White Horse visitor turned up at Service's cage in the Canadian Bank of Commerce bearing a copy and asking him to autograph it. Service had taken the name Sam McGee from the bank ledger, and one day Mr. McGee, who was a local businessman, also turned up. "You used my name in one of your poems," he said, with the air of a man who had been at least slightly singed. Service had written:

The flames just soared, and the furnace roared—such a blaze you
    seldom see;
And I burrowed a hole in the glowing coal, and I stuffed in Sam
    McGee.

McGee walked out without either making a deposit or asking for an autograph. A year or two later he moved to Great Falls, Montana, and in 1937 he went to Beiseker, Alberta, where, in September, 1940, he died. For the last twenty-three years of his life, wherever he happened to be, he was scarcely able to get through a day without someone's asking him whether it was warm enough for him. The press is not what it was in the times of Dana, Greeley, Bennett, and the elder Pulitzer, and of all the New York papers only the *Times* and *Herald Tribune* gave Mr. McGee an obituary and even they muffed the main point; they didn't tell whether he had been cremated.

At the end of 1907, Service was transferred by his bank to its branch in Dawson. Dawson was accustomed to rich miners but not to rich poets, and Service laid the foundation for a rather unusual reputation by freely exhibiting his first royalty check, which was for a thousand dollars. Dawson's Gold Rush population was on the wane, too, but there were enough ninety-eighters still around and the atmosphere was still reminiscent enough of the mighty past to stimulate Service, now conscious of the rewards of literature and a deliberate seeker after local color, to further verse.

At midnight [he has written] I wandered the streets of the abandoned town, with the light still strong enough to read by. I tried to summon up the ghosts of the Argonauts. The log cabins, in their desolation, were pathetic reminders of a populous past. I loved the midnight melancholy of the haunted streets. . . . As I pensively roamed these empty ways, a solitary and dreamful mourner, ghosts were all about me, whispering and pleading in the mystic twilight. Thus I absorbed an atmosphere that eluded all others; thus I garnered material for another book. Oh, my Dawson of those days was a rich soil from which I reaped a plentiful harvest!

Service's Dawson harvest, published in 1909 under the title of "Ballads of a Cheechako" by Briggs in Canada and in this country by Barse & Hopkins, a New York company no longer in existence, brought him an initial royalty check of three thousand dollars. Service flashed this at parties for a while, bought a few beers for his close friends, took midnight walks in the rural parts of the Klondike, and in 1909, at the age of thirty-five, having saved his first ten thousand dollars, abandoned banking, and all regimented work, forever. At the request of Dodd, Mead, he wrote a novel about the Gold Rush called "The Trail of '98." This contains a strikingly virtuous heroine, a girl called Berna, whom Service named after a brand of condensed milk to which he was partial. Berna's character is revealed in the following passage:

Once I asked of her, "Berna, if you had to choose between death and dishonour, which would you prefer?"
"Death, of course," she answered promptly.
"Death's a pretty hard proposition," I commented.

"No, it's easy; physical death, compared with the other, compared with moral death."

Rather than entrust Berna to the mails, Service personally escorted the manuscript to New York, where an artist he had met in the Yukon put him up at the National Arts Club. It was his first visit to Manhattan, and he hated it. Although he now had twenty thousand dollars in the bank and a like amount in royalties was coming in every year, he dined, by preference, in the Bowery, generally alone. After three or four months in town, he decided to stroll to New Orleans. He made Philadelphia in three weeks, and then, having caught a bad cold, irritably got aboard a train and rode the rest of the way. From there he went to Cuba. In 1912 he made a nostalgic trip back to Dawson, where, he discovered, "The Trail of '98" had stirred up considerable interest. The Dawson *Weekly News* had given it a lead editorial, which said, in part:

Klondikers who revel in fiction and those who venture into the realm only when there is special inducement in the way of a home product have been devouring of late "The Trail of '98," the first literary creation of Robert W. Service aside from his delightful verse. The new work burst into the midst of the Yukon winter during the dogged spell of extreme temperature in the fifties below, when Klondikers were in the receptive mood and not altogether busy wrestling with the burden of spring pokes. In this respect it came at a time to receive all-round reading by the Klondike family. Coming from the pen of a writer who makes his home in Dawson and writes of scenes with which most Klondikers have a personal and historic familiarity, the work of Mr. Service was received with that tremulous expectancy inspired by all home creations which are out of the ordinary. The local sales of the book have, according to book dealers, made a record.

As a painter who strives to put in all that might be seen, regardless of whether it be a point of ugliness or of beauty, Service has told the story of none too flattering freedom among the earlier comers—particularly in relations between man and woman. As told in his picture, no doubt there was a world of sin in early Klondike. His emphasis is strong enough to impress a careless stranger to Yukon who goes slashing through the book that eventually the best must fall and that there was no pure woman or untarnished man in Yukon at that time and no regard of the marital relations; that all Klondike was stained too deep to ever be blanched. But the careful reader will discern that toward the end the writer declares the days of loose morality and debauchery have passed.

The editorial ended on a note of hope:

All that Dawson is concerned in is that the world not hold against Klondike, because of the work, any impression that belongs merely to history, and that it accord to many of Klondike of that day and her men and women of today that same sweet flavor of life and peaceful and law-abiding pursuit which would justify the most refined coming here with full assurance that nowhere is womankind more honored with knightly chivalry and nowhere are laws more strictly and rigidly enforced.

Service stayed in Dawson long enough to read this editorial over a couple of times and to write "Rhymes of a Rolling Stone," a book which impelled the Toronto *Star* to observe:

It was in 1907 that "Songs of a Sourdough" made every Canadian reader sit up and sense the fact that at last a native [sic] writer was giving us verse jumping with life instead of the old piffle concerning shady nooks and babbling brooks, and such-like jaded fancy's flowers about "this Canada of ours."
. . . He missed some tackles and fumbled considerably with his story, "The Trail of '98." But he's over the line for a Carlisle Indian touchdown with "Rhymes of a Rolling Stone." . . . They are the real "Sourdough" stuff!

Service's life since 1913, when he settled in France, has been one long Brittany-Paris-Riviera dream, except for two violent interruptions—the first World War, in which he drove a Red Cross ambulance and then served as an intelligence officer in the Canadian Army; and the second World War, which he weathered in this country. He has now resumed his dream, though not precisely on the comfortable, prewar basis. "I've always lived out of the world altogether and I've certainly enjoyed it," he told a friend in New York, shortly before he sailed again for France this winter. "I've never voted, and I've avoided all responsibilities, as far as possible. My place in Brittany was one of the most beautiful spots I've ever seen. Our house stood on a rock jutting out into the sea, between two golden sandy coves. When the sun came up, the glitter of the waves was reflected on the walls of the house. I used to follow the tide out every morning, for about two miles, catching lobsters and spearing conger eels in the shallows. I'd swim half a mile to sea, float and rest, swim back, take a two-hour siesta, and then play the accordion. Evenings, I'd loaf and read from a library of five thousand books I bought in London—biography and autobiography. No fiction, hardly any poetry. I'm not a poetry man, though I've written a lot of verse. It was an ideal life, absolutely in touch with nature, and healthy; that's why I'm so fit and fine for my age today. My neighbors in Brittany never knew who I was. They simply knew I was the wealthiest man in that part of the country. I put up a war memorial after 1918 in the village, gave liberally to the church, although I'm an agnostic, and helped the poor, and I think I was held in high esteem. The Germans were about to overrun my place in 1940 when I left, with my wife and daughter. My property was included in Hitler's fortification system. It's bristling with pill-boxes and I'm told it is still mined. The house was sacked and destroyed, and the library burned, along with a seventy-thousand-word unconventional travelogue I'd written about Russia, which I visited in 1938 and 1939 and which, on the whole, disappointed me. My caretaker has written me that nothing was saved. I've given orders to have the house rebuilt and I hope to go back there. I have an apartment in Monte Carlo, part of one of those pink stucco villas just over the beach, but Monte Carlo is really too sophisticated for me as a steady diet. I'll go up in the hills and have a little hideaway and come to town to play roulette every so often." Service has a secret roulette system that he claims invariably enables him to win enough to pay for lunch. When he wins that much, he quits.

In addition to "Rhymes of a Red Cross Man" and "Ballads of a Bohemian," Service's irresponsible years on the Continent were punctuated by the writing of five novels, none of which did well enough to persuade the New York Public Library to stock them. The first of these, "The Pretender," which is written in the first person, deals with a rich and famous American writer who goes to live in Paris, where he pretends to be poor and obscure, a curious parallel to Service's way of life at the time he wrote it. "To have omnibus tastes and an automobile income—how ironic!" it begins, and goes on to such passages as:

With positive joy I watched my money filter away. "Good!" I reflected. "I shall soon be penniless, reduced to eating stale crusts and sleeping on . . . iron benches. . . . Who can divine the dazzling possibilities of vicissitude? All my life I have battled with prosperity; now, at last, I shall achieve adversity. I will descend the ladder of success. I will rub shoulders with Destitution. I may even be introduced to Brother Despair." . . . We make a mistake when we pity the poor. It is the rich we should pity, those who have never known the joy of poverty, the ecstasy of squeezing the dollar to the last cent. . . . Never to have been desperately poor —ah! that is never to have lived.

The joys of poverty are an old literary preoccupation of Service's, and he has celebrated them in verse as well as prose. "Let others sing of gold and gear, the joy of being rich. But oh, the days when I was poor, a vagrant in a ditch!" he wrote in "Ballads of a Bohemian" twenty-six years ago, and continued:

We've limousines, and marble halls, and flunkeys by the score,
We play the part . . . but say, old chap, oh, isn't it a bore?
We work like slaves, we eat too much, we put on evening dress;
We've everything a man can want, I think . . . but happiness.

Since Service began to make his pile, he has done very little work, has hardly ever worn a dinner coat, and has, in general, lived with considerable simplicity. During his stay in New York this winter, he guided his family to cafeterias for most of their meals. On one occasion, however, he did take his wife and daughter to lunch at the National Arts Club. Service took them on the supposition, acquired from his stay there as a guest thirty-six years ago, that he was an honorary member. He confided this belief, and his name, to a club factotum, who turned out to be an admirer of "The Shooting of Dan McGrew" and suavely escorted the Services to the dining room.

Service rested up as a novelist for eight years after "The Pretender." He then dashed off "The Poisoned Paradise," an extravaganza about the Monte Carlo gaming set, full of scenes like:

"I've had enough," he cried, and his black eyes flashed in his white face. He wrenched the bottle from the man's hand. "You swine, you! Where I come from there are men who would give their heart's blood for a mouthful of that wine you're wasting like filthy water."

Service thinks that Monte Carlo really *is* a poisoned paradise, but on the whole it suits him. "I *like* to live in a poisoned paradise," he once said. "It's probably the most wicked little spot in the world, but we live there very quietly and respectably." "The Roughneck," written a year later, has a Tahitian background, which it owes to a couple of months Service spent on the island in 1920. It was made into a movie in 1925. In 1926,

Service turned out "The Master of the Microbe," a slums-of-Paris number, and in 1927, "The House of Fear," a mystery thriller whose scene was Brittany. Except for its geographical background, this novel, his last, reflects its author's experience only in that its hero has heart trouble. A few years before writing it, Service, then in his late forties and a bug on health, embarked on a vigorous course of gymnastics in Paris. He boxed in a gym and bought a bicycle exercise machine for his home. His muscles hardened, his chest expanded, his waistline contracted, his step became springier and springier, and then one day he fell down in a faint. His exercise had strained his heart rather badly. He gave up drinking, smoking, chocolates, coffee, red meat, and strenuous exercise, sold his bicycle machine, and took thermal baths at a French spa. He got to feeling better and better, and in 1928, in "Why Not Grow Young? Or, Living for Longevity," he told how fine he felt and offered a few health hints to his readers. "I hummed like a top with health," he said of his condition when he wrote the book. "I vibrated with vitality, I laughed like a lunatic in sheer joy of living."

According to Service, he was assisted to this state of lunacy, to which he still clings, by never reading at meals and never writing letters to the papers, by insisting that his cheese be "mild, not mellow," by chewing every mouthful thirty times, by brushing his teeth three times a day, by keeping his feet warm in bed, and by eating a lot of vegetables. It was shortly before writing this book that the author of "Dan McGrew" began to eat twenty-two thousand potatoes a year, or 60.27 a day, as well as a good deal of cabbage and onions. "The potato is my standby," he wrote. "I love the candor of the cabbage and the inquisite irony of the onion." Service intimated that his readers should do the same, and he also advised them to cut out worrying, Limburger cheese, and red meat.

Service wrote this at a time when hedonism was less unfashionable than it is today, but his views haven't changed, judging by some remarks he made just before he sailed for France. "Shirk responsibility—that's my philosophy," he said one afternoon while sipping ginger ale. "I do feel a sense of responsibility to the poor, but I don't want to go beyond writing a check. I don't want to go to meetings, I don't want to hold office, I don't want to be important. The world is in such a damnable mess I want to forget the whole thing. Books, music, and nature—that's all I ask."

Service's philosophy of life is all over "Why Not Grow Young?," between directions for arm jerking ("Shoot the arms out in front on a level with the shoulder, then jerk them back again to the shoulder"), liver squeezing ("With your body below the waist quite rigid, bend the trunk sideways, first to right then to left"), and double leg oscillation ("Pivot on the small of the back. This excellent spine strengthener . . ."). It is presented at its clearest in the passage entitled "Simplicity and Soup":

It is my great misfortune that I cannot live according to my means. I am the owner of an inferiority complex acquired by thirty years of oppression. The need to work for sustenance so that I might be able to work for more sustenance has left its mark on me. I always feel safest, and consequently happiest, in modest surroundings. I prefer a brown teapot and a Bath bun on a marble-topped table to the glittering sophistication of the Savoy. . . . In my Breton home I see the peasants sitting on their doorsteps, eating their bowls of soup. . . . I envy the peasant as he sups his soup so placidly, while the setting sun gilds the drops that linger on his whiskers.

In recent decades the backdrop of Service's life has often been one of luxury and glamour, but he has resolutely cleaved to his simplicity. During his many winters on the Riviera, he never met Somerset Maugham, Bernard Shaw, or the late

Maxine Elliott. "Oh, my, I'd be scared to meet Shaw," he says. "Somerset Maugham was a neighbor of mine, but I'm scared of these big fellows. I think I'd even be scared to meet Sinclair Lewis. I like eating in pubs and wearing old clothes. I love low life. I sit with all the riffraff in cafés and play the accordion for them." During Service's last stay in America, he spent most of his time living quietly in Hollywood, breathing deeply, admiring sunsets, pivoting on the small of his back, and occasionally reciting some of his verse at monthly get-togethers of an organization called the Chaparral Poets, the Hollywood chapter of which was formed in his honor. He gave a few poetry readings for a local radio station and played himself, briefly, in a picture made from Rex Beach's "The Spoilers." In this, sitting in a box in a Nome dance hall, he is busily scribbling "The Shooting of Dan McGrew" as girls on the stage do a can-can. "It wasn't really a faithful reflection of how I used to work," Service said, after completing this assignment, which brought him three hundred dollars for three days' work. "The Universal people said I wasn't the type to play myself, and I guess they were right. I should have been a big, husky six-footer."

In "The Spell of the Yukon," the ballad which gave his first book its second, and enduring, name, Service wrote:

> There's a land—oh, it beckons and beckons,
> And I want to go back—and I will.

Actually, Service never did succumb to all these beckons, but his wife, an attractive white-haired woman with intense blue eyes, and their daughter, Iris, made a sentimental pilgrimage to Dawson in 1942. Service's cabin, which had been nearly dismantled by souvenir hunters, has been restored and kept up by a patriotic Canadian society, the Daughters of the Empire, and its local members gave Mrs. Service and Iris a reception.

Mrs. Service, a practical Frenchwoman, was unfavorably impressed by the cabin. "*Ça m'a fait triste,*" she said when she saw her husband again. "So primitive, the floor of uneven boards. I thought, 'Oh, the cold.' "

Mrs. Service is as interested in her husband's health as he is, and believes, as he does, that he looks young for his age. When they stopped off in New York on their way back to France, she was walking along the street one day with Frank Dodd, while Service, with another friend, strolled jauntily a few paces ahead. "Isn't he wonderful for a man of his age?" she said. Mr. Dodd, who is thin and wiry and only a year Service's junior, nodded pleasantly. "I'm damned near his age and I still take on the younger fellows at golf," Dodd said later. "*He* wasn't doing anything but walking to a cab."

March, 1946

Intimations of Immortality
VI

Eleven Years with the Wendell Willkies

MAINLY because I felt they would never enjoy a very large sale, win me the Pulitzer Prize, the attention of William Saroyan, or a $3,000-a-week contract in Hollywood, I have never had the slightest desire to write my memoirs. The world's great who have crossed my path, generally rather hurriedly, have done so secure in the knowledge that their secrets, even had I known them, would go no further; what Bernard Shaw might have said to me in Antibes in the summer of 1928, had we only met, will certainly never be divulged by *me*, though I cannot, of course, speak for Shaw. Recently, however, circumstances of my life have caused me to abjure this attitude; the dovetailing of one aspect of my existence with that of a certain person has seemed to me a sign from heaven, or at any rate from the Republican Party, to tell all and never calculate the royalties.

By one of those purely fortuitous coincidences that make living in an apartment so much more exciting than living in a private house, tent, or old shoe, I not only reside in the same apartment house in the East Eighties as Mr. Wendell Willkie, the Republican candidate for the Presidency, but I dwell on precisely the same landing, in the apartment adjoining that of the Willkies. The building contains four apartments on each floor, but there are two elevators, one for the side of the house which faces Fifth Avenue and one for the side which faces Eighty-second Street, so the Willkie apartment and that of my family, which are on the street, or cheaper, side, share the exclusive use of an elevator landing on the sixth floor. I hope

I have made myself clear; these two apartments are the *only* ones opening on this elevator landing, and if Mr. Willkie and I leave our homes at the same time, we go down in the elevator together—unless, of course, he ducks back into his foyer and lets me go down first. Incidentally, the apartments in our section of the building not only do not face Fifth Avenue but they are more modest in size than those on the other side. The Willkies, for example, have seven rooms, whereas John F. Curry, former leader of Tammany Hall, who lives on the Avenue, or Metropolitan Museum of Art, side, has twelve.

For the past few months, ever since it looked as though Mr. Willkie might be nominated, I have been buttonholing people and appraising them of my juxtaposition to the Willkies, hoping to shine in a kind of reflected glory. "Wendell Willkie lives in Apartment 6 D and I live in 6 C," I tell them. "We both look out on Eighty-second Street. He is nearer Fifth Avenue than I am and can see Central Park from his place, whereas I have to crane my neck out of the window to get even a glimpse of the Metropolitan Museum, but we share approximately the same view of Mrs. Mary Duke Biddle's house, the old Albert Gould Jennings house, and the old David Helier mansion, which is now a rooming house, and it is probably even easier for me than it is for Mr. Willkie to look up the block toward Madison Avenue and see the Hamilton School, formerly Mrs. Harry Hamlin's house; the spacious abode of Mr. and Mrs. Hall Park McCullough; the William J. Ryan house, currently occupied by the Roussy de Saleses; and the gray façade of Mrs. Casimir I. Stralem's residence." This sort of talk has tided me over several dinner parties, or at least over the soup, but now that Mr. Willkie *has* been nominated I'm not sure that it isn't turning out to be a boomerang. I find that people are not satisfied with my real-estate observations but ask me how Mr. Willkie shapes up as a neighbor, what his apartment looks like, whether he sings in his shower, and which he prefers for breakfast—honey or marmalade. Just the other day *Life* Magazine called me up to ask how much rent I supposed the Willkies paid, and it is clearly only a matter of how long it takes M. Lincoln Schuster to get through his reminder files before Simon & Schuster will commission me to write a book called "How to Live Next Door to a Presidential Candidate."

While I am now in the right frame of mind to cast all reticence aside, the embarrassing fact is that, although the Willkies and I have been neighbors for eleven years, my relations with Mr. Willkie have been confined to going up or down in the elevator with him four or five times, or about once every other year. On these occasions we generally nod to each other, but it is hard to do much in a literary way with a nod, even a possibly Presidential nod. Recently I have taken to spending hours in my coat closet, which practically juts into the Willkie apartment, trying to find out whether or not Mr. Willkie sings in his shower, but either the building is solidly constructed or the Willkies have been away; I haven't heard a sound. I did, however, have an encounter with a member of the Willkie family a week or so before the Convention. As I was waiting for the elevator, Mr. Willkie's son, a nice-looking young man in shirtsleeves, poked his head out of 6 D and handed me a letter. "Would you mind giving this to the elevator man to mail?" he asked. "Not at all," I replied, feeling a strong sense of history. For all I know, it was a letter written by the candidate himself, perhaps to Kenneth Simpson. The elevator came up so quickly I had no time to look at the address, let alone steam open the envelope. Moreover, three or four years ago, when I gave a cocktail party, I had a rather oblique contact with the Willkie ménage. A number of guests, leaving after my party, rang the Willkie bell instead of the elevator bell, and the next day I noted a sign pasted on the elevator door which read "This Is the Elevator." Probably this was placed there by the Willkie maid; in any case, I haven't given a cocktail party since, and the sign has long ago fallen off or been removed by some farsighted souvenir hunter.

The last time I met Mr. Willkie in the elevator was several weeks ago, on a morning when I had got up particularly early in order to see some early birds catching worms in Central Park. "That was a fine piece you had in *Fortune*," I volunteered, referring to an article called "We, the People," which he had contributed to a recent issue. Mr. Willkie thanked me cordially. "Someone send it to you?" he asked. As you may know, the Republican candidate has two subscriptions to *Fortune* himself, and his campaign manager is Russell W. Davenport, former managing editor of that publication. I submit that any man in Mr. Willkie's position who takes it for granted that his neighbor is *not* a *Fortune* subscriber (clearly established by polls taken by *Fortune's* circulation department as enjoying an executive post in a large corporation, an earned income of $30,000 a year, and an unearned income of $15,787) is both tolerant and realistic, and perhaps deserves the vote of all thoughtful men.

When the Moon Comes Over the
Raymond Fosdick Mountains

WHEN I saw in the papers not so long ago that Charles V. Bob had been sentenced to jail, I began to wonder how the Charles V. Bob Mountains and all those other geographical features which Byrd discovered at the South Pole were standing up. I got in touch with a member of the second Byrd Expedition, who produced an official National Geographic map of the South Polar regions and informed me that except for the Bobs all the names given to mountains, etc., at the Pole have stuck. It seems that the National Geographic Society, after Byrd had named the Bob Mountains, discovered they were part of the Queen Maud Range and not separable mountains at all. The Admiral had just looked at them from the wrong side at first.

On the whole, however, the features of the South Pole have been named for the ages, and those names—mostly familiar— which you read in the papers several years ago are now being taught to children at school. Rockefeller Mountains, Raymond Fosdick Mountains, and the Gilbert Grosvenor Range, which is named after the editor of the *National Geographic*, are as rugged as ever. The waters of Paul Block Bay are lapping softly at the foothills of the Edsel Ford Range and friends of the late Rear Admiral William A. Moffett who wish to take a memorial slide down Moffett Glacier may do so, at their own risk. Readers of the *Times*, visiting the South Pole on pleasure bent, have their choice of Arthur Sulzberger Bay; Adolph Ochs Glacier; Mt. Iphigene, named after Mrs. Sulzberger; and Mt. Marujupu, called after the three Sulzberger daughters, Marian, Ruth, and Judith, and the Sulzberger son, whose nickname is Punch. The three girls are getting to be young ladies now and I personally think they are big enough to have individual mountains named after them, just like Dr. Finley, who is represented by Mt. Finley in the Crown Prince Olav Mountains. For that matter, I don't know why Dr. Finley and Mr. Sulzberger should be out-mountained by Frederick T. Birchall, a *Times* correspondent who is down on the map for Birchall Peaks. Just a case of the management being bulldozed by the Newspaper Guild, I suppose.

I spotted Mt. Kennett Rawson near Moffett Glacier, and Mr. Rawson, another member of the Expedition whom I happen to know, was inclined to be modest about this. "The Admiral told me one day he'd named a mountain after me," he explained. "I said I appreciated it. You can't lose on having a mountain named after you." Mr. Rawson, who looks young to have a mountain named after him, called my attention to several modest mountains at the Pole, including Tennant Peak, which was named after a cook on the expedition, and Charles Gould Peak, named after a carpenter. Tennant and Gould are both in the Rockefeller Mountains. There's a Mt. Bumstead, named after Albert H. Bumstead, a National Geographic cartographer; and a Mt. Ralph D. Paine, Jr., named after a man whose brother was on Byrd's sledging party. Byrd encouraged members of the expedition to name individual mountains themselves but attended to the more important mountains and glaciers personally. He is responsible for Mts. Clarence Mackay, Vincent Astor, Paul Block, Jr., Rosenwald, James Farley, Louis McHenry Howe, and Cohen. The last was named after Mannie Cohen, formerly associated with Paramount, which sent a couple of newsreel men along. I later learned from others close to the Expedition that Byrd put his foot down at calling a mountain Lydia Pinkham. The Lydia Pinkham people had contributed $5,000 to the Expedition in the expectation that some adequate geographical feature would be named after the founder of their business, and following Byrd's veto the money was returned. "Nothing of a permanent nature was named commercially," I was told, "although the Admiral did name an autogyro the Pep Boys' Snow Man after the Pep Boys, who make an anti-freeze mixture."

I love all these rocks and glaciers and only regret they're so far away. It seems a pity that we have to put up with impersonal names like the Adirondacks, the Appalachians, and the Berkshires, for the most part, or else with stodgy Presidential mountains like Garfield and McKinley. I suggest we exchange geographic names with the South Pole. I want to be able to tell people I'm going up to the Rockefellers for the summer, to see the view from Paul Block, Jr., and to picnic on Vincent Astor, without going to a lot of trouble and expense.

How to Lose Your Self-Confidence

LIKE so many men of my generation, I was brought up with the theory that the system of trial by jury was a democratic institution, a tribute to human dignity and equality, and a pretty good thing all round. "Trial by one's peers!" my Andorran governess used to sigh. "If only we'd had that, I'd never have left Andorra, begorra! It's a pretty good thing all round." At school in Connecticut the same point of view was dinned into me. "Cheer up, my boy," Mr. Taft would say on the rare occasions when I sat at the headmaster's table. "Someday you'll be well out of this morass of algebra, geometry, and corrective posture and sitting on a jury with your peers, or better. It's a crackajack democratic institution." At college it was the same story. "The sacred responsibilities of the juror," Professor Chauncey Brewster Tinker would murmur over tea and cookies at the Elizabethan Club. "It's a cliché, but there it is. If only I weren't so ridden with prejudices, I'd get to serve on a jury myself from time to time."

Thus indoctrinated, I felt a glow of solemn anticipation a few weeks ago when I received a summons to serve as a juror in the Supreme Court. "I'm off to the jury," I said to my wife, who at once set about packing up a partially consumed Hershey bar for me to take with me. "It will mean getting up a little earlier and a considerable financial loss," I said, "but it's a capital opportunity to do God's work—to acquit the innocent, convict the guilty, and study human nature at first hand." Several friends came to the subway to see me off on my first day of service, and it was with a lively sense of human dignity and equality that I turned up at the County Court House on Foley Square.

As luck would have it, I was accepted for a jury that very morning, following a searching questioning by the two contending lawyers which established me as a man owning no insurance stocks and capable of viewing family squabbles with equanimity. The judge came in, the jurors were sworn in, and I listened intently as a sordid little tale unfolded itself of a thirteen-year-old girl suing her aunt for damages sustained by the plaintiff in a three-year-back accident involving the defendant's car. Attorney vied with attorney in seeking to gain my, and my fellow-jurors', sympathy. Pre-accident photographs of the little girl were flashed at the jurors; the little girl herself allowed her doctor to pull back her post-accident lips to expose her more esoteric ravages; the aunt's solicitude was outlined by various witnesses and her driving habits vignetted. I entered intimately into the lives of the litigating families and their neighbors. Lunching alone in nearby Chinatown, soberly conscious of my responsibilities as a fact-judging citizen, I sipped my tea as though it were nectar. By the end of the afternoon, swollen with the evidence of wreckers, motorcycle cops, surgeons, and friends of the families, I felt just, omniscient, and as capable of weighing evidence as Felix Frankfurter. The next morning, fresh from the subway, I sat vacantly in court two hours until the judge appeared from an antechamber and briefly informed the jurors that the case had been settled out of court and that we were dismissed. "Thank you for your services," said the judge, with what it seemed to me could only be irony. No word as to the terms of the settlement or the reasons leading to them was vouchsafed us.

I felt miffed but game, and my next impanelment, after a day or so of unemployed waiting in a large room adorned with historical murals, followed by a legal cross-examination which established me as a signer of no unpaid promissory notes and a comparative stranger to the Fulton Fish Market, found me eagerly listening to a case in which a young man, through his lawyers, sought to show that his signature on an unpaid promissory note had been obtained by fraud. For the better part of two days I entered into the lives of a brand-new set of characters, most of them connected with the Fulton Fish Market. Counsel vied with counsel in seeking to invoke my sympathies; witnesses directed their remarks deferentially to the jury box; conscientiously I sifted the gold from the dross; and again, human fate in my hands, I felt the equal at least of Felix Frankfurter. Scarcely had I reached this conclusion when the judge, intimating clearly that the issues had been too complicated for the jury to follow, directed the verdict himself, ignoring me and my fellow-jurors completely. "Thank you for your services," he said blandly, and we were herded back to the waiting room.

The third and last case on which I was found acceptable as a juror, since I was a man who had never figured in accident litigation, owned no office buildings, and was unacquainted with any Phippses, involved a lady who was suing the Phipps estate for damages resulting from injuries sustained when she fell over a sand receptacle in an office building owned by the defendant. After a couple of days, in which we jurors were showered with photographs, floor plans, hospital bills, and appeals to our reason; treated to the vexing spectacle of the plaintiff, a lady no longer young, displaying the precise condition of her left shoulder muscles; and admonished by both lawyers to deliver a fair and square verdict, the judge, on the plea of the Phipps attorney, threw the case out of court all by himself, on the ground that there was insufficient evidence of the building people's negligence.

The fact that the judge's opinion coincided with mine and, as I gathered from their acrimonious comments in the elevator afterward, with that of none of the other jurors has done nothing to help me regain my self-confidence. My frustrated curiosity (a holdover from the first case) and my plummetlike descent from a feeling of being powerful and useful to one of being something akin to a crasher at a Knickerbocker Assembly have left me shaky, subject to doubts, and incapable of looking my uptown friends in the eye. Three dollars a day is small pay for being broken like a Cecropia moth on a setting board, and I suggest that jurors thus abruptly denied their function ("to give a true answer, or verdict, on some matter submitted to them, and to render a verdict according to the evidence"— Webster) be additionally furnished with the price of six months' consultation with a competent analyst, a new hat, and a double brandy.

How to Get Along With Professors:
An Ad-Hoc Modus Vivendi

For the better part of the past year, during which I have been engaged in projects so mysterious that I do not know the combination of my own safe, my work in the government service has thrown me increasingly into the company of professors. My immediate office is shared by two of them. One is, in normal times, a professor of biography and political science at Dartmouth, the other a professor of history at Harvard. Both are Rhodes scholars and both, of course, possess degrees which entitle them to be called doctor. Their attitude toward me is sympathetic and they have encouraged my ambitions to acquire an honorary degree so as not to be the only non-doctor in the room.

These two colleagues are the soul of tact, and they frequently inquire into the mysteries of the newspaper world, which they believe I represent, but it cannot be denied that both in conversation and in their federal writings, which it is my occasional duty and pleasure to read, they often employ such Latin tags as *sui generis, ibid, de facto, ad hoc,* and *imperium in imperio,* and that this makes me extremely nervous. It has also made me competitive, since I have become anxious to meet them on their own ground. "I am going to be *in absentia* tomorrow," I said to one of them the other day, in an effort to fit in. "How's that?" "Ah, yes, it's the locative, if you like," he replied. If I like! I'm crazy about it. On another occasion, after a good deal of thought, I concluded a remark about the weather with the phrase *mirabile dictu.* "Let's see— it's the supine, isn't it?" said my colleague, giving me an encouraging nod. You can imagine in what condition this left me.

Two other colleagues are on the Harvard and University of Michigan faculties, respectively, and the man who stands *in loco parentis* to us, as it were, is a big Elizabethan and Tudor authority from the University of Pennsylvania. This professor, whose attitude toward me is that of a kindly sage who has rescued a promising younger person from a rather doubtful environment, is a veritable Roman candle of expressions like *in medias res, modus vivendi,* and *pari passu.* Another University of Pennsylvania professor whom I sometimes have occasion to consult in line of duty enjoys the multiple distinction of being a former Guggenheim Fellow, president of the American School of Indic and Iranian Studies, Inc., a past president of the American Oriental Society, the author of "Manuscript Illustration of the Uttaradhyayana Sutra," and the second generation of his family to be a Sanskrit scholar. I do not wish, in this little canvas, to overemphasize the *oscuro* at the expense of the *chiaro,* if I may lapse into Italian for the moment, and it is only fair to add that this particular pundit has never thrown any Sanskrit in my direction and that he is a reliable judge of bourbon. Still another professor who occupies a commanding position in the hierarchy in which I work is the Coolidge Professor of History at Harvard. And so it goes. It does no violence to truth to say that in my present line of business I am practically the only male civilian whose *status quo* and *modus vivendi* is not, *ipso facto, ad hoc, pari passu,* and very nearly *ab initio* that of a professor. *In propria persona,* I am in a hell of a fix.

I mention all this because it has been on my mind for some time and because it probably explains how I came to peek at the *American Historical Review,* the official periodical of the American Historical Association. Many of my colleagues are members of this association and some of them have regaled me with anecdotes of its doings, so when I caught sight of the July, 1944, issue of its quarterly *omnium-gatherum* in the office last week, I took it home with me, hoping for a kind of indoctrination that would enable me to stop flinching during working hours. My eye was at once caught, *nolens volens,* by the lead article, "Abraham Lincoln and the Tariff," by Reinhard H. Luthin, identified in a footnote as a "lecturer in history in Columbia University and joint author with Harry J. Carman of the volume on *Lincoln and the Patronage.*" This article commenced as follows:

The controversy between "high-tariff" and "low-tariff" groups has remained constant in American history.[1]

I traced that [1] down to the bottom of the page, and this is what I found:

[1] Orrin L. Elliott, *The Tariff Controversy in the United States,* 1789–1833 (Palo Alto, 1892); Carl W. Kaiser, jr., *History of the Academic Protectionist-Free Trade Controversy before 1860* (Philadelphia, 1939); Robert R. Russel, *Economic Aspects of Southern Sectionalism,* 1840–1861 (Urbana, 1924), pp. 37–40, 65–66, 151–56; John G. Van Deusen, *Economic Bases of Disunion in South*

Carolina (New York, 1928), pp. 19–21, 59–103, 328; Jesse T. Carpenter, *The South as a Conscious Minority*, 1789–1861 (New York, 1930), pp. 19, 29–30, 56; Ulrich B. Phillips, *The Life of Robert Toombs* (New York, 1913), p. 148; Avery Craven, *The Coming of the Civil War* (New York, 1942), pp. 215–16, 224, 321, 401; James C. Ballagh, "Southern Economic History: Tariff and Public Lands," American Historical Association, *Annual Report*, 1898 (Washington, 1899), pp. 223 ff.

Well, in point of sober fact, I never got beyond this first sentence and accompanying footnote, although, as a matter of courtesy to Dr. Luthin, I appointed a *locum tenens* to finish the article for me.[1] I never got beyond this sentence because I realized that, despite my increasingly relentless mastery of the Latin tag, there was still a big obstacle to my associating on equal terms with my professorial colleagues—my propensity for making undocumented remarks. I resolved to cure this. "Old Father Sun is certainly out today," I said to the first man I ran into in my office the next morning, and before he had a chance to reply, I continued, "Charles Greeley Abbot, dir. since 1907, Smithsonian Astrophys. Obs., *The Sun, The Sun and the Welfare of Man, The Earth and the Stars, Fundamentals of Astronomy*, pp. ff. *et seq., passim, pari passu*, and *ad astra per aspera*." [2] The man I addressed looked at me with delight. " 'Truly the light is sweet, and a pleasant thing it is for the eyes to behold the sun,' " he said. "*Ecclesiastes* XI, 7, c. 200 B. C. We're having a little lunch today at the Brookings Institution, old man—just a few kindred spirits. I hope you'll answer *adsum* to our roll call."

I suppose I should have taken this *cum grano salis*, for when I showed up at the Institution it appeared that no lunch had

[1] This *locum tenens*, a Yale man, ended up with a bad case of *delirium tremens* and I had to appoint another *locum tenens* in his place, all of which ran into money. Ah, *lacrimae rerum!*

[2] Actually, I said a whole lot more than this, but I am omitting full documentation in this account in order to leave room for the rest of this book.

been scheduled. It turned out that the man I had been talking to was not a professor but someone who had come in to fix the radiator. Tomorrow is another day, however.[3] Plainly I am in the groove, and the first Rhodes scholar I meet is going to get both barrels, rain or shine. Abbot [4] also has quite a lot to say about rain.

[3] Thursday.
[4] *Cf. supra.*

Who Do You Think You Are—Jay Gould?

LUNCHING noisily at a midtown hotel the other day, I over-
heard a lady at the adjoining table say to her companion,
"Will wonders never cease?" The lady thus addressed nodded
sympathetically but volunteered no direct reply, and this
recalled to my mind an intention I have long nourished: to
answer, once and for all, those questions that people are continually asking one another without getting a civil reply, or, as
a rule, any reply at all. Some of these questions have been left
dangling for generations; I hope in this article not only to
satisfy the curiosity of living men and women who have asked
them but—by arranging for carbon copies of this treatise to be
buried, along with a number of gifted interpreters, in time
capsules all over the world—to make it unnecessary for any-

one to ask them again for several thousand years. The time thus saved can be used for small talk of a witty, agreeable nature, for the concoction of practical jokes, or for the manufacture of munitions, muffins, or mufflers, as the particular period may seem to require.

The answer to "Will wonders never cease?," for example, is no. Wonders will never cease. Wonders have been going on for centuries. If they should cease now, that in itself would constitute a wonder.

Again, take the question "Will it never stop raining?" The answer to this is yes. It always stops raining sooner or later.

"Is it hot enough for you?" and "Did you ever hear of such impudence?" are other questions that can be answered flatly, and seldom are. If anyone asks you whether it is hot enough for you, you may be sure that it is stifling. "Yes. Open the window if you like" is the correct reply to this question. As for prior tidings of similar impudence, unless you are a small child engaged in your first conversation, you undoubtedly have heard of an instance of commensurate effrontery. No one asks this question of small children, and the answer, therefore, is yes.

There are a good many interrogations that can't be answered yes or no, such as "Who ever heard of such a thing?," the reply to which is "Lots of people," "Practically no one," or "Aunt Minnie," depending on the context. I append herewith some other questions that have been cluttering up conversations, unanswered, for years, along with responses which are calculated to relegate them to limbo from now on.

"What's the world coming to?" The world is coming to its senses, but it will take a long time, as the world is not very bright. Meanwhile, there will be plenty of trouble.

"How's tricks?" Tricks in general are a terrible bore, the best ones being performed by members of the Society of American Magicians and A. E. Gallatin, an enthusiastic amateur who frequently mystifies a group of credulous friends by causing a coin to disappear in a goblet. Mr. Gallatin is listed in the *Social Register* but not in the telephone book, and there is no use trying to get him for parties.

"What's new?" The Tiffany building at Fifty-seventh Street and Fifth Avenue.

"What news on the Rialto?" See any Venice paper.

"Shoeshine?" No thanks, not today; according to Thorstein Veblen's "Theory of the Leisure Class," it's just snobbery that causes people to take an aesthetic pleasure in shiny shoes when they feel the opposite about shiny pants, coats, and noses.

"Shine the seat of your trousers?" Please.

I think this just about covers the list, but if you have any others, you might send them to me, care of the nearest time capsule. I asked a young man of my acquaintance who dropped in while I was writing this what question he most frequently heard going unanswered, and he said it was "Who do you think you are—Jay Gould?" Not moving much in robber-baron circles, I had never come across this, and I'm not sure how extensive its vogue is, but the answer, for any right-thinking person, is no—except, of course, when it's asked of the present Jay Gould.

Are there any more questions?

How Not to Get into "Who's Who"

EXCEPT for those times when I am drugging myself with movies, vanilla frosteds, the latest novel, or *crèmes de népenthe*, it is difficult for me to avoid the bothersome thought: Why haven't I amounted to anything, or at least to anything much? It is true that I am the owner of a small car and of two even smaller dinner coats, one eight years old and one three, and that I am the vice-president of a rather large garage in the Bronx, across the street from the Morrisania railroad station; on the other hand, I am not listed in the *Directory of Directors*, *Who's Who*, or "The Red Network," nor am I a member of the Racquet, Union, University, Knickerbocker, Brook, and

Garden City Golf Clubs, all of which are listed, with their telephone numbers, in an engagement diary I was given for Christmas by someone who probably has no idea of the obscurity of my position.

Thanks to an article in a recent issue of *Fortune* about William Bushnell Stout, builder of the first metal airplane in the United States and president of the Stout Engineering Laboratories in Dearborn, Michigan, the reason for my unsuccess has been made clear to me. Bill Stout, as *Fortune* and a few old friends call him, became a success in the airplane field as a result of the experience narrated in the following passage:

> One of his most vivid childhood memories is of a walk with his Methodist-preacher father. They strolled beside a lake and watched the flight of gulls. "Someday men will fly like that," said his father, "and you may be the one to bring it."

Well, the Wright brothers, who I suspect had a similar conversation with their father or one of their uncles in their youth, beat Stout to it, but Stout did get to the top in aeronautics, and he owes it all to his father and those gulls. I know he owes it all to his father and the gulls because this sort of thing happens too often to be coincidence. For example, Igor Sikorsky, another outstanding airplane designer, writes in his autobiography, "One of my earliest recollections was what my mother told me about Leonardo da Vinci and his attempts to design a flying machine." Sikorsky is a reticent man and doesn't quote his mother directly, but I can guess what she said. She said, "Igor Ivanovitch, someday you may successfully carry on the work of Leonardo in his attempts to design a flying machine," and there Igor is today, engineering manager of Vought-Sikorsky, the Leonardo da Vinci of Bridgeport, Conn.

Occasionally, I know, a man in full maturity will come along, voice his ambitions firmly, and attain them. The late Lord

Rosebery, who announced, and subsequently carried out, his intention of becoming Prime Minister, winning the Derby, and marrying the greatest heiress in England, was such a man. In general, though, the achievements of successful men have to be specifically outlined to them in early youth. It is a matter of record that George III was a mere child and a mere prince when his mother said to him, "George, be a King." George became King, but if it hadn't been for his mother, not to mention his grandfather, George II, the idea might never have entered his head. It is less generally known, but I think it has never been denied, that Wendell Willkie was only six when his father took him for a walk and showed him a flock of politicians. "Wendell," he said, "someday you will run for the Presidency of the United States."

Now and then, in the case of a perverse child, ambition is best stimulated in reverse. I quote from *Time*, February 1, 1932:

"Frank" Roosevelt saw his first President in 1887 when he was five. Sitting in the White House was large, grim, depression-ridden Grover Cleveland. James Roosevelt escorted his sailor-suited little son to Washington. President Cleveland put a fat hand on the yellow Roosevelt head and said: "I'm making a strange wish for you, little man, a wish I suppose no one else would make. I wish for you that you may never be President of the United States."

A word to young Roosevelt was sufficient, and we have Cleveland to thank for the turn American history has taken.

What I am getting at, of course, is that my elders never gave me anything important to shoot at. My mother never said a damned thing to me about Leonardo da Vinci; she simply read me the works of Jean Henri Fabre, and this sidetracked me into collecting insects until some people in Connecticut, mistaking me for a death's-head sphinx, tried to put me in a cyanide jar. My father used to take me for walks in the country, but he never advised me to grow up to be President of the United States, or even of Standard Brands. In fact, the only inspirational remark I recall his making was "My boy, your mother has a mortgage on a rather large garage in the Bronx, and if she should ever have to foreclose, you may grow up to be its vice-president."

Intimations of Immortality

I HAVE just found out, to my intense pleasure, that I am mentioned in the Westinghouse Time Capsule, which, as you may have read, was recently buried in the Immortal Well fifty feet below ground, in swampy soil, on the site of the World's Fair. There I am, along with a five-cent can opener, a woman's hat of the latest mode, a toothbrush, an alarm clock, a nail file, a specimen of Westinghouse urea plastic Beetleware, a Westinghouse Mazda electric lamp, a bactericidal Westinghouse Sterilamp, an electric razor with a Westinghouse motor, a photograph of the Westinghouse East Pittsburgh works, a Holy Bible, the Story of Rockefeller Center, a special message from Albert Einstein, and quite a lot of rubber, asbestos, coal, and cement. If I can believe David S. Youngholm, vice-president of the Westinghouse Electric & Manufacturing Company and chairman of the World's Fair Committee, I am going to be there for the next five thousand years, resisting ravages and doubtless getting mellower and mellower. I have been chosen out of any number of proposals submitted, and I am in a seven-foot torpedo-shaped tube of copper alloy. Mr. Youngholm says that I and my fellow-immortals have been put in this torpedo because of the Westinghouse Company's "desire to touch upon the principal categories of our modern life in all its variety and vigor." I was packed at the laboratories of the Westinghouse Lamp Division at Bloomfield, N. J., under the guidance of the United States Bureau of Standards, and with F. D. McHugh, managing editor of the *Scientific American*, and Grover Whalen looking on as official witnesses—enviously, I haven't a doubt. Moreover, I am twenty feet above sea level, which the Westinghouse people say is plenty to spare and which I say is good for my hay fever. They also say, "Archaeologists have been consulted to make certain that things included in the Time Capsule . . . will truly represent our vast and complex civilization." You can imagine how I feel. I feel insufferable.

I am not only in the Westinghouse Time Capsule but I am in what I consider the very best part of it. According to Westinghouse, there are five general categories—Small Articles of Common Use, Materials of Our Day, Miscellanous Items, Newsreel, and an Essay in Microfilm, which is also referred to as "the core of the cross-section of civilization." I am right in this microfilm core, under a subdivision entitled "How Information Is Disseminated Among Us." What's more, I am in it twice. I am in it on the masthead of the May 23, 1938, issue of *Life* Magazine, which it includes (I was a charter member of *Life's* editorial staff at the time), and I am in it in the September 3, 1938, issue of *The New Yorker*, having had an article about an Egyptian obelisk in that number—an archaeological subject which now seems almost implausibly appropriate. I hope the archaeologists of 6939 who dig me up will not fail to correlate my two appearances and give me credit for the rather wide scope of my activities.

Incidentally, I note that the inner crypt in which I repose is lined with an envelope of Pyrex glass set in a water-repellent petroleum-base wax and that it is filled with humid nitrogen, although how humid nitrogen gets along with water-repellent wax I can't imagine. I do not wish to complain, however. No one likes being in a special circular spun-aluminum container lined with rag ledger paper and carefully tied with linen twine more than I. Only one thing tends to cloud my happiness, and that is Mr. Youngholm's remark, "In the instances where several brands of items, equally good, were suggested but only one could be used, the one selected was chosen simply by lot." I do not like to feel that immortality can be pulled out of a hat.